Electronic Signatures for B2B Contracts

Aashish Srivastava

Electronic Signatures for B2B Contracts

Evidence from Australia

Springer

Aashish Srivastava
Business law and Taxation
Monash University
Melbourne, Victoria
Australia

ISBN 978-81-322-0742-9 ISBN 978-81-322-0743-6 (eBook)
DOI 10.1007/978-81-322-0743-6
Springer India Heidelberg New York Dordrecht London

Library of Congress Control Number: 2012946761

Printed on acid-free paper

Springer is part of Springer Science+Business Media (www.springer.com)

Preface

The speed with which commercial transactions are concluded with the Internet has hitherto been unknown. Yet, little success has been met in persuading businesses to adopt electronic signatures to manifest their consent and provide proof of their commitments for dealings via the Internet. Over the last decade, both on national and international fronts, various pieces of legislation have been enacted and policies developed in order to promote the usage of electronic signatures. However, paper-based signatures are still the preferred instrument to electronic signatures for entering into contracts and commercial transactions. What are the causes of this apathy on the part of the business community? Why is there a resistance towards electronic signatures in this era of e-business? This book presents the findings of an empirical study on large public-listed Australian companies. Respondents comprised of heads of the information technology and legal departments and senior management executives.

The book is essentially divided into two parts. The first half of the book provides a comprehensive description of the functions and the technology underlying electronic signatures. Using diagrams and hypothetical examples, the chapters explain the different types of electronic signature and provide a thorough description of digital signature (the most renowned form of electronic signature) highlighting its characteristics and the various kinds in which it is available to businesses, the process involved in applying and receiving digital signature certificates and the implementation process. It also discusses a few case laws on electronics signatures and the various pieces of legislation that have gradually developed both nationally and internationally in order to regulate and facilitate the use of electronic signatures.

The second half of the book presents the findings of the empirical study. Six key factors are identified that potentially create a disincentive to businesses to move from the practice of manuscript signatures to the new technology of electronic signatures. These are ignorance or lack of understanding of the electronic signature technology, the prevailing culture and custom associated with manuscript signatures, complexities with the use of electronic signatures, cost of the technology, legal concerns and security concerns. The book examines each of these factors thoroughly in light of participants' responses. As security and legality were the most important concerns among the business community, separate chapters have been dedicated to these two issues.

The book concludes by summarising the main findings of the empirical study and suggests a few measures that might help overcome businesses' low usage of electronic signatures for B2B contracts.

Acknowledgement

This study has benefitted from the assistance of several individuals. I owe my deep and sincere gratitude to Professor DK Srivastava, who has been my mentor and has provided me inspiration and guidance in every step of this research. Associate Professor Bruce Thomson, St. George's University, Grenada, provided invaluable guidance and support with the methodology used in the research. Special thanks to Paul Sugden and Professor Paul von Nessen in providing constructive comments and suggestions.

I would also like to extend my appreciation to the Department of Business Law and Taxation, Monash University, for graciously providing excellent work culture, computer facilities and other administrative support. To all my friends, thank you for your encouragement and support. I also thank Sagarika Ghosh at Springer for providing me an opportunity to publish my work.

I would especially like to thank my wife, Preety. Her love, constant encouragement and support acted as a pillar of strength during my writing up of this book. My most sincere gratitude goes to my family who has given me constant and unconditional support and shared my joys and sorrows. Finally, I would like to dedicate this book to my late father Shri DN Srivastava who would have felt very proud of me today.

Contents

List of Figures and Boxes

Glossary

ABN-DSC	Australian Business Number-Digital Signature Certificate – issued to businesses and organisations that have an ABN.
Accreditation	A formal statement by an authority that a given information system, professional or organisation is approved to carry out certain duties and to perform certain functions.
AGIMO	Australian Government Information Management Office – a business group developed in the Department of Finance and Deregulation. AGIMO replaced NOIE in April 2004 taking over its functions relating to the promotion and coordination of the use of new information and communications technology to deliver Government policies, information, programs and services.
Applicant	An individual or an organisation (represented by an authorised officer) which has applied for a digital signature certificate before the keys and certificate are issued to him/it.
Asymmetric-key cryptography	See public-key cryptography.
ATO-DC	Australian Taxation Office Digital Certificate – ATO-DC is a part of closed loop PKI. They can only be used by businesses for dealing electronically with the ATO and not with other or businesses.
Authentication	The act of proving that something such as a document is true or genuine.
Authorised officer	The person who: 1. Is issued with, and accepted, keys and a digital signature certificate on behalf of the organisation 2. Is authorised by the organisation to perform the functions associated with the keys and the digital signature certificate.
B2B	Business to business: online interaction between businesses.
B2C	Business to consumer: online interaction between businesses and consumers.

B2G	Business to government: online interaction between businesses and the government.
CA	Certification authority – normally an accredited agency which, after verifying the identity of applicants and other relevant information, issues digital signature certificates to them.
Certificate applicant/applicant	A person or authorised officer of a business organisation that applies for a digital signature certificate.
Closed PKI	Compared to open PKI, it limits the use of digital signature certificates to a known set of relying parties where parties are normally contractually bound. For example, ATO-DC is a closed loop PKI.
Compromise	A violation or suspected violation of a security policy that results in an unauthorised revelation or loss of control over sensitive information.
Confidentiality	The obligation of a person not to disclose sensitive data such as his/her private key to third parties.
Cryptography	A branch of applied mathematics that involves transforming message into seemingly incomprehensible form and back again into the original and easily recognisable form.
Data	Files, programs and other information communicated, processed by or stored in a computer.
Data integrity	Data which has not been altered or damaged in an unauthorised way.
Data message	Information generated, sent, received or stored by electronic, optical or similar means.
Digital signature	One form of electronic signature that is created and verified by using cryptography.
Digital signature certificate/digital certificate	An electronic file that contains at least the following set of information: the name of the applicant or the authorised officer, details of the business including its contact address, the public key of the business, the serial number of the certificate, the validity period of the certificate and the name of the CA.
DSC/DC	See digital signature certificate/digital certificate.
ECEG	Electronic Commerce Expert Group – an expert group set up in 1998 to recommend to the attorney general the type of ETL Australia needed to adopt.
Electronic signature	Data in electronic form, affixed to or logically associated with, a data message, which may be used to identify the signatory in relation to the data message and to indicate the signatory's approval of the information contained in the data message.
Electronic signatures directive	European Union Directive on a Community Framework for electronic signatures legislation drafted in 1999 with an aim to promote e-commerce among the EU member states through uniformity.

Encryption	The process of changing ordinary text data into a garbled form (ciphertext) so that the original data either cannot be read (one-way encryption) or cannot be read without using a decryption process (two-way encryption).
EOI	Evidence of identity – evidence (e.g. documents) produced by an applicant at the time of application to substantiate his/her identity.
E-sign	*Electronic Signatures in Global and National Commerce Act 2000* – a legislation aimed to pre-empt any inconsistent state laws and ensure uniform ETL across all US states.
ETA	*Electronic Transactions Act 1999* (Cth) – Australia's federal ETL on electronic signatures. Note all Australian states and territories have adopted a similar ETL, and the discussion in this thesis is confined to the provisions of the federal ETL.
ETL	Electronic transactions law – a general term referring to laws on electronic transactions, including electronic signatures.
Gatekeeper	A strategy employed by the Commonwealth Government for the use of public-key technology.
Gatekeeper-accredited CA or RA	A CA or RA that has been accredited by Gatekeeper Competent Authority after successful evaluation in accordance with accreditation criteria.
Key	A variable value that is applied using an algorithm to the unencrypted text to produce an encrypted text or to decrypt an encrypted text.
Key generation	A process which generates private key/public key pair to a subscriber.
Key pair	A pair of asymmetric cryptographic keys (public key and a private key) – one to decrypt messages that have been encrypted using the other.
MLEC	UNCITRAL *Model Law on Electronic Commerce 1996* – a set of rules for national legislators for conducting electronic commerce.
MLES	UNCITRAL *Model Law on Electronic Signatures 2001* – a set of rules for national legislators focusing exclusively on electronic signatures.
NOIE	National Office for the Information Economy – an executive agency of the Commonwealth of Australia which was replaced by AGIMO in April 2004.
Non-Individual DC	A digital signature certificate issued to businesses and organisations which can be used to deal electronically with the Commonwealth and state entities as well as for entering into online transactions with other businesses and organisations.
Non-repudiation	Used more in a technical than legal sense, it prevents a person from denying having used his/her digital signature.

Open PKI	Open PKI deployments anticipate the widespread acceptance of digital signature certificates where relying parties may not be known and where the parties are not generally contractually bound.
Password/PIN	A string of characters used to access data stored on a computer or a PISD.
PISD	Portable Information Storage Device – a portable device on which electronic data can be stored, for example, smart card and flash disk.
PKC	See public-key cryptography.
PKI	See public-key infrastructure.
PKI entity	One of the following: 1. CA 2. RA 3. A subscriber 4. Relying party
Private key	The part of a key pair that is required to be kept secret by its owner to ensure authenticity and integrity of a data message.
Public key	The part of a key pair that can be made public and published in a digital signature certificate.
Public-key cryptography	A cryptography process that involves two keys: a private key and a public key. The two keys are unique to the user and work together as a functioning key pair. A data message encrypted with a private key can only be decrypted by the corresponding public key and vice versa.
Public-key infrastructure	The combination of hardware, software, people, policies and procedures required to create, manage, store, distribute and revoke certificates based on public-key cryptography.
RA	Registration authority – an entity in the PKI framework which, among other functions, acts for CAs to register applicants for keys and certificates.
Recipient (of a digital signature)	A person who receives a digital signature and is in a situation to rely (regardless whether such a reliance occurs) on that digital signature.
Relying party	A recipient who acts in reliance on a digital signature certificate and digital signature.
Repudiation (see also non-repudiation)	Occurs when a person denies or attempts to deny participation in all or part of an electronic transaction involving electronic signatures.
Smart card	Similar in shape and size to a bank credit card, it is embedded with a microprocessor chip, can store a larger amount of data and has powerful processing capability.
Subscriber agreement	An agreement that outlines the responsibilities of the key holder and/or organisation.

Subscriber/owner/ key holder	The authorised officer in a business organisation who holds and uses key pairs and digital signature certificate on behalf of the organisation.
The Convention	United Nations Convention on the use of electronic communications in international contracts – drafted in 2005, the law predominantly focuses on issues arising in international contracts effected by electronic means, including electronic signatures.
Token	A hardware security device that contains a user's confidential data (e.g. a private key and digital signature certificate).
UETA	*Uniform Electronic Transactions Act 1999* – legislation drafted with an aim to promote a uniform ETL across all US states.
UNCITRAL	United Nations Commission on International Trade Law – the Commission formulates and regulates international trade in cooperation with the World Trade Organisation.

Chapter 1
Introduction

The explosive growth of the Internet in the last two decades has fuelled a revolution in the way commerce is conducted. Electronic commerce allows businesses to reach out to global markets that are no longer bound by geography or time. Increasingly, governments, businesses and consumers are using information technology and the Internet to electronically exchange information, produce, market, buy, sell and even deliver products and services to places virtually unreachable before. Relative to traditional practices and procedures, e-commerce increases convenience and choice, fosters competition and more importantly generates new business opportunities and market efficiencies.

The advent of the Internet transformed the world of commerce in the 1990s.[1] To enable e-commerce to achieve its full potential required the use of a new mechanism that could allow online authentication. Electronic signatures,[2] in particular, digital signatures,[3] were established with the objective to authenticate and facilitate commercial transactions in the electronic environment. However, one key issue facing global communication and trade was the legal recognition of electronic signatures

---

[1] In 2007, on average, 95 % of medium and large businesses in OECD countries and 85 % of businesses in non-OECD countries were using the Internet. On average, about four out of five businesses with 10 or more employees in OECD countries had a broadband connection in 2007, and three out of four had their own website. On average, one-third of such businesses used the Internet for purchasing and 17 % for selling goods and services.

[2] '"Electronic signature" is defined as data in electronic form in, affixed to or logically associated with, a data message, which may be used to identify the signatory in relation to the data message and to indicate the signatory's approval of the information contained in the data message'. See UNCITRAL *Model Law on Electronic Signatures 2001* art 2(a).

[3] Digital signature is a type of electronic signature, which is 'created and verified by using cryptography, the branch of applied mathematics that concerns itself with transforming messages into seemingly unintelligible form and back into the original form'. See UNCITRAL, *Guide to Enactment of the UNCITRAL Model Law on Electronic Signatures* (2001) [36]. http://www.uncitral.org/pdf/english/texts/electcom/mlelecsig-e.pdf. at 5 August 2011. Note a detailed explanation of these technologies is provided in Chap. 2.

A. Srivastava, *Electronic Signatures for B2B Contracts: Evidence from Australia*,
DOI 10.1007/978-81-322-0743-6_1, © Springer India 2013

so that they would emulate the same assurance and trust that traditional paper-based signature offered. This required the crafting of a legal framework.

The mid-1990s marked the emergence of a few legislative enactments governing electronic transactions. The first legislation was enacted in 1995 by the United States (US) State of Utah.[4] This was a technology-specific legislation that focused solely on cryptography-based digital signatures. The same year California passed its own legislation[5] using a more minimalist and technology-neutral, market-based approach.[6] These two model laws were later adopted by several other US states and countries.[7]

However, no matter what systems or legal principles were adopted at a state or national level, to promote global e-commerce, there was a need for a mechanism to provide international recognition to electronic signatures. In an attempt to create a more harmonised set of laws, several initiatives were implemented at both regional and global levels. The European Union (EU) enacted the Electronic Signatures Directive in 1999 to ensure consistency and legal validity of electronic signatures within its member states.[8] At a global level, the United Nations Commission on International Trade Law (UNCITRAL) has provided model laws that offer a legislative guide to countries on the framing of their national electronic signature legislation.[9] Typically, legislation have taken one of three types of approaches[10]: a minimalist or technology-neutral approach where any technology can be used as an electronic signature provided it satisfies the legal function of a signature,[11] a digital signature

[4] R J Richards, 'The Utah Digital Signature Act As "Model" Legislation: A Critical Analysis' (1999) 17(3) *The John Marshall Journal of Computer & Information Law* http://www.jcil.org/journal/articles/217.html at 12 September 2011.

[5] See *California Secretary of State, California Digital Signature Regulations: California Government Code Section 16.5*, http://www.sos.ca.gov/digsig/code-section-16-5.htm at 28 January 2011.

[6] See note 10 for the definition of technology-neutral or minimalist approach legislation.

[7] The US states such as Minnesota, Mississippi and Missouri followed the Utah model. Other states such as Alabama, Arizona, Colorado, Connecticut and Delaware followed the Californian model. Note that all of these legislation were superseded by the *Uniform Electronic Transactions Act 1999* (UETA) and the *Electronic Signatures in Global and National Commerce Act 2000* (E-Sign). This has been discussed in detail in Chap. 3.

[8] See *Directive 1999/93/EC of the European Parliament and of the Council of 13 December 1999 on a Community Framework for Electronic Signatures [2000] OJ L13/13*. The text of the Directive can be found at http://eur-lex.europa.eu/LexUriServ/LexUriServ.do?uri=CELEX:31999L0093:EN:HTML at 12 May 2011.

[9] See UNCITRAL *Model Law on Electronic Commerce 1996* and *Model Law on Electronic Signatures 2001*. The text of these model laws can be found on the UNCITRAL website at http://www.uncitral.org/uncitral/en/uncitral_texts/electronic_commerce/1996Model.html and http://www.uncitral.org/uncitral/en/uncitral_texts/electronic_commerce/2001Model_signatures.html at 15 January 2011.

[10] See Minyan Wang, 'Do the Regulations on Electronic Signatures Facilitate Electronic Commerce? A Critical Review' (2007) 23 *Computer Law & Security Report* 32; Paul R Schapper, Mercedes Rivolta and Joao Veiga Malta, 'Risk and Law in Authentication' (2006) 3(1) *Digital Evidence Journal* 10; Babette Aalberts, and Simone van der Hof, 'Digital Signature Blindness' (2000) 7 *The EDI Law Review* 1.

[11] Most common law countries have adopted a minimalist approach legislation. These include the USA, the United Kingdom (UK), Canada and New Zealand. Note the legal functions of a signature have been discussed in detail in Chap. 2.

or technology-specific approach[12] that recognises the use of only digital signatures[13] and lastly a two-pronged approach that provides an evidentiary presumption in favour of validity of an electronic signature if the parties use specific technologies, in particular, digital signatures, issued by recognised certification authorities.[14]

Both at national and international level, several policies have been developed by governments to provide a legal framework for promoting the usage of electronic signatures. Yet, anecdotal evidence and reports in the media indicate that there has been a very low usage of the technology worldwide. A 2006 progress report on the EU Electronic Signatures Directive expressed concern with regard to the slow take-up of digital signatures among its 25 member states.[15] 'The reluctant take-up of electronic signature tools is slowing down the growth of trade in goods and services via the internet',[16] noted the report. Other countries such as Malaysia, Germany and Thailand have also reported low acceptance of electronic signatures in recent years.[17] Scholars in the field have expressed concern that the culture of non-acceptance of electronic signatures by individuals and businesses is hard to change.[18]

Note that while the legislation was enacted to give an impetus to e-commerce at all levels, digital signatures are mostly used, if at all, for government online

---

[12] The technology-specific approach has also been referred as a prescriptive approach in the literature.

[13] These digital signatures are usually based on public-key infrastructure (PKI). See *Digital Signature Act 1997* (Malaysia). Note some countries initially adopted a technology-specific approach but later amended their legislation to either a two-pronged or minimalist approach. For example, Italy, India and Germany, a technology-specific legislation was initially enacted but was later amended to a two-pronged approach legislation.

[14] EU's Electronic Signatures Directive is a good example of a two-pronged approach legislation. Most countries in the EU have adopted the Electronic Signatures Directive. The legislation of China is also considered as a two-pronged approach legislation. See *Electronic Signature Law 2004* (China); See also Wang, above n 10, 36.

[15] See Commission of the European Communities, *Report on the operation of Directive 1999/93/EC on a Community framework for electronic signatures* (2006). http://ec.europa.eu/information_society/eeurope/i2010/docs/single_info_space/com_electronic_signatures_report_en.pdf at 11 May 2011.

[16] Ibid.

[17] See H Saripan and Z Hamin, 'The Application of Digital Signature Law in Securing Internet Banking: Some Preliminary Evidence from Malaysia' (2011) 3 *Procedia Computer Science* 248; eGovernment, *Take-up of electronic signatures remains low in Germany* (2004) epractice.eu. http://www.epractice.eu/document/1276 at 12 March 2011; Pascale Prud'homme and Hassana Chira-aphakul, E-Commerce in Thailand: A Slow Awakening, *Thailand Law Forum*. http://thailawforum.com/articles/e-commerce.html at 14 December 2010.

[18] See Heiko Roßnagel, 'On Diffusion and Confusion – Why Electronic Signatures Have Failed'. In S Fischer-Hübner et al. (Eds) *Trust and Privacy in Digital Business* (2006) 71; Jane K Winn, 'The Emperor New Clothes: The Shocking Truth about Digital Signatures and Internet Commerce' (2001) 37(2) *Idaho Law Review* 353; Raymond Perry, 'Digital Signatures – Security Issues And Real-World Conveyancing' (2001) 151 *New Law Journal* 1100. See also in the Australian context, Drugs and Crime Prevention Committee, Parliament of Victoria, *Inquiry into Fraud and Electronic Commerce* (2004) (180). http://www.parliament.vic.gov.au/dcpc/Reports/DCPC_FraudElectronicCommerce_05-01-2004.pdf at 21 April 2011.

delivery services.[19] Anecdotal evidence shows that there has been a low usage of the technology among businesses when dealing with other businesses for contracts and commercial transactions despite governments' effort to promote it as a valid form of authentication for enabling and sealing e-commerce transactions.

Against the above background, there arises a need to understand the reasons driving businesses' reluctance to use electronic signatures. What could be the likely factors to impede the use of electronic signatures, in particular, the well-renowned digital signature technology in a regulated environment? *Why is there a lack of acceptance of electronic signatures by the business community for entering into contracts and commercial transactions with each other?*

While answering the above question, a range of subsidiary questions arises. Are businesses reluctant to use electronic signatures because of security concerns? Are they concerned about the legal implications of using the technology? Is cost an impediment? Is the technology too complex to understand and use? Or is the reluctance to use the technology emanating from an ignorance or lack of understanding of the technology and/or the legislation?

This book attempts to answer the above questions based on academic writings, case laws and an empirical study relying predominantly on views and experiences of stakeholders. The primary focus of this work is on *digital signature*, which is the most renowned and entrusted form of electronic signature. The study uses a *framework analysis* methodology and is based on a sample of 27 participants interviewed from large public-listed Australian companies.[20] Respondents comprised of heads of the information technology (IT) and legal departments and senior management (SM) executives.[21]

The outline of the book is as follows: Chapter 2 essentially provides a comprehensive description of the functions and technology underlying electronic signatures. It starts with an outline of the history and background of manuscript signature

---

[19] Drugs and Crime Prevention Committee, Parliament of Victoria, *Inquiry into Fraud and Electronic Commerce* (2004) 180. http://www.parliament.vic.gov.au/dcpc/Reports/DCPC_FraudElectronic Commerce_05-01-2004.pdf at 21 April 2011.

[20] A five-stage framework analysis method was adopted for analysing the interview data. In stage 1 (familiarisation), the author familiarised himself with the interview transcripts and obtained an overview of the collected data. In stage 2 (identifying a thematic framework), an initial coding was conducted from the issues emerging from stage 1 to set up a thematic framework. The thematic framework at this stage was only tentative, and further refining was made at subsequent stages of analysis. In stage 3 (indexing), the initial coding or in other words the thematic framework was applied to the collected data through the use of textual codes to identify those segments of the interview transcripts that reflected a particular theme. In stage 4 (charting), specific pieces of data corresponding to a particular theme were pulled out from the interview transcripts and arranged in charts with each chart representing a specific theme. After all the indexing and charting were done in accordance with the themes, in the final stage 5 (mapping and interpretation), the author examined the key characteristics of the collected data with a view to mapping and interpreting the data set as a whole. The above five steps were carried out with the help of NVivo, a software package well known for the analysis of qualitative data.

[21] Note that semi-structured interviews were conducted face-to-face or through telephone to collect participants' views on the potential issues associated with the low usage of electronic signatures.

and the various functions it serves. The discussion is then extended to electronic signatures. Next, the chapter gives a thorough description of digital signature highlighting its characteristics and the various forms in which it is available in Australia, the process involved in applying and receiving digital signature certificates and the implementation process. It then discusses other forms of electronic signature such as password, personal identification number (PIN), biometrics and e-mail. Also discussed in this section are a few cases associated with e-mail as a form of signature.

Chapter 3 is made up of two sections. The first section outlines the various legislation that were gradually developed in order to regulate and facilitate the use of electronic signatures both nationally and internationally. The next section of the chapter explores the issues raised in the literature with regard to the usage of electronic signatures, focussing on those ones, which provide insights on the lack of acceptance of the technology.

Chapter 4 examines the factors that has led or can potentially contribute to a low usage of the electronic signature technology in the business community. Six key factors are identified that can potentially create a disincentive to businesses to move from the practice of manuscript signatures to the new technology of electronic signatures. These are ignorance or lack of understanding of the electronic signature technology, the prevailing culture and custom associated with manuscript signatures, complexities with the use of electronic signatures, cost of the technology, legal concerns and security concerns. This chapter focuses on the first four factors.

Given an extensive list of security concerns regarding the electronic signature technology and its usage, Chap. 5 addresses this issue separately. It examines businesses' perceived concerns with the three basic ways electronic signatures are stored. These include the use of passwords where an electronic signature is stored on the hard disk of a computer, on portable information storage devices (PISDs) and using biometric devices. A thorough discussion and comparison of these three methods of electronic signature storage is carried out based on empirical data. Access to the Internet is prerequisite for the use of electronic signatures, and therefore, the vulnerabilities stemming from the use of the Internet are likely to be a subject of concern for businesses. Businesses' perceptions are sought in order to determine whether security risks associated with the Internet can represent a disincentive for them to use the electronic signature technology.

Chapter 6 conducts a thorough examination of the legal issues associated with electronic signatures. In particular, the following issues are explored: ignorance of the legislation governing electronic signatures, complexities arising with evidentiary matters when proving authenticity of electronic signatures in the court of law and complexities in the development of contracts with international partners because of lack of harmony in legislation across countries.

Finally, Chap. 7 summarises the main findings of the study. In light of these findings, it discusses some policy implications and proposes a few measures that if implemented may overcome businesses reluctance to use electronic signatures.

Chapter 2
From Manuscript to Electronic Signature: Background, Technology and Case Laws

History and Background of Signature

A common dictionary definition of a signature is 'the name of a person written with his or her own hand'.[1] We use our handwritten signature as a part of several of our daily life activities such as when signing for a courier delivery or when purchasing goods and services using our credit card. In the business realm, a signature also plays a very important role. It is used by businesses to enter into contracts and commercial transactions. However, it is important to note that for the enforceability of such contracts and commercial transactions, a signature is not a mandatory requirement under most laws, particularly, under English law and common law systems. Under such systems, 'the requirement for a signature originated not as a pre-requisite for the contract to be binding but for it to be enforceable in the Courts – a fine distinction'.[2]

The concept of a signature was first introduced in England in the seventeenth century. Because of political and social instability and inadequate legal procedures, a lot of opportunists had started making fraudulent claims. Some clear and concise legislative provisions were warranted to prevent such abuses, and this led to the

[1] For example, *Merriam-Webster Online Dictionary*, (2011). http://www.m-w.com/dictionary/signature at 20 January 2011.

[2] Lorna Brazell, *Electronic Signatures Law and Regulation* (2004) 14.

A. Srivastava, *Electronic Signatures for B2B Contracts: Evidence from Australia*,
DOI 10.1007/978-81-322-0743-6_2, © Springer India 2013

enactment of the *Statute of Frauds 1677* (Imp).[3] This legislation was later received in many common law countries.[4]

What may constitute a signature drew a lot of attention in the English Courts in the latter half of the nineteenth century, predominantly with regard to the execution of wills. In the case of *Jenkins v Gaisford & Thring*,[5] the court held that a mark of any kind made by the testator or someone else will meet the requirements of a legally valid signature on a will under the *Wills Act 1837* provided there are sufficient surrounding circumstances to show the intent of the testator.[6] Sir C Cresswell noted that:

> [t]he word signed ... must have the same meaning whether the signature is made by the testator himself or by some other person in his presence and by his direction. ... Whether the mark was made by a pen or by some other instrument cannot make any difference, neither can it in reason make a difference that a facsimile of the whole name was impressed on the will instead of a mere mark X.[7]

A similar issue arose in the case of *Bennett v Brumfitt*[8] whereby Sir William Bovill CJ said that a stamped signature is a good signature within the meaning of the *Statute of Frauds 1677* (Imp). The leading English authority on the form and validity of a signature is *Goodman v J Eban*[9] where the issue was whether a rubber stamp

---

[3] Of the 15 sections of the *Statute of Frauds 1677* (Imp), two have been important in the history of contracts, notably s 4 and s 17. In particular, s 4 states that 'No action shall be brought whereby to charge any executor or administrator upon any special promise to answer damages out of his own estate; or whereby to charge the defendant upon any special promise to answer for the debt, default or miscarriage of another person; or to charge any person upon any agreement made upon consideration of marriage; or upon any contract or sale of lands, tenements or hereditaments, or any interest in or concerning them; or upon any agreement that is not to be performed within the space of 1 year from the making thereof; unless the agreement upon which such action shall be brought, or some memorandum or note thereof, shall be in writing and signed by the party to be charged therewith or some other person thereunto by him lawfully authorized'. Further, s 17 states that 'No contract for the sale of goods, wares or merchandises for the price of £10 sterling or upwards shall be allowed to be good except the buyer shall accept part of the goods so sold and actually receive the same, or give something in earnest to bind the bargain or in part payment, or that some note or memorandum in writing of the said bargain be made and signed by the parties to be charged by such contract or their agents thereunto lawfully authorized'.

[4] In Australia, it is under s 24 of the *Australian Courts Act 1828* (Imp) that was passed on 25 July 1828. Section 24 states that '[a]ll laws and statutes in force within the realm of England at the time of the passing of this Act ... shall be applied in the administration of justice in the courts of New South Wales ... so far as the same can be applied within the said colonies'. The current position in Australia is as follows: Provisions of the original statute relating to guarantees and dealings in land still apply in Western Australia. Otherwise, the section has been re-enacted in whole or in part in other states and territories with only land contracts being required to be evidenced by writing in all jurisdictions. Section 17 of the original statute was repealed and re-enacted in the various Sale of Goods Acts of the respective states and territories. Note that the requirement of writing in sale of goods transactions has since been abolished in all jurisdictions except for Western Australia and Tasmania. See N C Seddon and M P Ellinghaus, *Cheshire and Fifoot's: Law of Contract* (8th ed, 2002) 734.

[5] (1863) 3 SW & TR 93. Also available at *The English Reports* (1921) CLXIV, 1208.

[6] *Wills Act 1837* (UK) c 26.

[7] *The English Reports*, above n 5, 1208.

[8] (1867) LR 3 CP 28.

[9] [1954] 1 QB 550.

could be a legally valid form of signature. In the decision, Sir Raymond Evershed MR stated that 'the essential requirement of signing is the affixing, either by writing with a pen or pencil or by otherwise impressing on the document, one's name or "signature" so as personally to *authenticate* the document'.[10] While Romer LJ said:

> The first reaction of many people, I think, would be that the impression of a name produced by a rubber stamp does not constitute a signature, and, indeed, in some sense, is the antithesis of a signature. When, however, the matter is further considered in the light of authority and also of the *function* which a signature is intended to perform one arrives, I think, at a different result.[11]

Apart from the above cases, the English Courts have also considered the legality of other forms of signature. A signature on a document impressed upon by a printing machine,[12] by typewriting[13] and by putting one's initials[14] has been accepted as a valid signature under the *Statute of Frauds 1677* (Imp). The answerback of a telex machine[15] and dividend cheques containing the printed signature of a company's secretary[16] also satisfy the statutory requirement of a signature.

In all the above cases, the critical underlying legal principle was that (a) it is the *function* that a signature performs that is important rather than the *form* it adopts and (b) by simply affixing a person's name on a document without the signatory approving and adopting the contents of the document will not constitute a legally valid signature. By not approving and adopting the contents of the document, the signatory has not effectively *authenticated* the document. Also, what is important is that the signatory intends to approve and adopt the contents of the document even if he or she does not personally affix the signature.[17] A similar practice has taken place in the Australian Courts.[18] The *Electronic Commerce Expert Group* (Australia) stated that:

> [w]ith a view to the functions that a signature performs, courts have held that signature signals endorsement or acknowledgement of the document to which the signature is

[10] Ibid., 557 (emphasis added).

[11] Ibid., 563 (emphasis added). Romer LJ also cited *Stroud's Judicial Dictionary* (3rd ed) where the definition of a signature is 'the writing, or otherwise affixing, of a person's name, or a mark to represent his name by himself or by his authority with the intention of authenticating a document as being that of, or binding on, the person whose name or mark is so written or affixed'. See also *British Estate Investment Society Ltd v Jackson (HM Inspector of Taxes)* (1956) TR 397.

[12] *Brydges (Town Clerk of Cheltenham) v Dix* (1891) 7 TLR 215.

[13] *Newborne v Sensolid (Great Britain) Ltd* [954] 1 QB 45.

[14] *Phillimore v Barry* (1818) 1 Camp 513.

[15] *Clipper Maritime Ltd v Shirlstar Container Transport Ltd* [1987] 1 Lloyd's Rep. 546. See also *Standard Bank London Ltd v Bank of Tokyo Ltd* (1995) CLC 496.

[16] *Re a debtor (No 2021 of 1995), Ex parte Inland Revenue Commissioners* [1996] 2 All ER 345, 349 (Laddie J).

[17] Note that it may not be necessary for the signatory to affix the signature himself. It may be done by someone else with his authorisation. See *Re Whitley Partners Ltd* (1886) LR 36 ChD 337; *Halley v O'Brien* (1920) 1 IR 330. However, in those circumstances where a document is required by the statute to be made under a person's hand or signed by him, the person needs to personally sign it either with his name or a mark, by a pen or by a stamp. See *Electronic Rentals Pty Ltd v Anderson* (1971) 124 CLR 27, 42 (Windeyer J).

[18] *Farrelly v Hircock (No 1)* [1971] Qd R 341, 356 (Wanstall J). See also *Regina v Moore; Ex parte Myers* (1884) 10 VLR 322, 324 (Higinbotham J).

appended or which is signed, as well as identifying the party who signed. The signature does not necessarily have to be handwritten.[19]

Thus, for a signature to be legally valid, there must be an expressed or implied indication that the person who has written his/her name or initials on a document has approved and adopted the contents of the document.[20] In other words, the purported signature will be valid if it can provide *evidence of authentication* of the document by the signatory, that is, satisfy the evidentiary function.[21]

Meeting the Law's Functional Requirement

As shown above, the legal stance under the English and Australian laws purports that the validity of a signature is determined not by its form but by the function it performs. Thus, if a signature on a document is challenged in the court of law, evidence will be required to demonstrate (a) the identity of the signer affixing the signature, (b) the intention of the signer to sign the document and (c) the signer approves and adopts the contents of the documents.[22] Professor Reed considered these three requirements as the *primary* function of a signature.[23] The following section demonstrates how these three evidential requirements apply to a manuscript signature.

---

[19] Electronic Commerce Expert Group, *Electronic Commerce: Building the Legal Framework-Report of the Electronic Commerce Expert Group to the Attorney General* (1998) [2.7.29]. http://www.ag.gov.au/www/agd/agd.nsf/Page/e-commerce_Electroniccommerceexpertgroupsrepor at 15 January 2011.

[20] See Sharon A Christensen, William Duncan and Rouhshi Low, 'The Statute of frauds in the Digital Age – Maintaining the Integrity of Signatures' (2003) 10(4) *Murdoch University of Electronic Journal of Law* [8]. http://www.murdoch.edu.au/elaw/issues/v10n4/christensen104.html at 24 March 2011.

[21] Electronic Commerce Expert Group, above n 19 [2.7.29], states that there are five main functions of a signature. Evidentiary function ensures the availability of admissible and reliable evidence. The other main functions of a signature are cautionary, reliance, channelling and record-keeping.

[22] Another important function that a signature performs is that the signer has authority to bind the person or entity against whom the document is to be enforced.

[23] Chris Reed, 'What is a Signature?' (2000) 3(1) *Journal of Information, Law and Technology* [3.1.2]. http://www2.warwick.ac.uk/fac/soc/law/elj/jilt/2000_3/reed at 29 January, 2011. For a detailed description of the functions a signature performs, see Stephen Mason, *Electronic Signatures in Law* (2nd ed, 2007) 20; Mark Sneddon, 'Legislating to Facilitate Electronic Signatures and Records: Exceptions, Standards and the Impact on the Statute Book' (1998) 21(2) *University of New South Wales Law Journal* 59; Adrian McCullagh, Peter Little and William J Caelli, 'Electronic Signatures: Understand the Past to Develop the Future' (1998) 21(2) *University of New South Wales Law Journal* 452; UNCITRAL, *Guide to Enactment of the UNCITRAL Model Law on Electronic Commerce* (1996) [48] [53]. http://www.uncitral.org/uncitral/en/uncitral_texts/electronic_commerce/1996Model.html at 3 July 2011; UNCITRAL, *Guide to Enactment of the UNCITRAL Model Law on Electronic Signatures* (2001) [29]. http://www.uncitral.org/pdf/english/texts/electcom/ml-elecsig-e.pdf at 5 August 2011; American Bar Association, *Digital Signature Guidelines* (1996) 4–9. http://www.abanet.org/scitech/ec/isc/dsgfree.html at 28 January 2011.

Identity of the Signer Affixing a Signature

Where a manuscript signature is affixed on a document, identifying the signatory is the most fundamental matter to be evidenced. Evidence will be adduced to show that the signature in question corresponds to that of the alleged signatory's normal signature. With the help of a handwriting analyst, the signature is compared with a sample of the signatory's signature signed naturally in other circumstances. Handwriting analysts generally look into two main aspects: pictorial representation and construction of letters. Forgers tend to focus on the pictorial details such as slope, size, and spacing but often fail to copy the way the letters are constructed such as the direction of the letters. The signature is also further verified on the basis of the attributes of the instrument used to affix the signature such as how smooth the signature has been signed and whether it is jagged or confident.[24]

Intent of the Signer to Sign the Document

Evidence will be adduced to show that the signatory who affixed his/her manuscript signature on the document had the intent to sign that document. Two cases need mention in this regard. First, in the English case of *L'Estrange v F Graucob Ltd*,[25] it was held that under the general rule with regard to signature, once a person signs a contract, he/she is bound by its terms because he/she had the intention to sign the contract. It is immaterial whether he/she read the terms of the contract or not. Scrutton LJ stated that '[w]hen a document containing contractual terms is signed, then, in the absence of fraud, or … misrepresentation, the party signing it is bound, and it is wholly immaterial whether he/she has read the document or not'.[26] This decision and principle was recently upheld by the High Court of Australia in the *Toll (FGCT) Pty Limited v Alphapharm Pty Ltd*[27] case where the Full High Court unanimously agreed on the following:

> The general rule, which applies … is that where there is no suggested vitiating element [eg duress or misrepresentation], and no claim for equitable or statutory relief, a person who signs a document which is known by that person to contain contractual terms, and to affect legal relations, is bound by those terms, and it is immaterial that the person has not read the document.[28]

On the other hand, in the *Pyror v Pyror*[29] case where a father asked his daughter to sign her husband's name as a witness to the will, the court held that the signature

---

[24] Mason, above n 23, 17.

[25] [1934] 2 KB 394. See also *Parker v South Eastern Railway Company* (1877) 2 CPD 416; *Foreman v Great Western Railway Company* (1878) 38 LT 851.

[26] Ibid., 403.

[27] (2004) 219 CLR 165. This was a unanimous decision of Gleeson CJ, Gummow, Hayne, Callinan and Heydon JJ.

[28] (2004) 219 CLR 165, 185 (emphasis added).

[29] (1860) LJR 29 NS P, M & A 114.

was not legally valid. Although the daughter had put her mark on the will, she had no intention to sign as a witness.

The Signer Approves and Adopts the Contents of the Document

The most important evidence that needs to be adduced when a manuscript signature is disputed is that the intended signatory had the intention to authenticate and adopt the contents of the document as his/her own. In the *Ringham v Hackett and Another*[30] case, Lawton LJ said that 'a printed name accompanied by a written signature was prima facie evidence that the cheque was being drawn on the account it purported to be drawn on'.[31] In another case – *Central Motors (Birmingham) Ltd v P A & SNP Wadsworth*[32] – the court held that the 'signature involve[d] a mental element and … it [was that] that distinguishe[d] it as mere writing of the name'.[33]

Electronic Signature and the Law's Functional Requirements

The emergence of the Internet as an expeditious commercial transaction tool raised concern among the business and legal community that the use of paperless signatures could be hindered by legal obstacles or by uncertainty with regard to their legal effect or validity. In a number of countries, the legislature responded to this concern by drafting their own electronic signature legislation. The drafters considered the evidential function of a manuscript signature (as described above) and incorporated similar provisions in the electronic signature legislation.[34] This is known as a functional-equivalent approach. The *Model Law on Electronic Commerce 1996* (MLEC) is an example of such legislation.[35] Consequently, the *Electronic*

---

[30] (1980) 124 SJ 201.

[31] Ibid., 202.

[32] (1982) 133 NLJ 555, Court of Appeal (Civil Division).

[33] Ibid., 555.

[34] This approach looks into what are the functions of writing and signature in a traditional paper-based document and then establishes how such functions can be satisfied in the electronic environment.

[35] UNCITRAL, above n 23 [53], states that 'Article 7 is based on the recognition of the functions of a signature in a paper-based environment. In the preparation of the Model Law, the following functions of a signature were considered: to identify a person; to provide certainty as to the personal involvement of that person in the act of signing; to associate that person with the content of a document'. Note that the enactment further states that 'in addition, a signature could perform a variety of functions, depending on the nature of the document that was signed. For example, a signature might attest to the intent of a party to be bound by the content of a signed contract; the intent of a person to endorse authorship of a text; the intent of a person to associate itself with the content of a document written by someone else; the fact that, and the time when, a person had been at a given place'.

Transactions Act 1999 (ETA) of Australia which is based on the MLEC has also adopted a functional-equivalent approach.[36] The two legislative approaches are discussed in detail in the next chapter.

Digital Signature

Among the various forms of electronic signatures, digital signature has been increasingly considered as the most secure and robust form of electronic signature[37] and is known to have 'no serious contender'.[38] Digital signature is created and verified using cryptography,[39] a branch of applied mathematics that involves transforming a message into seemingly incomprehensible form and back again into the original and easily recognisable form.[40] However, in order to understand how a digital signature functions, it is important to first understand some key terms associated with the technology. They are described below.

Key Terms Associated with a Digital Signature

Hash Function

A hash function is a process where a data message is passed through an algorithm, which can be considered as a formula or a series of mathematical steps to achieve a particular task. Applying a hash function to a data message results in a number

[36] Electronic Commerce Expert Group, above n 19 [4.5.43]. According to Christensen, Duncan and Low, under the *Statute of Frauds 1677* (Imp), one of the functions of a signature is also to ensure the integrity of the document. However, this has not been incorporated in the ETA. See Sharon A Christensen and William D Duncan and Roushi Low, 'The Statute of Frauds in the Digital Age-Maintaining the Integrity of Signatures' (2003) 10(4) *Murdoch University Electronic Journal of Law*. http://www.murdoch.edu.au/elaw/issues/v10n4/christensen104.html at 20 May 2011.

[37] Henry H Perritt Jr, 'Legal and Technological Infrastructures for Electronic Payment Systems' (1996) 22(1) *Rutgers Computer and Technology Law Journal* 1; K H Pun et al., 'Review of the Electronic Transactions Ordinance: Can the Personal Identification Number Replace the Digital Signature?' (2002) 32 *Hong Kong Law Journal* 241; Christopher P Keefe, 'A Law student's Guide to the Future of Transactions over the Internet: A Review of the Digital Signature Guidelines' (1997) 1 *Virginia Journal of Law and Technology*. http://www.vjolt.net/vol1/issue/vol1_art6.html at 28 January 2011.

[38] James Backhouse, 'Assessing the Certification Authorities: Guarding the Guardians of Secure E-Commerce' (2002) 9(3) *Journal of Financial Crime* 217, 217.

[39] Cryptography is the art and science of keeping a message secret. See 'Electronic Frontiers Australia', *Introduction to Cryptography* (2001). http://www.efa.org.au/Issues/Crypto/crypto1.html at 12 May 2011. For a history of cryptography, see David Kahn, *The Codebreakers: The Story of Secret Writing* (1996).

[40] For a comprehensive understanding of the technical procedures involved in cryptography and the various types of cryptography, see Javek Ikbel, 'An Introduction to Cryptography', in Harold F Tipton and Micki Krause (eds), *Information Security Management Handbook* (5th ed, 2004) 1333; Sharon K Black, *Telecommunications Law in the Internet Age* (2002) ch 9.

which is substantially smaller than the data message, and is called a *message digest* or *hash value*, or the digital fingerprint of the data message.[41] The process of a hash function can be considered similar to the process of creating yoghurt from milk. Milk (data message) can be converted through the use of bacteria (algorithm) into yoghurt (message digest). However, the reverse process (i.e. creating milk from yoghurt) is not possible. It is imperative to note that two identical data messages if passed through the same algorithm will give the same hash value. However, if one data message is changed even by a single letter, the hash value will change.

Key

A key in cryptography is a variable value that is applied using an algorithm to the unencrypted text to produce an encrypted text or to decrypt an encrypted text. The length of a key is measured in bits and determines the complexity in encrypting or decrypting a text in a given message. The length of a key can be considered similar to the number of levers in a padlock. The higher the number of levers (bits) a lock (algorithm) has, the greater the strength of that lock.

Symmetric-Key Cryptography

Symmetric-key cryptography is a process where a single key is shared between the sender and the recipient. The key is not known to the third person. The sender encrypts the data message to be sent to the recipient through a key and the recipient decrypts the data message through the same shared key. It works like a lock with two duplicate keys, one with the sender and another with the recipient.

Asymmetric-Key Cryptography

In asymmetric-key cryptography also known as public-key cryptography (PKC), there are two keys: a private and a public key. The two keys are unique to the user and work together as a functioning key pair. A private key can be considered as an electronically generated random number which is secret to the user just like a password or PIN. On the other hand, a public key is known to the public and can often be found on a designated web server following a similar process to finding a person's name in a telephone directory but in an online world.[42] It is important to note that unlike symmetric-key cryptography here, the keys are not duplicates but

---

[41] For more insights on the technical procedure involving hash, see Keith Pasley, 'Hash Algorithms: From Message Digests to Signatures', in Harold F Tipton and Micki Krause (eds), *Information Security Management Handbook* (5th ed., 2004) 1349.

[42] A public key is also available on a subscriber's digital certificate. This is discussed further in this chapter.

correspond to each other. A data message encrypted with a private key can only be decrypted by the corresponding public key and vice versa. A detailed technical explanation on how PKC works and its usage in digital signature is explained in Appendix A.

Certification Authority (CA)

Just as in the physical world the identity of an individual is established through the issuance of documents such as passport, identity card or credit card, the identity of an individual in cyberspace can be established through a digital signature certificate[43] issued by a CA also known as a 'trusted third party'. It is the CA that links the public and private key pair to an individual. This association is confirmed in a certificate known as a digital signature certificate. A digital signature certificate is nothing but an electronic file containing all necessary information (including public key) to identify the creator of a digital signature.[44]

Registration Authority (RA)

A RA works in association with CAs and performs the necessary checks and formalities required for the issuance of a digital signature certificate. Once the RA has completed such checks and formalities, its outcome is reported to the corresponding CA. A RA's job can be considered similar to an agent providing mobile telecommunication services to the public on behalf of a parent company. The applicant requiring a mobile connection (digital signature certificate) visits the agent's office (RA) which verifies the applicant's identity as well as performs other checks and formalities and reports it to the parent telecommunication company (CA). The parent telecommunication company (CA) then grants the applicant a mobile connection (digital signature certificate). A CA can also act as a RA.

Characteristics of a Digital Signature

A digital signature is commonly considered as the most secure and robust form of electronic signature because of its ability to ensure authentication, integrity and non-repudiation in the electronic environment. Later in this chapter is discussed

---

[43] A digital signature certificate is also referred to as a digital certificate.

[44] A digital signature certificate issued to a business is an electronic file which generally contains the following information: the name of the applicant or the authorised officer, details of the business including its contact address, the public key of the business, the serial number of the digital signature certificate, the validity period of the digital signature certificate and the name of the CA that issued the digital signature certificate.

how these functions are satisfied by a digital signature in an electronic environment. To facilitate understanding on this matter, the three functions are explained below.

Authentication

Black's law dictionary defines authentication broadly as 'the act of proving that something (as a document) is true or genuine'.[45] The identification of a sender who signed a data message is provided through his/her digital signature. It also expresses the sender's authorisation to the content of the data message and his/her intention to be legally bound by that document.[46]

Integrity

In the digital world, integrity means ensuring that a communication has not been altered in the course of its transmission. Integrity is critical to e-commerce transactions particularly where contracts are executed electronically. The recipient of a data message must be confident of its integrity before he or she can rely and act on it.[47] A data message signed using a digital signature provides this confidence. It ensures that the data message retains its entirety during transmission from the sender's computer to the recipient's computer and that any alteration is detected.

Non-repudiation

In the context of digital signature, the term non-repudiation is used more in a technical rather than legal sense. Non-repudiation means 'a property achieved through cryptographic methods which prevents an individual or entity from denying having performed a particular action'.[48] The sender of a message cannot falsely repudiate that the message was not sent by him. However, in the legal realm, a signature can always be repudiated for a number of reasons such as forgery or where the signature

[45] Bryan A Garner (ed), *Black's Law Dictionary* (8th ed, 2004), 142.

[46] For a comprehensive understanding about authentication and the various technologies through which authentication can be achieved, see Richard E Smith, *Authentication: From Passwords to Public Keys* (2002).

[47] Yee Fen Lim, 'Digital Signature, Certification Authorities and the Law' (2002) 9(3) *Murdoch UniversityElectronicJournalofLaw*[12].http://www.austlii.edu.au/au/journals/MurUEJL/2002/29.htmlat 20 June 2011.

[48] OECD, *OECD Guidelines for Cryptography Policy* (2000) Department of Justice. http://www.justice.gov/criminal/cybercrime/oeguide.htm at 10 June 2011.

is not a forgery, it was obtained by unconscionable conduct by a party to the transaction or undue influence exerted by a third party.[49] It is to be noted that where technical people use the word non-repudiation, 'it should not be mistaken that they are using it in the legal context, despite their misunderstanding that the term, in their view, should have a legal meaning'.[50]

Types of Digital Signature Certificate

As mentioned above, digital signatures are created using PKC. They are generally used within an overarching infrastructure known as public-key infrastructure (PKI). PKI can be defined as 'the combination of hardware, software, people, policies and procedures needed to create, manage, store and distribute keys and certificates based on PKC'.[51] There are many different PKIs worldwide. As this study focuses on Australia, it looks into the *Gatekeeper*[52] PKI project launched in May 1998.[53] Currently, the *Gatekeeper* PKI framework primarily facilitates government online service delivery, but digital certificates are also available to businesses through *Gatekeeper*-accredited CAs[54] for entering into contracts and commercial transactions with other businesses.[55] There are two main types of *Gatekeeper*-accredited digital signatures certificates available to businesses in Australia. These are the Non-Individual Digital Certificate (Non-Individual DC) and the Australian Business Number-Digital Signature Certificate (ABN-DSC). Non-Individual DCs and ABN-DSCs are

---

[49] McCullagh and Caelli provide an excellent overview on the distinction between the legal and technical meanings of non-repudiation. See Adrian McCullagh and William J Caelli, 'Non-Repudiation in the Digital Environment' (2000) 5(8) *First Monday*. http://firstmonday.org/issues/issue5_8/mccullagh/index.html at 28 January 2011.

[50] Mason, above n 23, 471. See also Les Owens, *Hack Proofing your Wireless Network* (2002) 87.

[51] Australian Government Information Management Office, *Gatekeeper PKI Framework: Glossary* (2009). http://www.finance.gov.au/e-government/security-and-authentication/gatekeeper/docs/Glossary.pdf at 12 May 2011.

[52] The *Gatekeeper* project was released in 1998 as the Australian Government's strategy for PKI use by the government. However, 'the strategy is now much more than a PKI scheme for Australian Government use; it also addresses industry and international needs'. See Australian Government Information Management Office, *Gatekeeper PKI Framework: Cross Recognition Policy* (2008). http://www.gatekeeper.gov.au/data/assets/file/0004/52276/Cross_Recognition_Policy.rtf at 20 May 2011.

[53] See A. Jancic and M.J. Warren, 'PKI-Advantages and Obstacles' (Paper presented at 2nd Australian Information Security Management Conference on Securing the Future, Perth, Australia, 26 November 2006); Kate Boyle, 'An Introduction to Gatekeeper: The Government's Public Key Infrastructure' (2000) 11(1) *Journal of Law and Information Science* 39.

[54] For a list of *Gatekeeper*-accredited CAs and RAs, see *Directory of Accredited Service Providers* (2012) Australian Government Information Management Office. http://www.finance.gov.au/e-government/security-and-authentication/gatekeeper/accredited/index.html at 21 February 2012.

[55] See, for example, VeriSign Authentication Services, *Gatekeeper Digital Certificates Overview* (2011). http://www.verisign.com.au/gatekeeper/overview/index.html at 17 February 2012.

available to businesses and organisations, which they can use to deal electronically with the Commonwealth and state entities (CSE) as well as for entering into online transactions (contract and commercial transactions) with other businesses and organisations that accept *Gatekeeper*-accredited digital certificates.[56] Apart from *Gatekeeper*-accredited digital signatures, under the ETA, businesses are also allowed to use other forms of electronic signature (such as PIN/password/biometrics) when dealing with each other, including digital signature certificates issued by CAs which are not necessarily *Gatekeeper* accredited.[57]

Issuance of Accredited Digital Signature Certificates

Australian businesses can either apply for a Non-Individual DC or an ABN-DSC from a *Gatekeeper*-accredited CA.[58] To apply for an accredited Non-Individual DC or an ABN-DSC, an organisation first needs to submit an online application form through a *Gatekeeper*-accredited CA's website.[59] The applicant (an authorised officer for an ABN-DSC) will then have to personally appear at a RA's office (designated by the CA) and undergo a personal identification check, that is, provide documentary proof of his/her personal information so that he/she satisfies the 'evidence of identity' (EOI) points criteria, as is required when opening a bank account. The applicant is also required to fulfil an EOI check for his/her organisation known as an organisation identification check.[60] After verification of the requisite documents, if the requirements are complied with, the RA sends its approval to the CA. Next, the CA sends an e-mail to the applicant giving instructions on how the digital signature certificate and the key pairs (private and public keys) are to be imported from the CA's website and installed on his/her computer.

Two essential building blocks for e-commerce are trust and confidence. Digital signature certificates are believed to provide both of these with a high degree of security as they include stringent identity checks prior to their issue. Thus, three

[56] For example, Non-Individual DCs and ABN-DSCs can be used with the Australian Customs Service. See VeriSign, *VeriSign Gatekeeper: Customs Digital Certificates*. http://www.verisign.com.au/gatekeeper/customs/ at 20 May 2011.

[57] As mentioned above, the researcher is not aware of any PKI set up exclusively in Australia that can be used by businesses for B2B transactions. However, the process of applying for and implementing a digital certificate would presumably be similar to that under a *Gatekeeper* accredited CA. Therefore, in the absence of any other PKI, this thesis explains the *Gatekeeper* process.

[58] For the purpose of explaining this process, the *Gatekeeper*-accredited CA, *VeriSign*, has been chosen. See VeriSign, *VeriSign Gatekeeper*. http://www.verisign.com.au/gatekeeper/overview.shtml at 23 March 2011.

[59] Ibid.

[60] The applicant/authorised officer is also required to sign the subscriber's agreement and pay the requisite fee.

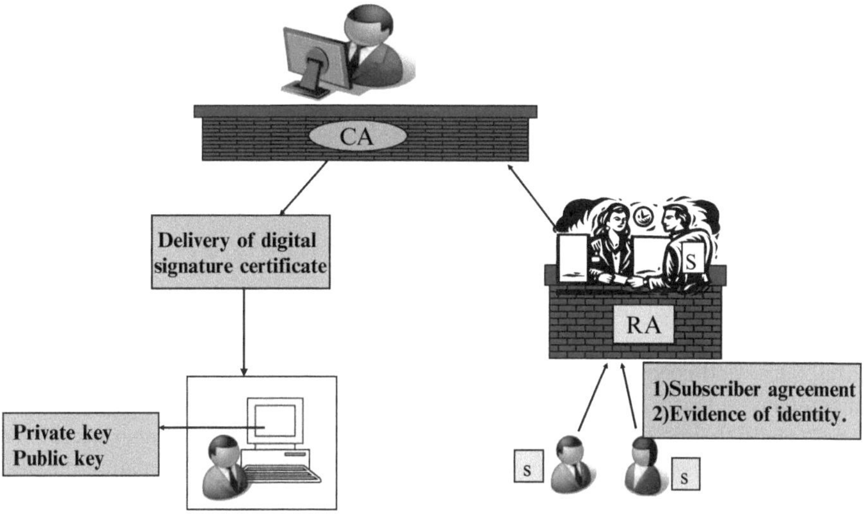

Fig. 2.1 The process of applying and receiving a digital signature certificate and key pairs

grades of Non-Individual DC are issued based on EOI checks.[61] The higher the grade, the greater the level of reliability an applicant can expect in its usage.

The applicant, now a subscriber, imports the digital signature certificate[62] and generates the key pairs in accordance with the instructions provided by the CA. The private key generated and installed by the subscriber is held in secret by the user, and nobody, not even the subscriber's CA, knows what the subscriber's private key is. However, the public key which is available on the digital signature certificate can also be made publicly available on the CA's web server. The key pairs and digital signature certificate can then be installed on the hard disk of the applicant's computer or stored on portable information storage devices (PISDs) such as a smart card or a flash disk protected via a password or a pass phrase (see Fig. 2.1).

---

[61] The personal identification check comprises the following: 50 EOI points are required for Non-Individual DC (Grade 1), 100 EOI points are required for Non-Individual DC (Grade 2) and 150 EOI points are required for Non-Individual DC (Grade 3). An ABN-DSC is treated as equivalent to a Non-Individual DC (Grade 2) for the purpose of identification and therefore requires 100 EOI points from the authorised officer of a business applying for an ABN-DSC. Similarly, the organisation identification check also needs to satisfy some EOI point criteria: Non-Individual DC (Grade 1 and Grade 2) and ABN-DSC require 1 EOI document, and Non-Individual DC (Grade 3) requires 1 EOI document along with a certificate from the Australian Business Register. For example, see VeriSign, *VeriSign Gatekeeper: Non-Individual (Type 2) Certificate*. http://www.verisign.com.au/gatekeeper/nonindividual.shtml at 23 November 2010.

[62] As mentioned in above, the digital signature certificate issued is an electronic file which generally contains the following information: the name of the applicant or the authorised officer, details of the business including its contact address, the public key of the business, the serial number of the digital signature certificate, the validity period of the digital signature certificate and the name of the CA that issued the digital signature certificate.

Once the private key is generated and stored by the subscriber, it is ready for use. The subscriber should now be able to send a data message by affixing his/her digital signature that is created through his/her private key. The following section describes this process with the help of a hypothetical example.

Implementation of a Digital Signature

The implementation of a digital signature is best illustrated using the following scenario. Let us suppose that Paul is the CEO of a multinational company in Melbourne and needs to e-mail a merger proposal to Abe, the managing director of a company in Perth. In order for Paul to use his digital signature, both organisations need to have their respective digital signature certificates from a *Gatekeeper*-accredited CA.[63] Paul wants the data message not only to contain his digital signature but also to remain confidential during transmission from his computer in Melbourne to Abe's computer in Perth.

To sign the data message (merger proposal) through the use of digital signature and to secure the data message's confidentiality, four things will be required by Paul: (1) data message to be signed, (2) hash algorithm to create message digest, (3) the sender's private key and (4) the recipient's public key. It is essential to mention here that only if the sender requires the data message to be confidential (i.e. encrypted transmission) will the public key of the recipient be required.

Paul has the merger proposal in the form of an electronic file and a hash algorithm as a software stored on his computer. Paul, as an authorised officer of his company, also has his private key from a *Gatekeeper*-accredited CA. He can access Abe's public key either by asking him to send his digital signature certificate or from the web server of Abe's *Gatekeeper*-accredited CA.[64] Figure 2.2 demonstrates how the digital signature is implemented.

First, the data message – the unencrypted merger proposal – to be sent is passed or hashed through a hashing algorithm. The message digest (output) is then locked or encrypted using Paul's private key to obtain a digital signature.[65] Once the digital signature is created, Paul has two choices. Either he can attach the digital signature to the data message and send it to Abe, the recipient, or Paul may choose to send a confidential data message to Abe.[66] However, as mentioned before, Paul would like the data message to remain confidential during its transmission from Melbourne to

---

[63] Note that a problem of interoperability may arise if the two CAs do not operate within the *Gatekeeper* PKI domain.

[64] As mentioned in above, a digital signature certificate contains a subscriber's public key.

[65] This is a reversible process. If Paul's public key is applied to the digital signature, it will generate the message digest.

[66] Note that often, the digital signature certificate is also attached to the data message so that it is easy for the recipient to know the identity and other details of the sender.

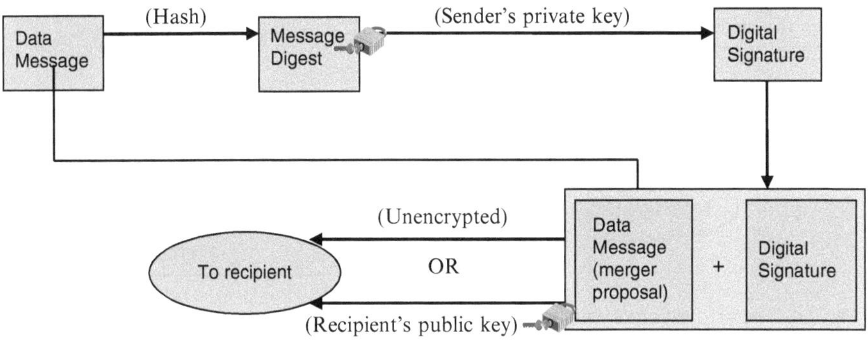

Fig. 2.2 The implementation of a digital signature

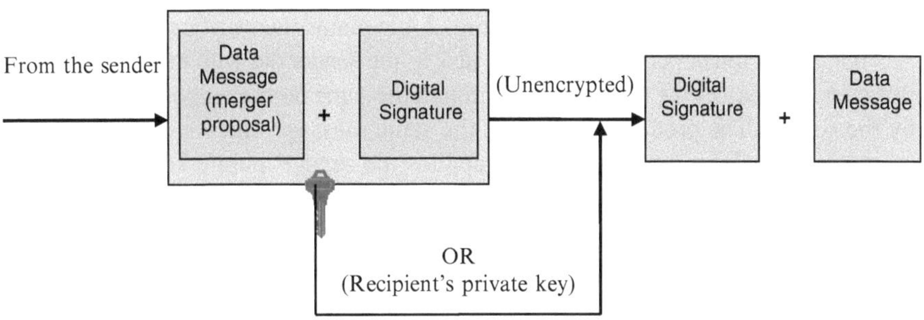

Fig. 2.3 The verification of a digital signature

Perth and that nobody other than Abe should be able to read it. In such case, the unencrypted data message together with the digital signature is locked/encrypted using Abe's public key before it is sent to him.

Once the data message affixed with Paul's digital signature reaches Abe's computer, the latter can unlock or decrypt the data message and digital signature (if an encrypted version has been sent by Paul) using his private key. This way, Abe can read the data message sent by Paul and verify that the digital signature belongs to him (see Fig. 2.3).

Achieving Authentication, Integrity and Non-repudiation Functions

As mentioned above, a digital signature is often considered to be the most secure and robust form of electronic signature because of its ability to ensure authentication, integrity and non-repudiation in the electronic environment. *Authentication* is achieved as the sender's digital signature is attached to the data message he/she would like to send. The recipient can be assured that the data message has come from the sender and not anyone else as the private key used to generate the digital signature is only known to the sender. The *integrity* of the data message can be

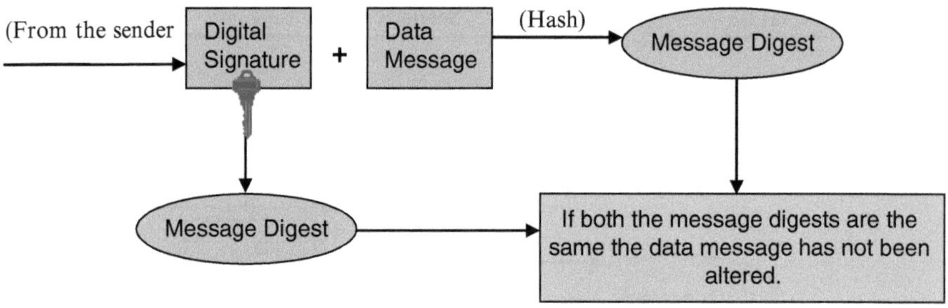

Fig. 2.4 The verification of data integrity

checked by the recipient without contacting the sender, that is, the sender can make sure that the data message has not been altered after its despatch from the sender's computer. The procedure described in Fig. 2.4 explains this verification process.

First, the recipient performs the same task as the sender did with the data message, that is, he/she passes the data message through the same hashing algorithm as applied by the sender. The product obtained is the same message digest as was generated by the sender. Secondly, the recipient applies the sender' public key to his digital signature. The product generated is another message digest. The two message digests are then compared, and if they are exactly the same, the recipient can be ensured that the message has not been altered during transmission from the sender's computer to his own.

The process or cryptography used to sign an electronic document with a digital signature also ensures *non-repudiation* from a technical standpoint. As the private key is held in secret by the user and the process involved in signing with a digital signature is highly secure, it 'can be used to prove that some kind of event or action has taken place [and] ... that ... event or action cannot be repudiated later'.[67] As mentioned above, where technical people use the word non-repudiation, it should not be mistaken that it is being used in the legal context.[68] From a legal stance, a digital signature may be repudiated.

Other Forms of Electronic Signature

Other than digital signature which is considered to be the most secure form of electronic signature, there exists a range of other electronic signatures such as password; PIN; biometric indicators in the form of fingerprint, iris scan, hand geometry and dynamic signature verification; and e-mail. However, such forms of signature are

[67] Sigfried Herda, 'Non-Repudiation: Constituting Evidence and Proof in Digital Cooperation' (1995) 17 (1) *Computer Standard and Interfaces* 69.

[68] See above, n 50.

considered valid in the eyes of the law only if they meet the functional requirements of a signature.[69] A brief outline of these various forms of electronic signature is given below. This section also highlights a few cases associated with e-mail as a form of electronic signature.

Password

A password is the most common form of electronic signature used for authentication. Passwords are generally used to log onto a computer or a network or online service. A single computer can be used by many users, each owning a username and a password. Each time a user wants to access the computer, he/she has to enter his/her username and password. The computer then checks the password file containing the list of all usernames and corresponding passwords. Only if the entry matches the username to the corresponding password will the login be successful; otherwise, the user is denied access.

However, when more than one computer is connected via a shared network and resources are stored on a remote server, passwords used to access such remote resources are generally different from those used to log onto the individual computers. For example, it is very common to use a username and a password to access a network printer or to access the Internet. In this case, the password file is stored at a centrally located server containing a list of usernames and corresponding passwords (see Fig. 2.5).

However, in both situations mentioned above (i.e. a stand-alone computer and a shared network), there is a risk that someone could access the password file that contains the list of usernames and passwords. In order to secure the password file from unauthorised access, passwords are generally encrypted or hashed through the hashing algorithm. Once passwords are hashed even if they are extracted by hackers, they are of no use because it is almost impossible to retrieve the actual password from a hashed password.[70]

PIN

PINs are generally issued by banks to their customers to allow them to access automatic teller machines (ATMs) securely and carry out a range of banking transactions. Nowadays, many other institutions issue PINs as a form of electronic signature. Figure 2.6 depicts the US Department of Education's website that provides PIN to students as a form of electronic signature.

---

[69] See above, n 23.

[70] Hashing has been discussed above in n 41.

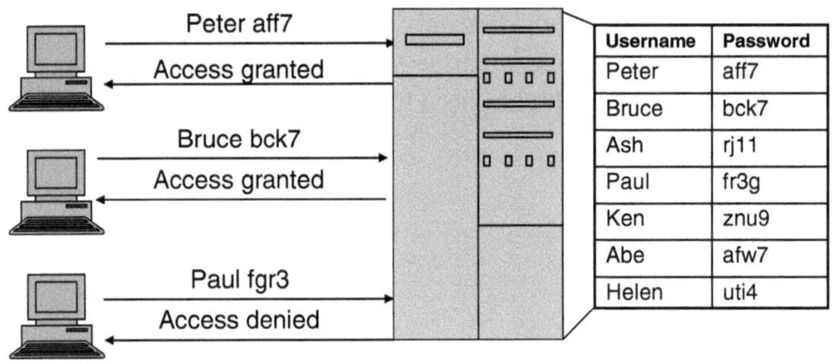

Fig. 2.5 Password verification process

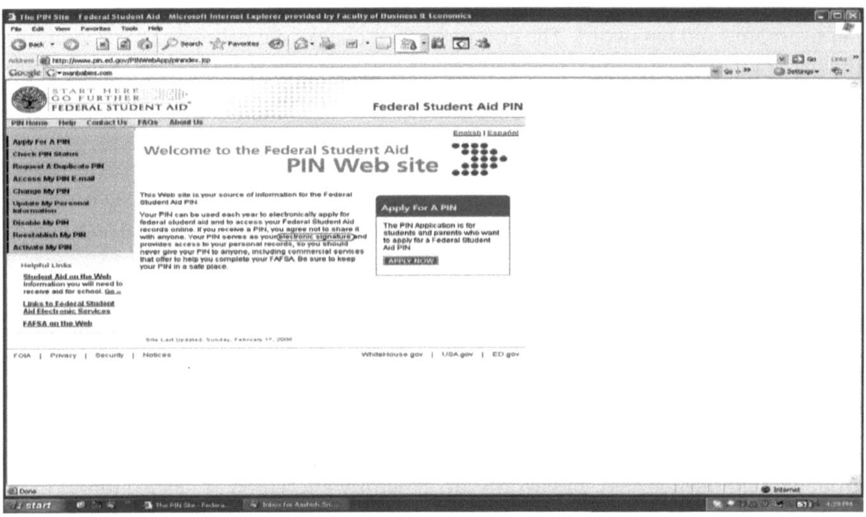

Fig. 2.6 PIN as an electronic signature (US Department of Education, *Federal Student Aid PIN* (2011). http://www.pin.ed.gov/PINWebApp/pinindex.jsp. 6 September 2011)

Biometrics

In biometrics, 'the body is the password'.[71] Biometrics uses features of the body or a person's behaviour for authentication. Some examples of biometrics are fingerprint,

[71] Smith, above n 46, 193. The history of biometrics can be traced back to 2600 BC when Egyptians used to keep records of workers' body measurements to keep a track of their identification so that they cannot apply for double rations or try to shift their workplace to easier locations. However, it was Alphonse Bertillon, the first director of Paris Bureau of Identification, who in 1892 conceived the idea of using human body measurement for classifying people. See Mark Lockie, *Biometric technology* (2002) 6, 58.

iris,[72] retina,[73] voice,[74] keystroke dynamics[75] and signature dynamics.[76] The mandatory use of such biometrics has been in existence for many years in institutions such as prisons and military bases. However, the use of biometrics as a form of electronic signature is voluntary rather than compulsory. Also, biometric indicators used as electronic signature generally represent an authentication by verification rather than an authentication by identification.[77]

How Does Biometric Work?

Biometric works in a similar way as a password. Despite the various forms of biometric fundamentally, they all function in a similar way. All biometric systems

[72] The iris is a colourful ring that surrounds the pupil of the eye. The visual texture of the iris is considered to be unique for each individual and for each eye as it is the result of the chaotic morphogenetic process that takes place during the embryonic development. The use of iris as a biometric authentication measure is a latest form of authentication. For recording the distinctive characteristics of the iris, a camera is used as a biometric reader. The camera is placed at a particular distance from the eye for recording the image of the iris. The unique characteristics of the iris is extracted and recorded in a database. Next time the user uses his or her iris for authentication, the unique characteristics of his or her iris are extracted and compared against the one that are stored in the database. See Davide Maltoni et al., *Handbook of Fingerprint Recognition* (2003) 10.

[73] The retina is the back portion of an individual's eyeball and contains a number of blood vessels. The pattern of these blood vessels is highly complex and distinctive in each and every individual. Its unique characteristics can be judged by the fact that the pattern of veins in the retina is more distinctive than any other biometric features in twins. The biometric reader for the retina is a scanning device. It requires a person to place his or her eye close to the device that shines a low powered infrared light and record the pattern of the blood vessels that is reflected. The unique characteristics of blood vessels are extracted and stored in a database. The next time the user presents his or her eye for authentication, the unique patterns of the blood vessels in the retina are again extracted and compared with those stored in a database. See Maltoni, above n 73, 10.

[74] In voice biometrics, the distinctive characteristics of the sound of a human voice are recorded. In this process, the user speaks either a selected phrase (text dependent) or any phrase (text independent) on a microphone, and the biometric reader extracts the unique sound to create a biometric signature or template which is stored in a database. Next time the user uses his or her voice for authentication, it is checked against the recorded template for a match or non-match. See Maltoni, above n 73, 11.

[75] Keystroke dynamics is based on the habitual pattern rather than the physical feature of an individual. Here, the user's rhythm pattern in typing the keys on a keyboard is analysed. A biometric signature or the template of the rhythm in which an individual types on a keyboard is extracted and stored in a database. Next time when the user types on the keyboard, the rhythm pattern is again extracted and checked against the stored database for a match or non-match. See Maltoni, above n 73, 10.

[76] Signature dynamics, as keystroke dynamics, is also based on the habitual pattern rather than the physical feature of an individual. Here, the biometric reader is the digitised pad or tablet attached to a computer, and the user is required to sign on that pad using a pen or stylus. Either the pen or the tablet is fitted with a sensor to record the pattern of the signature. The sensor records the angle at which the pen is held, the velocity and acceleration of the signature and the stroke of the signature. The template is then stored in a database and checked for verification the next time the user signs on the electronic pad. See Maltoni, above n 73, 11.

[77] To understand the difference between authentication by verification and authentication by identification, see Lockie, above n 72, 30.

use a biometric reader that collects the trait of a particular biometric. For example, a camera will be a biometric reader for an iris or retina, and a fingerprint reader will be a biometric reader for a fingerprint. The biometric reader will extract the trait associated with a particular biometric to generate a data item known as a biometric signature. This biometric signature is then stored in a database in an electronic form. Henceforth, whenever the user presents his/her biometric, it is verified with the biometric signature stored in the database.

The most common form of biometric used is the fingerprint.[78] The fingerprint pattern of an individual is in the shape of whorls, loops and arches that are formed before birth and is unique to every individual. These minutiae determine the characteristics of an individual. The unique fingerprint is extracted to create a biometric signature or template which is stored electronically in a database. Thereafter, whenever the user uses his or her fingerprint for authentication, it is checked against the stored template for a match or non-match.

E-mail

A typed name at the end of an e-mail is also a form of electronic signature. For example, 'hotmail™' provides an option to its users to create a personal signature which they can attach to their e-mail message (Fig. 2.7).

The user can enter his/her name, address or any other personal details in a designated box and that is used as a form of signature. This signature is then attached to the user's e-mails. In addition, the e-mail header which prints the sender's name and address (e.g. 'xyx', xyz@hotmail.com) can also be used as a form of electronic signature. However, both forms of signature – e-mail and e-mail header – are considered valid subject to whether they meet the law's functional requirements of a signature.[79]

E-mail as a Form of Electronic Signature: A Few Cases

The functional requirements of an e-mail as a signature have been examined before courts in a few countries. Four such cases worthy of discussion that appeared in the courts in Singapore, the UK and Australia are illustrated in this section. However, there appears to be no case law that has dealt specifically with the issue of digital signature, particularly in Australia.

[78] It was in 1893 after the UK Home Ministry Office recognised that two individuals cannot have the same fingerprint that this form of identification measure gained wide popularity especially with major law enforcement departments. See Maltoni, above n 73, 1.

[79] See above, n 23.

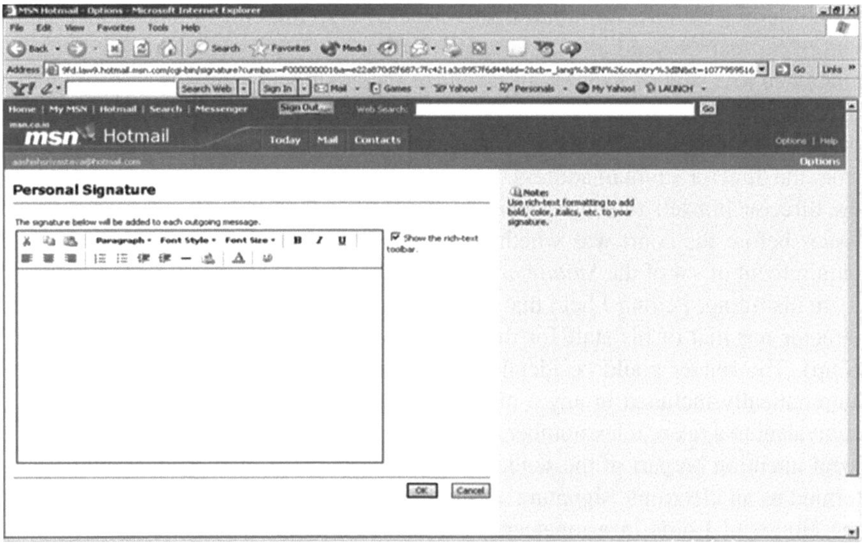

Fig. 2.7 E-mail as an electronic signature (See www.hotmail.com)

In *SM Integrated Transware Pte Ltd v Schenker Singapore (Pte) Ltd*,[80] a case dealing with negotiations of a lease by e-mail, many e-mails were exchanged between the parties. On one occasion, a staff member of the defendant company sent a memorandum through an e-mail to a staff member of the plaintiff company without typing his name or any pseudonym at the bottom of the text. His name appeared only in the header of the e-mail which printed the sender's name and address, for example, 'From: xyx xyz@abc.com.hk'. The issue raised in this case was whether or not the alleged e-mail could be considered as signed by the sender within the meaning of s 6(d) of the *Civil Law Act* of Singapore which is the modern re-enactment of the *Statute of Frauds 1677* (Imp) (c3).[81]

In this case, the court held that, in general, where law requires a signature an unsigned e-mail is usually not sufficient. It requires an electronic signature which can be in any form including a name next to the e-mail header provided there is an appropriate authentication and a suitable intention. Prakash J held that, in this particular case, the sender omitted to affix his name at the bottom of the text in the e-mail because he knew that his name would appear at the head of the message next to his e-mail address. In these circumstances, there could be no doubt that the sender of the message had the intention to be identified.[82]

---

[80] [2005] 2 SLR 651.

[81] Section 6(d) of the *Civil Law Act* (Singapore), which is the modern re-enactment of the *Statute of Frauds 1677* (Imp) (c3), states that for land lease to be enforceable, the document must be signed. Further, s 8 of the *Electronic Transactions Act 1998* (Singapore) states that where a rule of law requires a signature, an electronic signature will be satisfy the requirement.

[82] The court considered two US cases relevant to its decision: *Cloud Corporation v Hasbro Inc* 314 F 3d 289 (7th Cir, 2002); *Shattuck v Klotzbach* 14 Mass L Rep 360 (Mass Super Ct, 2001).

While in *J Pereira Fernandes SA v Mehta*,[83] the director of a company asked one of his staff to send an e-mail to its creditor's solicitors confirming a personal guarantee to a sum of £25,000 in favour of the creditor. There was no dispute that the e-mail was sent under the director's authority. The director's name did not appear in the body of the e-mail although the e-mail header showed that the message came from the director's e-mail address. This e-mail address had previously been used by the director himself to send e-mails to the creditor and his solicitors. One of the issues before the court was whether the e-mail was adequately signed as per the requirement of s 4 of the *Statute of Frauds 1677* (Imp).

In his ruling, Pelling J held that the e-mail contained neither the signature of the director nor that of his staff for the purpose of s 4 of the *Statute of Frauds 1677* (Imp). The sender could be identified only through his e-mail header which was automatically included in any e-mail communication. Such an e-mail header was equivalent to a fax or telex number and was therefore not a sufficient indicator of the legal intention on part of the sender. Consequently, the e-mail header could not be termed as an electronic signature. Pelling J relied, in particular, on the decision of the House of Lords in a nineteenth century case *Caton v Caton*[84] which distinguished between signatures providing authentication to an entire document and those that appeared incidentally or in relation to only a part of it. Pelling J noted that in the absence of evidence to contrary, an automatic insertion of the sender's e-mail address in the e-mail header by the Internet service provider (ISP) came under the incidental category. It could not be deemed as an intention to provide authentication to an entire document. However, he opined that if the name had been typed into the body of the e-mail, it would have constituted a valid signature.

The above judgement has been criticised by scholars on the ground that the name of the sender in the e-mail header, for example, abc@xyz.com, could provide appropriate and suitable authentication and thus represented a valid signature for the purpose of s 4 of the *Statute of Frauds 1677* (Imp).[85] The judgement thus gives a wrong signal that if a person fails to type his/her name in the body of his/her e-mail, he/she may no longer be held liable for his/her promise.[86]

In Australia, the case of *Faulks v Cameron*[87] dealt with e-mails as electronic signatures in a de facto relationship. In this case, the plaintiff and the defendant

---

[83] [2006] 1 WLR 1543.

[84] (1867) LR 2 HL 127.

[85] Mason argues that all the functional requirements of a signature were satisfied in the following cases: (a) the e-mail was from Mr Mehta, (b) Mr Mehta was aware of the fact that his e-mail address or e-mail header would appear in the e-mail and the recipient could reply to Mr Mehta on this e-mail address which made it a unique mark, (c) there has been many past correspondences through the same e-mail account between the parties, (d) the e-mail contained a promise from Mr Mehta or under his authority and (e) Mr Mehta admitted that the e-mail was sent by him which indicated that he approved and adopted the content of the e-mail. See Mason, above n 23, 319.

[86] Mason, above 23, 319. See also Clive Freedman and Jake Hardy, 'J Pareira Fernandes SA v Mehta: A 21st Century E-Mail Meets a 17th Century Statute', (2007) 23(1) *Computer Law & Security Report*, 77.

[87] [2004] NTSC 61.

lived together in a de facto relationship for a couple of years before their separation. In 2003, the plaintiff wrote an e-mail to her former partner informing him that she was in the process of preparing a separation statement. A series of e-mail correspondence took place between the parties in this regard. In his e-mails to the plaintiff, the defendant would type his name at the bottom of the text. In her application to the court, the plaintiff submitted that the defendant's e-mails constituted a signed separation agreement for the purposes of the *De Facto Relationship Act 1999* (NT). One of the issues before the Supreme Court of the Northern Territory was whether a name typed at the bottom of the text in an e-mail constituted an electronic signature within the meaning of the *Electronic Transactions (Northern Territory) Act 2000* (NT).

Acting Master Young concluded in this case that the printed signature on the defendant's e-mails successfully identified him and indicated his approval of the information communicated, that the method was as reliable as was appropriate and that the plaintiff consented to the method. He expressed his satisfaction that the agreement was signed for the purpose.[88] However, this decision has also been criticised for not providing enough judicial reasoning and guidance with regard to the potential scope and application of the *Electronic Transactions (Northern Territory) Act 2000* (NT).[89]

In another case – *McGuren v Simpson*[90] – the New South Wales Supreme Court examined the validity of an e-mail header as an electronic signature. In this case, Ms McGuren and Mr Simpson were in a relationship from 1992 to 2000. Mr Simpson claimed that Ms McGuren had used up his motor accident compensation without his permission and sought recovery of the money from her. On the other hand, Ms McGuren argued that she spent the money in accordance with Mr Simpson's instruction and with his approval. Mr Simpson brought his claim before the court on the basis of an e-mail sent to him by Ms McGuren in which she had admitted spending the money without his permission. The name of Ms McGuren was not written in the body of the e-mail but appeared in the e-mail header as McGuren Kim, Kim.Mcguran@air.gov.au. One of the issues in the case in the Supreme Court of New South Wales appeal was whether the e-mail sent by Ms McGuren to Mr Simpson constituted an acknowledgement that was signed for the purpose of the *Limitation Act 1969* (NSW).

In his ruling, Master Harrison held that McGuren's e-mail header was a signature for the purpose of the *Limitation Act 1969* (NSW). Master Harrison concluded that:

> As Ms McGuren's name appears in the e-mail and she expressly acknowledges in the e-mail as an authenticated expression of a prior agreement, the e-mail is recognisable as a note of a concluded agreement. Accordingly, the Magistrate was correct at law to conclude that Ms

---

[88] Ibid., 64.

[89] See Sharon Christensen, Stephen Mason and Kathryn O'Shea, 'The International Judicial Recognition of Electronic Signatures – Has your Agreement been Signed?' 2006 11(5) *Communications Law*, 150.

[90] [2004] NSWSC 35.

> McGuren signed the e-mail and that the requirements of s 54(4) of the Act were met. It was open to the Magistrate to find that Ms McGuren acknowledged the claim and she has admitted her legal liability to pay Mr Simpson that which he seeks to recover.[91]

The above decisions confirm that with regard to an electronic signature – in particular with an e-mail and in general with other forms of electronic signature – courts will examine its functions in using accepted signature principles.[92] In other words, courts will require evidence that proves the identity and the intent of the signer.

Conclusion

Digital signature, through functions such as authentication, integrity and non-repudiation, can be a reliable alternative to a manuscript signature in the online environment and provides a secure form of authentication for businesses entering into online transactions with other businesses. Other forms of electronic signature such as PIN, password, e-mail and biometrics can also be used as alternatives to manuscript signature in the electronic environment. However, more important than the form of a signature is the function it performs. The legal validity of these various forms of electronic signature relies exclusively on whether they satisfy the functional requirements of a signature.

---

[91] Ibid., [22]. In coming to the decision, Master Harrison also looked into *Halsbury's Laws of Australia* 110 Contract at [110-1030] which states that:

> Where the name of the party to be charged appears on the alleged note or memorandum, for example, because it has been typed in by the other party, the so-called 'authenticated signature fiction' will apply where the party to be charged expressly or impliedly acknowledges the writing as an authenticated expression of the contract so that the typed words will be deemed to be his or her signature. This principle has no application to a document which is not in some way or other recognisable as a note or memorandum of a concluded agreement.

[92] As discussed in above n 23.

Chapter 3
Electronic Signatures: Legislative Developments and Acceptance Issues

Historical Development of Electronic Signature

The origin of the electronic signature technology, in particular, digital signature, can be traced back to 1976 when the concept of public-key cryptography (PKC) was introduced by Diffie and Hellman.[1] Two years later, the idea of PKC was extended to third party intermediary and digital signature certificates by Kohnfelder.[2] Coincidentally, during the same period, the *United Nations Convention on the Carriage of Goods by Sea 1978 (the Hamburg Rules)* was drafted. Article 14(3) of the *Hamburg Rules* states that:

> The signature on the bill of lading may be in handwriting, printed in facsimile, perforated, stamped, in symbols, or made by any other mechanical or *electronic means*, if not inconsistent with the law of the country where the bill of lading is issued.[3]

The *Hamburg Rules*, however, did not explicitly explain the meaning of a signature affixed by *electronic means*. However, they indicated that as far back as 1978, there existed an international law that validated the use of signatures affixed by electronic means although the term *electronic signature* was not employed by the *Hamburg Rules*.

A year later, in March 1979, the *Hamburg Rules* were examined by the Working Party No. 4 (WP4) on the *facilitation of international trade procedures*.[4] The WP4

---

[1] Whitfield Diffie and Martin E Hellman, 'New Directions in Cryptography' (1976) 22(6) *IEEE Transactions on Information Theory* 644.

[2] Loren M Kohnfelder, *Towards a Practical Public-key Cryptosystem* (Bachelor's thesis, Massachusetts Institute of Technology, 1978).

[3] *United Nations Convention on the Carriage of Goods by Sea 1978* (The Hamburg Rules) Art 14(3) (emphasis added).

[4] The WP4 was set up by the *United Nations Economic Commission for Europe* while looking into the problems associated with the signing of electronic documents and its legal implications.

A. Srivastava, *Electronic Signatures for B2B Contracts: Evidence from Australia*,
DOI 10.1007/978-81-322-0743-6_3, © Springer India 2013

concluded that 'the increasing use of electronic and other automatic methods of data transfer [meant] that ... new ways of'[5] authenticating the data was required. It recommended that:

> Governments and international organisations responsible for relevant intergovernmental agreements [should] study national and international texts which embody requirements for signature on documents needed in international trade and [should] give consideration to amending such provisions, where necessary, so that the information which the documents contain may be prepared and transmitted by electronic or other automatic means of data transfer, and *the requirements of a signature may be met by authentication guaranteed by the means used in the transmission.*[6]

In 1981 the Customs Co-operation Council (CCC)[7] considered the recommendations of the WP4 and construed that instead of a handwritten signature, various technological means, such as automated data processing and the electronic data interchange (EDI), could be used by international traders for declaring customs regulatory information on entry to a country. However, they were acceptable only if they were supported by an appropriate national legislation.[8] The technological means could 'include the use of unique passwords linked to the declarant and transmitted with the information; software keys for the encryption of data; and the generation of *electronic signature*'.[9] This was probably the first time that the term *electronic signature* was legally used.

The 1980s was an era in which along with the CCC, other bodies[10] promoted the use of automatic data processing and the EDI.[11] Against such developments, it was predicted that the early 1990s would be marked by a global EDI revolution with the EDI technology replacing paper-based transactions.[12] However, some experts in this field cautioned that there were a few legal issues associated with the use of EDI that were required to be resolved before such a revolution could take place. One of these issues related to the validity of a signature in the context of the EDI.[13]

---

[5] United Nations Economic Commission for Europe, *Recommendation No. 14 Adopted by the Working Party on Facilitation of International Trade Procedures* (1979). http://www.unece.org/cefact/recommendations/rec14/rec14_1979_inf63.pdf at 30 January 2011.

[6] Ibid 85 (emphasis added).

[7] The CCC made recommendations to its members, United Nations organisations and its specialised agencies and Customs and Economic Unions.

[8] See Customs Co-operation Council, *Recommendation of the Customs Co-operation Council Concerning the Transmission and Authentication of Customs Information which is Processed by Computer*, (1981). http://www.wcoomd.org at 22 at June 2011.

[9] Ibid (emphasis added).

[10] These include the trade electronic data interchange systems, the Caddia and the Coordinated Development. See D Naezer, 'EDI: A European Perspective', in H B Thomsen and S B Wheble (eds) *Trading with EDI: The Legal Issues* (1989) 86, 89.

[11] Ibid.

[12] H B Thomsen and S B Wheble (eds) *Trading with EDI: The Legal Issues* (1989) 1.

[13] E Bergsten and R M Goode, 'Legal Questions and Problems to be Overcome', in H B Thomsen and S B Wheble (eds) *Trading with EDI: The Legal Issues* (1989) 125, 138.

They believed that an apposite technology and cryptography could authenticate a message and therefore replace manuscript signatures in the electronic environment.[14] However, the extent to which such technologies or cryptographic techniques would be legally recognised was uncertain.[15]

Similar concerns were raised with regard to the authentication of electronic communications by another eminent scholar though not in the context of EDI but rather with e-mail messages. However, unlike his predecessors, Professor Reed did not confine his argument to the authentication of a message but extended it to two authentication measures associated with a message: (a) authenticating the identity of the sender and (b) the contents of the electronic documents. He argued that in any agreement or contract, there was a possibility of two dispute scenarios.[16] The sender could either deny that he/she sent the message when he/she did or that he/she sent the message to the recipient with the alleged contents when he/she did not.[17] Professor Reed claimed that unless these two issues were addressed in the electronic environment through the use of an appropriate technology – as in the case of a handwritten signature on a physical document – it was highly unlikely that contracts or other transactions would be performed electronically.[18] He believed that the lack of these two authentication measures acted as a powerful brake in the extensive usage of electronic communication for commercial and legal purposes.[19]

National and International Initiatives in Electronic Signature Legislation

On 9 March 1995, the American state of Utah was the first jurisdiction in the world to pass an ETL known as the *Utah Digital Signature Act 1995*.[20] This legislation was technology specific as only digital signatures involving PKC issued by a licensed certification authority (CA) were considered equivalent to a manuscript signature. Approximately 6 months later, using a more liberal approach, the state of California passed its own technology-neutral ETL. The Californian law defined a digital signature as 'an electronic identifier, created by computer, intended by the party using it to

---

[14] Ibid.

[15] Ibid.

[16] Chris Reed, 'Authenticating Electronic Mail Messages – Some Evidential Problems' (1989) 52(5) *The Modern Law Review* 649, 650.

[17] Ibid.

[18] Ibid.

[19] Ibid.

[20] R J Richards, 'The Utah Digital Signature Act As "Model" Legislation. A Critical Analysis' (1999) 17(3) *The John Marshall Journal of Computer & Information Law* http://www.jcil.org/journal/articles/217.html at 12 September 2011. Please note here it refers to the previous Act which was superseded by the *Uniform Electronic Transactions Act 1999* (UETA) and the *Electronic Signatures in Global and National Commerce Act 2000* (E-Sign). See below n 57 and 68.

have the same force and effect as the use of a manual signature'.[21]Thus, this law did not make any distinction between an electronic signature and a digital signature, and anything that could replace a traditional signature in the electronic environment could be termed as a digital signature.

After Utah and California enacted their legislation, several other US states adopted their own ETLs during 1995 and 1996. Some of these, such as the Washington's *Electronic Authentication Act,* were substantially similar to the Utah Act,[22] while others such as Wyoming's ETL adopted a more liberal approach similar to the Californian legislation.[23] However, Florida's *Electronic Signature Act,*[24] which was enacted on 31 May 1996, was perhaps one of the earliest ETLs that defined and distinguished the term electronic signature from digital signature. It described an electronic signature as 'any letters, characters, or symbols, manifested by electronic or similar means, executed or adopted by a party with an intent to authenticate a writing'[25] and a digital signature as a type of electronic signature that uses an asymmetric cryptosystem.[26] The Act clearly favoured the digital signature approach and outlined a framework with regard to the use of digital signatures.[27]

A further development in the field of electronic signatures was marked by a comprehensive dossier prepared by the American Bar Association (ABA) on digital

---

[21] *California Secretary of State, California Digital Signature Regulations: California Government Code Section 16.5,* http://www.sos.ca.gov/digsig/code-section-16-5.htm at 28 January 2011. Please note here it refers to the previous Act which was superseded by the *Uniform Electronic Transactions Act 1999* (UETA) and the *Electronic Signatures in Global and National Commerce Act 2000* (E-Sign). See below n 57 and 68.

[22] The US states such as Minnesota, Mississippi and Missouri followed the Utah model. All of these states' legislation have been superseded by the *Uniform Electronic Transactions Act 1999* (UETA) and the *Electronic Signatures in Global and National Commerce Act 2000* (E-Sign). See below n 57 and 68.

[23] The US states such as Alabama, Arizona, Colorado, Connecticut and Delaware followed the Californian model. All of these states' legislation have also been superseded by the *Uniform Electronic Transactions Act 1999* (UETA) and the *Electronic Signatures in Global and National Commerce Act 2000* (E-Sign). See below n 57 and 68.

[24] *Electronic Signature Act 1996* (Florida). http://www.bocaagency.com/MLS/Electronic%20Signature%20Act%20of%201996.htm at 25 January 2011. Please note here also it refers to the previous Act which was superseded by the *Uniform Electronic Transactions Act 1999* (UETA) and the *Electronic Signatures in Global and National Commerce Act 2000* (E-Sign). See below n 57 and 68.

[25] Ibid § 4(4).

[26] Ibid § 4(3).

[27] Later on in order to provide uniformity across all US states, two technology-neutral initiatives were adopted: the *Uniform Electronic Transactions Act 1999* (UETA) and the *Electronic Signatures in Global and National Commerce Act 2000* (E-Sign). Both the Acts aimed to provide a uniform e-signature law for the use of e-signature and records. See below n 57 and 68. See also John S Stolz and John D Cromie, 'E-Commerce Gets a Boost with E-Sign' (2001) 10(4) *Business Law Today.* http://www.abanet.org/buslaw/blt/bltmar01cromiestolz.html at 12 July 2011.

signatures in 1996 known as the *Digital Signature Guidelines*.[28] The guidelines dissipated the confusion that long existed among legal, IT and business professionals as to what is the difference between an electronic signature and a digital signature. The guidelines stated that:

> [t]he term 'electronic signature' is sometimes used, generally with a meaning including all legally recognisable signatures under the currently prevalent, broad definitions of 'signature' U.C.C. § 1–201(39) (1990). An 'electronic signature' thus includes digital signatures ... as well as digitised images of paper-based signatures, typed notations such as 's/James Jones', and perhaps addressing information such as the 'From' headers in electronic mail.[29]
>
> From an information security viewpoint, these simple 'electronic signatures' are distinct from the 'digital signatures' described ... in the technical literature, although 'digital signature' is sometimes used to mean any form of computer-based signature.[30]

In an attempt to promote e-commerce at a global level and provide legal recognition and greater certainty to online contracts, a number of efforts were initiated by the United Nations (UN). The first of such initiatives was the *Model Law on Electronic Commerce* 1996 drafted by the United Nations Commission on International Trade Law (UNCITRAL).[31]

Model Law on Electronic Commerce 1996 (MLEC)

The aim of the MLEC was to ensure that members of the United Nations enjoyed harmonious economic relations. The MLEC provided 'essential procedures and principles for facilitating the use of modern techniques for recording and communicating information'.[32] It proposed a set of rules to national legislators that would remove legal obstacles and secure the legal environment for e-commerce. The MLEC has been very well accepted as many countries have adopted its provisions when drafting their national law on electronic commerce and electronic signatures.[33]

However, the MLEC defines neither an electronic signature nor a digital signature. It only provides certain general provisions which grant legal effect and recognition to electronically produced messages and signatures. Article 5 states that '[i]nformation shall not be denied legal effect, validity or enforceability solely on the grounds that it is in the form of a data message'.[34] Data message is defined in Art 2 to include

---

[28] American Bar Association, *Digital Signature Guidelines* (1996). http://www.abanet.org/scitech/ec/isc/dsgfree.html at 28 January 2011.

[29] Ibid 42.

[30] Ibid 3 (emphasis added).

[31] See UNCITRAL *Model Law on Electronic Commerce 1996*. The text of the *Model Law on Electronic Commerce* can be found on the UNCITRAL website at http://www.uncitral.org/uncitral/en/uncitral_texts/electronic_commerce/1996Model.html. 15 January 2011.

[32] Amelia H Boss, 'Electronic Commerce and the Symbiotic Relationship between International and Domestic Law Reform (1998) 72 *Tulane Law Review* 1931, 1954.

[33] Countries that have adopted the MLEC include Singapore, Philippines, Brunei and Australia.

[34] MLEC Art 5.

information generated, sent, received or stored by electronic, optical or similar means.[35] Note that Art 5 embodies the principle that there should not be any discrimination between paper and electronic mediums. However, it also states that its provisions should not be misinterpreted as 'establishing the legal validity of any given data message or of any information contained therein'.[36]

Article 7 of the MLEC deals with the use of signatures in the electronic environment. It states that where there is a legal requirement of a signature, such requirement is fulfilled in relation to a data message if:

1(a) A method is used to identify that person and to indicate that person's approval of the information contained in the data message.
1(b) That method is as reliable as was appropriate for the purpose for which the data message was generated or communicated, in the light of all the circumstances, including any relevant agreement.[37]

The provision in Art 7(1) (a) is similar to Professor Reed's stipulation discussed above regarding authentication measures.[38] Article 7(1) (b) imposes some additional requirements for the validity of a signature in the electronic environment. In order to determine that the method used was appropriate, several factors may be considered, including (a) the sophistication of the equipment used by the parties, (b) the nature of the trade activity and (c) the frequency at which commercial transactions take place between the parties.[39] However, under Art 7(1) (b), 'a possible agreement

[35] The term data message is defined as 'information generated, sent, received or stored by electronic, optical or similar means including, but not limited to, electronic data interchange (EDI), electronic mail, telegram, telex or telecopy': Art 2(a) MLEC.

[36] UNCITRAL, *Guide to Enactment of the UNCITRAL Model Law on Electronic Commerce* (1996) [46]. http://www.uncitral.org/pdf/english/texts/electcom/05-89450_Ebook.pdf at 3 July 2011. Further in [61], the *Guide to Enactment* states that 'under the Model Law, the mere signing of a data message by means of a functional equivalent of a handwritten signature is not intended, in and of itself, to confer legal validity on the data message. Whether a data message that fulfilled the requirement of a signature has legal validity is to be settled under the law applicable outside the Model Law'.

[37] MLEC Art 7.

[38] Reed, above n 16.

[39] UNCITRAL, above n 36, [58] states that '[i]n determining whether the method used … is appropriate, legal, technical and commercial factors that may be taken into account include the following: (1) the sophistication of the equipment used by each of the parties; (2) the nature of their trade activity; (3) the frequency at which commercial transactions take place between the parties; (4) the kind and size of the transaction; (5) the function of signature requirements in a given statutory and regulatory environment; (6) the capability of communication systems; (7) compliance with authentication procedures set forth by intermediaries; (8) the range of authentication procedures made available by any intermediary; (9) compliance with trade customs and practice; (10) the existence of insurance coverage mechanisms against unauthorised messages; (11) the importance and the value of the information contained in the data message; (12) the availability of alternative methods of identification and the cost of implementation; (13) the degree of acceptance or non-acceptance of the method of identification in the relevant industry or field both at the time the method was agreed upon and the time when the data message was communicated; and (14) any other relevant factor'.

between originators and addressees of data messages as to the use of a method of authentication is not conclusive evidence of whether that method is reliable or not'.[40]

It is worthwhile noting that Art 7(3) provides jurisdictions with an option to exclude the application of Art 7 to certain communications and transactions when drafting their electronic signature law. Also, with regard to evidentiary issues, Art 9 states that in any legal proceedings, data message should not be denied admissibility as evidence solely on the ground that it is a data message.[41]

However, a few issues have been raised with regard to the MLEC. [42] First, it does not provide a definition of an electronic signature.[43] Also, the term data message that is repeatedly used tends to create confusion because it encompasses electronic signatures affixed to an electronic communication.[44] Second, the MLEC, including Art 7, imposes certain requirements on an electronic signature to determine its validity based on a functional-equivalent approach.[45] In particular, this approach considers the functions of writing and signature in a traditional paper-based document to determine whether such functions can be satisfied in the electronic environment.[46] Third, the MLEC is a technology-neutral legislation which does not specify or recommend any particular electronic signature technology. [47]

The European Union Directive on a Community Framework for Electronic Signatures (Electronic Signatures Directive)

Wary that divergent rules on the legal recognition of electronic signatures and the accreditation of certification service providers[48] across its member states might create a significant barrier to e-commerce, the European Union (EU) enacted the *Directive on a Community Framework for Electronic Signatures* in 1999.[49] The Electronic Signatures Directive was part of a series of directives aimed at promoting e-commerce among the EU member states through uniformity.[50] The Electronic

---

[40] UNCITRAL, above n 36, [60].

[41] MLEC Art 9.

[42] Brian Fitzerald et al., *Internet and E-Commerce Law* (2007) 545.

[43] Ibid.

[44] Ibid.

[45] Ibid.

[46] Ibid.

[47] Ibid.

[48] A certification authority (CA) is also known as certification service provider in some countries particularly the European Union countries.

[49] See *Directive 1999/93/EC of the European Parliament and of the Council of 13 December 1999 on a Community Framework for Electronic Signatures [2000] OJ L13/13*. The text of the Directive can be found at http://eur-lex.europa.eu/LexUriServ/LexUriServ.do?uri=CELEX:31999L0093:EN:HTML 12 May 2011.

[50] Lance C Ching, 'Electronic Signatures, A comparison of American and European Legislation' (2002) 25 *Hastings International and Comparative Law Review* 199, 212.

Signatures Directive allows a wide range of electronic signature technologies. It defines an electronic signature as 'data in electronic form which are attached to or logically associated with other electronic data and which serve as a method of authentication'.[51] It also defines an *advanced electronic signature* as one that satisfies the following four criteria:

(a) It is uniquely linked to the signatory.
(b) It is capable of identifying the signatory.
(c) It is created using means that the signatory can maintain under his sole control.
(d) It is linked to the data to which it relates in such a manner that any subsequent change of the data is detectable. [52]

While the Electronic Signatures Directive does not specify what forms of electronic signature fall under the ambit of *advanced electronic signatures*, there is currently only one technology, namely, digital signature with public-key infrastructure (PKI), that can satisfy the above criteria. In particular, Art 5 of the Electronic Signatures Directive states that member states must ensure that only *advanced electronic signatures* which are based on a qualified certificate[53]and created by a secure signature-creation device[54]are given a presumption of validity, considered legally equivalent to a manuscript signature and admissible as evidence in legal proceedings. On the other hand, other electronic signatures shall not be given a presumption of validity, and therefore, parties shall have to prove the validity of the electronic signature and the intention of the signer to be bound by his/her signature.

In view of the legal effects of an electronic signature and *advanced electronic signatures*, scholars have argued that the Electronic Signatures Directive takes a two-tiered approach. The first tier requires member states to prohibit invalidation of electronic signatures on the ground that they are in electronic form. The second tier provides certain legal benefits and obligations to *advanced electronic signatures*.[55]

As mentioned above, the Electronic Signatures Directive implicitly recommends digital signatures by giving them a special legal status. Such recommendation is likely to enhance the use of digital signatures in its member states since individuals

---

[51] Electronic Signatures Directive Art 2(1).

[52] Electronic Signatures Directive Art 2(2).

[53] A qualified certificate is a certificate that meets specific security standards and is issued by recognised certification service providers.

[54] A 'signature-creation device means configured software or hardware used to implement the signature-creation data': Art 2(5) of the Electronic Signatures Directive.

[55] Andrew Barofsky, 'The European Commission's Directive on Electronic Signatures: Technological "Favoritism" Towards Digital Signatures' (2000) 24(1) *Boston College International and Comparative Law Review* 145, 154; Anda Lincoln, 'Electronic Signature Laws and the Need for Uniformity in the Global Market' (2004) 8(1) *Journal of Small and Emerging Business* 67, 76; Jennifer L Koger, 'You Sign, E-Sign, We all Fall Down: Why the United States Should not Crown the Market Place as Primary Legislator of Electronic Signatures' (2001) 11(2) *Transnational Law & Contemporary Problems* 491, 505.

and businesses will favour that technology which grants them higher legal protection and certainty. However, granting a special status to one particular technology has certain drawbacks. As the technology gets outdated the law becomes ineffective. In addition, it becomes a threat to other present and future technologies.[56]

The US Uniform Electronic Transactions Act 1999 (UETA)

As mentioned above, after Utah and California, several other US states adopted their own ETLs during the mid-1990s. However, there were several inconsistencies across the various legislation. The UETA, which is based on the MLEC, was enacted with the objective to address such inconsistencies.[57] To date, almost all jurisdictions in the USA have adopted the UETA either in its original form or with some amendments.[58]

The UETA is a technology-neutral legislation only applicable to transactions related to business, consumer transactions and governmental matters.[59] The aim of the UETA is to ensure that electronic signatures represent a valid method for entering into contracts. The UETA states that 'a contract may not be denied legal effect or enforceability solely because an electronic record was used in its formation'.[60] It further states that if a law requires a signature, an electronic signature satisfies that requirement.[61] An electronic signature is defined in the UETA as 'an electronic sound, symbol, or process attached to or logically associated with a record and executed or adopted by a person with the intent to sign the record'.[62] Note that the UETA focuses on the intention of the parties and thus enforces any form of electronic

---

[56] Barofsky, above n 55, 158.

[57] The text of the Act can be found on the National Conference of Commissioners on Uniform State Laws (NCCUSL) website at http://www.ncsl.org.

[58] For a current list of US states that have adopted the *Uniform Electronic Transactions Act 1999,* see the National Conference of State Legislatures, *The Uniform Electronic Transactions Act* (2008). http://www.ncsl.org/programs/lis/CIP/ueta-statutes.htm at 11 May 2011. See also Christopher William Pappas, 'Comparative US and EU Approaches to E-Commerce Regulation: Jurisdiction, Electronic Contracts, Electronic Signatures and Taxation' (2002) 31(2) *Denver Journal of International Law & Policy* 325, 341. It is believed that there still exist some inconsistencies across jurisdictions. See Allison W Freedman, 'The Electronic Signatures Act: Preempting State Law by Legislating Contradictory Technological Standards' (2001) 3 *Utah Law Review* 807.

[59] Comment 1 in § 3 of the UETA states that '[t]he scope of this Act is inherently limited by the fact that it only applies to transactions related to business, commercial (including consumer) and governmental matters. Consequently, transactions with no relation to business, commercial or governmental transactions would not be subject to this Act'. See also B A Pearlman, 'Finding an Appropriate Global Legal Paradigm for the Internet: United States and International Responses' (2001) 29(3) *Georgia Journal of International and Comparative Law* 597, 615.

[60] UETA § 7(b). Note this is similar to MLEC Art 5.

[61] UETA § 7(d).

[62] UETA § 2(8).

signature. Further, the UETA provides for the attribution and effect of an electronic record and an electronic signature. Section 9 of the UETA states that:

(a) An electronic record or electronic signature is attributable to a person if it was the act of the person. The act of the person may be shown in any manner, including a showing of the efficacy of any security procedure applied to determine the person to which the electronic record or electronic signature was attributable.
(b) The effect of an electronic record or electronic signature attributed to a person under subsection (a) is determined from the context and surrounding circumstances at the time of its creation, execution, or adoption, including the parties' agreement, if any, and otherwise as provided by law.[63]

Under the UETA, businesses need to ensure that the process (e.g. security procedure) through which an electronic signature is applied to a document is set up in a manner that the application of the signature evidences the intention of the signer. This is usually determined by the context in which the signature is applied and the surrounding circumstances.[64]

The US Electronic Signatures in Global and National Commerce Act 2000 (E-Sign)

By the end of 2000, only 22 out of the 50 US states had adopted some version of the UETA.[65] Many chose to retain their individual legislation which, however, lacked uniformity.[66] There were also a few states that had not enacted any electronic signature laws.[67] In order to avoid any inconsistent state laws and ensure uniform legislation across all its states, the US Congress passed the E-Sign.[68] E-Sign pre-empted state laws if they were inconsistent with the UETA. A state could avoid this pre-emption by adopting the official version of UETA as approved and recommended to the states by NCCUSL[69] or by adopting an electronic transactions law that established

[63] UETA § 9.

[64] Fitzerald et al., above n 42, 550. See also Thomas J. Smedinghoff, 'Seven Key Legal Requirements for Creating Enforceable Electronic Transactions' (2005) 9(4) *Journal of Internet Law* 3.

[65] Ian A Rambarran, 'I Accept, But Do They? 'The Need for Electronic Signature Legislation on Mainland China' (2002) 15 *Transnational Law* 405, 420.

[66] J E Stern, 'The Electronic Signatures in Global and National Commerce Act' (2001) 16(1) *Berkeley Technology Law Journal* 391, 399.

[67] Rambarran, above n 65, 420.

[68] See *Electronic Signatures in Global and National Commerce Act 2000* (E-Sign). The text of the Act can be found at http://frwebgate.access.gpo.gov/cgibin/getdoc.cgi?dbname=106_cong_public_laws&docid=f:publ229.106 at 22 May 2011.

[69] See above n 57.

the legal effect of *all forms* of electronic signature (i.e. does not give higher legal recognition to any particular form of technology) as defined by the E-Sign.[70]

The provisions of E-Sign reflect the core principles of the UETA.[71] It is a technology-neutral legislation similar to UETA because it does not mandate any particular technology for authentication. The technology-neutral approach allows the market to decide which technology to adopt for entering into e-commerce.[72] The E-Sign prohibits state or federal statutes from specifying any particular technology for electronic transactions.[73] It defines electronic signature exactly as UETA does, that is, an 'electronic sound, symbol, or process, attached to or logically associated with a contract or other record and executed or adopted by a person with the intent to sign the record'.[74] As with the UETA, the focus of E-Sign is on the intention of the parties and not on the technology that has been used as an electronic signature to substitute a handwritten signature in the electronic environment.[75]

While there are several similarities between UETA and E-Sign, they are also characterised by a few differences which are rather significant. E-Sign does not make provisions for the attribution and effect of an electronic record and an electronic signature. However, the UETA 'creates a framework for attributing an electronic signature'.[76] Also, under E-Sign there are certain transactions that must remain paper based such as the creation and execution of wills, codicils, testamentary trusts, court orders, notices or official court documents, cancellation or termination of utility services (including water, heat and power) and arrangements governing adoption and divorce.[77]

---

[70] Lincoln, above n 55, 74.

[71] However, it imposes additional requirements for the protection of consumers in electronic transactions. See Fitzerald et al., above n 42, 550.

[72] Amelia H Boss, Searching for Security in the Law of Electronic Commerce, (1998) 23(2) *Nova Law Review* 583, 623.

[73] Stern above n 66, 402 states that this approach was consistent with the *minimalist* principles laid down in the Framework for Global Electronic Commerce by the then president and vice president of the USA. See also William J Clinton and Albert Gore, *A Framework for Global Electronic Commerce* (1997) Technology Administration http://www.technology.gov/digeconomy/framewrk.htm at 21 March 2011.

[74] E-Sign § 7006(5).

[75] Rambarran, above n 65, 421.

[76] UETA § 9 states that: '(a) An electronic record or electronic signature is attributable to a person if it was the act of the person. The act of the person may be shown in any manner, including a showing of the efficacy of any security procedure applied to determine the person to which the electronic record or electronic signature was attributable; (b) the effect of an electronic record or electronic signature attributed to a person under subsection (a) is determined from the context and surrounding circumstances at the time of its creation, execution, or adoption, including the parties' agreement, if any, and otherwise as provided by law'.

[77] E-Sign § 7003(a)–(b).

The Model Law on Electronic Signatures 2001 (MLES)

After adopting the MLEC in 1996, the UNCITRAL decided to examine the issue of electronic signatures exclusively.[78] This led the UNCITRAL to develop the MLES[79] which dealt entirely with electronic signatures. The MLES applies where electronic signatures are used in the context of *commercial*[80] activities.[81] It is built on the fundamental principles laid down in Art 7 of the MLEC which deals with the fulfilment of the signature function in the electronic environment.[82] The MLES is also a technology-neutral legislation. However, unlike the MLEC, it provides a definition for electronic signature. Article 2(a) of the MLES defines an electronic signature as:

> data in electronic form in, affixed to or logically associated with, a data message, which may be used to identify the signatory in relation to the data message and to indicate the signatory's approval of the information contained in the data message.[83]

Article 6 of the MLES is a replication of Art 7[84] of the MLEC but inserts a new provision under Art 6(3) to indicate when an electronic signature will be considered reliable and appropriate for the purpose of that specific document.[85] Article 6(3) states that an electronic signature is considered to be reliable if:

(a) The signature-creation data are linked to the signatory.
(b) The signature-creation data were, at the time of signing, under the control of the signatory.
(a) Any alteration to the electronic signature, made after the time of signing, is detectable.

---

[78] UNCITRAL, *Guide to Enactment of the UNCITRAL Model Law on Electronic Signatures* (2001). http://www.uncitral.org/pdf/english/texts/electcom/ml-elecsig-e.pdf at 5 August 2011.

[79] See UNCITRAL *Model Law on Electronic Signatures 2001*. The text of the MLES can be found on the UNCITRAL website at http://www.uncitral.org/uncitral/en/uncitral_texts/electronic_commerce/2001Model_signatures.html at 15 January 2011.

[80] The term commercial has been given a very broad meaning under the MLES. The *Guide to Enactment of the UNCITRAL Model Law on Electronic Signatures*, above n 78, [87] states that '[t]he term "commercial" should be given a wide interpretation so as to cover matters arising from all relationships of a commercial nature, whether contractual or not. Relationships of a commercial nature include, but are not limited to, the following transactions: any trade transaction for the supply or exchange of goods or services; distribution agreement; commercial representation or agency; factoring; leasing; construction of works; consulting; engineering; licensing; investment; financing; banking; insurance; exploitation agreement or concession; joint venture and other forms of industrial or business cooperation; carriage of goods or passengers by air, sea, rail or road'.

[81] MLES Art 1.

[82] *Guide to Enactment of the UNCITRAL Model Law on Electronic Signatures*, above n 78, [7]. See also above n 37.

[83] MLES Art 2(a).

[84] See above n 37 for Art 7 of the MLEC.

[85] MLES Art 6(3).

(b) Where a purpose of the legal requirement for a signature is to provide assurance as to the integrity of the information to which it relates, any alteration made to that information after the time of signing is detectable.[86]

Further, Art 7 of the MLES allows the enacting state to determine which electronic signatures satisfy the provisions of Art 6. Although both the MLEC and the MLES are technology neutral, the latter has been specifically drafted with PKI (i.e. digital signatures and certification authorities) in mind.[87] Thus, the MLES defines the duties and standards of care for entities (such as the signatory, the certification authority and the relying party) in the PKI infrastructure.

Article 8 of the MLES provides guidelines regarding the conduct of the signatory. When using a signature-creation data for creating a legally binding signature, the signatory must, among other requirements, exercise *reasonable care*[88] to avoid its unauthorised use[89] and without undue delay inform any person relying on that signature that it has been compromised. Articles 9 and 10 address certain requirements for the conduct and trustworthiness of certification authorities.[90] Article 11 of the MLES provides for the conduct of the relying parties. Relying party is defined as 'a person that may act on the basis of a [digital signature] certificate or an electronic signature'.[91] Article 11 states that the relying party shall bear the legal consequences of its failure to take reasonable steps to verify the reliability of an electronic signature[92] or the suspension/revocation of a certificate supporting the electronic signature.[93]

The Australian Electronic Transactions Act 1999 (Cth) (ETA)

In Australia, an *Electronic Commerce Expert Group* (ECEG) was established in 1998 primarily to 'ensure that Australian business is given the opportunity to be at the forefront of electronic commerce'.[94] The ECEG's task was to identify the legal problems that businesses may potentially face when entering into online transactions and to recommend to the attorney general the type of legislative regime Australia

[86] MLES Art 6(3) (a)–(d). However, Art 6(4) does not restrict any person to prove to establish in any other way the appropriateness and reliability of the electronic signature in question.

[87] *Guide to Enactment of the UNCITRAL Model Law on Electronic Signatures*, above n 78, [12][28].

[88] The issue of *reasonable care* has been discussed by a few scholars. See below n 197.

[89] MLES Art 8(1) (a) and (b).

[90] Note these requirements are similar to those laid down in the Electronic Signatures Directive. See above n 49.

[91] MLES Art 2(f).

[92] MLES Art 11(a).

[93] MLES Art 11(b).

[94] Electronic Commerce Expert Group, *Electronic Commerce: Building the Legal Framework-Report of the Electronic Commerce Expert Group to the Attorney General* (1998) [Overview]. http://www.ag.gov.au/www/agd/agd.nsf/Page/e-commerce_Electroniccommerceexpert-groupsreport at 15 January 2006.

should adopt to regulate the use of electronic signatures. In March 1998, the ECEG submitted a report to the attorney general describing electronic signatures as one of the most complex issues associated with e-commerce. Due to a lack of any uniform legislative approach internationally on usage and validity of electronic signatures, laying down a detailed legislative model was discouraged.[95]

On the basis of the ECEG report, Australia enacted a technology-neutral legislation in 1999 known as the ETA.[96] The ETA is a federal legislation, and states and territories have adopted similar electronic signature and transactions legislation.[97] The provisions of the ETA are based on the MLEC. The ETA thus adopts a similar functional-equivalent approach and does not define the term electronic signature.[98] However, it lays down the requirements for signatures in s 10 of the Act. Section 10 states that if under a law of the Commonwealth, the signature of a person is required; that requirement is taken to have been met in relation to an electronic communication if:

(a) In all cases, a method is used to identify the person and to indicate the person's approval of the information communicated.
(b) In all cases, having regard to all the relevant circumstances at the time the method was used, the method was as reliable as was appropriate for the purposes for which the information was communicated.
(c) If the signature is required to be given to a Commonwealth entity, or to a person acting on behalf of a Commonwealth entity, and the entity requires that the method used as mentioned in paragraph (a) be in accordance with particular information technology requirements, the entity's requirement has been met.
(d) If the signature is required to be given to a person who is neither a Commonwealth entity nor a person acting on behalf of a Commonwealth entity, the person to whom the signature is required to be given consents to that requirement being met by way of the use of the method mentioned in paragraph (a). [99]

---

[95] Ibid.

[96] The text of the Act can be found on the Attorney General's Department website at http://www.comlaw.gov.au/comlaw/Legislation/ActCompilation1.nsf/0/11866D05A55BE8F6CA25730200002C72?OpenDocument at 15 February 2011.

[97] These legislation are *Electronic Transactions Act 2000* (NSW), *Electronic Transactions Act 2000* (SA), *Electronic Transactions Act 2000* (Tas), *Electronic Transactions Act 2000* (ACT), *Electronic Transactions Act 2003* (WA), *Electronic Transactions (Victoria) Act 2000* (Vic), *Electronic Transactions (Queensland) Act 2000* (Qld) *and Electronic Transactions (Northern Territory) Act 2000* (NT).

[98] However, s 3 of the ETA defines electronic communication. Note the ETA is argued to be a *light-touch* legislation because it does not define electronic signatures. See Fitzerald et al., above n 42, 552.

[99] Note, however, the ETA has recently been amended in accordance to the United Nations Convention on the Use of Electronic Communications in International Contracts 2005. Section 10 of the ETA that lays down the requirement for a signature in electronic environment is now similar to that provided in the Convention under Art 9(3), discussed in the following section. See Chap. 6 for further details.

The United Nations Convention on the Use of Electronic Communications in International Contracts 2005 (The Convention)

The Convention is the latest document in the field of electronic transactions that gives legal recognition to electronic contracts.[100] The focus of the Convention is predominantly on issues arising in international contracts conducted by electronic means, including electronic signatures. One major distinction from UNCITRAL's earlier two model laws is that the Convention is 'an instrument that is binding under international law upon states … that choose to become party to that instrument'.[101] A state that has become a party to the Convention is only permitted to depart from its provisions 'if the Convention permits reservations to be taken to its provisions'.[102] Member states are required to sign the Convention in order to become a party. In contrast to the Convention, it is neither a requisite for member states to sign the model laws nor are they binding. Instead, a 'model law is created as a suggested pattern for law-makers in national governments to consider adopting as part of their domestic legislation'.[103] As with the MLEC, the Convention does not define an electronic signature. However, it does define the terms *communication*,[104] *electronic communication*[105] and *data message*,[106] which are important for the use of electronic communications in international contracts.

Article 9(3) of the Convention specifically deals with the issue of signatures. In fact it reiterates the basic provision set down in Arts 6, 7 and 8 of the MLEC relating to the criteria for establishing functional equivalence between electronic communications and paper documents and between electronic authentication methods and handwritten signatures. It states that where the law requires that a communication or a contract should be signed by a party, that requirement is met if:

(a) A method is used to identify the party and to indicate that party's intention in respect of the information contained in the electronic communication.
(b) The method used is either:

---

[100] See UNCITRAL, *2005 – United Nations Convention on the use of Electronic Communications in International Contracts* (2005). http://www.uncitral.org/uncitral/en/uncitral_texts/electronic_commerce/2005Convention.html at 10 June 2011.

[101] UNCITRAL, *FAQ – UNCITRAL Texts* http://www.uncitral.org/uncitral/en/uncitral_texts_faq.html#model at 13 May 2011.

[102] Ibid.

[103] See above n 100.

[104] 'Communication means any statement, declaration, demand, notice or request, including an offer and the acceptance of an offer, that the parties are required to make or choose to make in connection with the formation or performance of a contract:' Art 4(a) of the Convention.

[105] 'Electronic communication means any communication that the parties make by means of data messages': Art 4(b) of the Convention.

[106] 'Data message means information generated, sent, received or stored by electronic, magnetic, optical or similar means, including, but not limited to, electronic data interchange, electronic mail, telegram, telex or telecopy:' Art 4(c) of the Convention.

(i) As reliable as appropriate for the purpose for which the electronic communication was generated or communicated, in the light of all the circumstances, including any relevant agreement; or
(ii) Proven in fact to have fulfilled the functions described in subparagraph *(a)* above, by itself or together with further evidence.[107]

While the above article looks quite similar to Art 7 of the MLEC,[108] it is augmented by an additional provision featuring as Art 9(3) (b). As per this provision, the method used under Art 9(3) does not need to be reliable and appropriate if it can be proven to have fulfilled the functions described in Art 9(3) (a) by itself or together with further evidence.

Electronic signatures represent an important tool for promoting e-commerce and international trade. The above section showed that a number of legislation have been developed both at national and international levels in an attempt to provide legal recognition to electronic signatures and facilitate their usage. However, these pieces of legislation also feature a number of salient differences. Despite such differences, the core message that emerges from the above initiatives and legislative developments is that electronic signatures have the same legal status as handwritten signatures in the electronic environment.

Acceptance Issues with Electronic Signatures

The legal developments in the realm of electronic signatures discussed above highlight the significance of the technology for the enhancement of global e-commerce. While governments and law framers have put in significant efforts to regulate and facilitate the use of the electronic signature technology through the enactment of various legislation, there still appears to be a low usage. The following section examines some of the issues raised in the literature.

Lack of Acceptance of Electronic Signatures

Despite significant efforts made by authorities to promote the use of electronic signatures as an alternative to pen and ink signatures, there still appears to be slow take-up of the technology.[109] Vogel claimed that '[h]ardly an area of law shows such

[107] Article 9(3) of the Convention.

[108] See above n 37 for a discussion on Art 7 of MLEC.

[109] Heiko Roßnagel 'On Diffusion and Confusion-Why Electronic Signatures Have Failed', in S Fischer-Hübner et al. (eds) *Trust and Privacy in Digital Business* (2006) 71. See also Asina Pornwasin, 'Drive for Greater Use of Digital Signatures' 8 January 2008 *The Nation*. http://www.nationmultimedia.com/2008/01/08/technology/technology_30061450.php at 10 May 2011; eGovernment, *Take-Up of Electronic Signatures Remains Low in Germany* (2004) epractice.eu.

imbalance between legislation and application as electronic signatures. The use of such signatures is essentially unknown'.[110] He noted that all earlier expectations with regard to the usage of electronic signatures had been disappointing and despite the technological and legal framework being well established for electronic signatures, the 'killer application that [would] launch the use of [such] signature devices seem to be yet undiscovered'.[111] A 2006 progress report on the operation of the 1999 EU Electronic Signatures Directive showed that there was a very low and disappointing take-up of advanced or qualified electronic signatures such as digital signatures in the European countries.[112]

Ackerman and Davis as well as Perry claimed that the usage of electronic signatures has been abysmally low.[113] Very few people seem to own digital signature certificates, and a therefore 'lack of widespread adoption of digital signature-based electronic commerce' was noted.[114] Perry remarked that the culture of non-acceptance of electronic signatures is unlikely to change and '[r]ather more worryingly the same observation seems to apply to businesses'.[115] He said that 'despite widespread promotion accompanied by tremendous enthusiasm for its potential',[116] the digital signature technology has not taken off in the business community. Winn shared Perry's views and noted that 'years of experimentation ha[d] revealed that digital signatures [were] poorly suited for use as a substitute for manual signature'[117] and that millions of dollars and ample amount of time spent on promoting the digital signature technology had been unable to encourage its widespread usage.[118]

---

http://www.epractice.eu/document/1276 at 12 March 2008; Commission of the European Communities, *Commission Frustrated that People Ignore Digital Signatures* (2006) OUT-LAW. COM. http://www.out-law.com/page-6751 at 22 May 2008; Prud'homme, Pascale and Chira-aphakul, Hassana, *E-Commerce in Thailand: A Slow Awakening*, Thailand Law Forum. http://thailawforum.com/articles/e-commerce.html at 14 December 2011.

[110] Hans-Josef Vogel, 'E-Commerce: Directives of the European Union and Implementation in German Law', in D Campbell and S Woodley (eds) *E-Commerce: Law and Jurisdiction* (2000) 29, 64.

[111] Ibid.

[112] Commission of the European Communities, *Commission Frustrated that People Ignore Digital Signatures* (2006) OUT-LAW.COM. http://www.out-law.com/page-6751 at 22 May 2011.

[113] M S Ackerman and D T Davis, 'Privacy and Security Issues in E-Commerce', in D C Jones (ed) *New Economy Handbook* (2003), 922; Raymond Perry, 'E-Conveyancing: Problems Ahead?' (2001) 151 *New Law Journal* 215, 215.

[114] Ackerman and Davis, above n 112, 922.

[115] Perry, above n 112, 219.

[116] Perry, above n 112, 219.

[117] Jane K Winn, 'The Emperor's New Clothes: The Shocking Truth about Digital Signatures and Internet Commerce' (2001) 37(2) *Idaho law Review* 353, 383.

[118] Ibid.

Ignorance and Confusion with the Terms Electronic Signature and Digital Signature

The terms electronic signature and digital signature have often been used interchangeably resulting in a great amount of misunderstanding. Aalberts and Hof remarked that such unfortunate terminological confusion has led to a wide range of laws and regulations worldwide, creating a legislative chaos.[119]

Difficulty in Understanding the Digital Signature Technology

Dumortier and Eecke claimed that the term digital signature is confusing.[120] 'Using cryptographic keys to sign a document is more difficult to explain and understand', and the 'abstract, almost invisible nature of the digital signature technique' was noted as one of the obstacles to widespread acceptance by end users.[121] Gripman believed that most people are unaware of the digital signature technology and the inherent benefits that it provides.[122] Schultz also remarked that there is a high level of ignorance about the digital signature technology.[123] He claimed that 'even the so called experts may not know the basics of encryption'.[124] Concurring with Schultz, Tuesday remarked that such ignorance exists at all levels. It is a fairly common belief among companies' directors that a digital signature is nothing but a scanned image of a handwritten signature.[125] Giving a few examples of situations where a digital signature had been wrongly believed to be a scanned image of a handwritten signature, Sharky also claimed that there is an immense lack of awareness among individuals as to what actually a digital signature is.[126]

---

[119] Babette Aalberts and Simone van der Hof, 'Digital Signature Blindness' (2000) 7 *The EDI Law Review* 1, 9.

[120] J Dumortier and Patrick V Eecke, 'The European Draft Directive on a Common Framework for Electronic Signature' (1999) 15(2) *Computer Law & Security Report* 106.

[121] Ibid 107.

[122] David L Gripman, 'Electronic Document Certification: a Primer on the Technology Behind Digital Signatures' (1999) 17(3) *The John Marshall Journal of Computer & Information Law* 769.

[123] Eugene Schultz, 'The Gap between Cryptography and Information Security' (2002) 21(8) *Computers & Security* 674.

[124] Ibid 675.

[125] Vince Tuesday, *User Indifference Thwarts Electronic Signature effort* (2002) Computerworld. http://www.computerworld.com/securitytopics/security/story/0,10801,67303,00.html at 28 January 2012.

[126] *Shark Tank: Not exactly what the doctor ordered* (2003) Computerworld. http://blogs.computerworld.com/sharky/20030129 at 22 March 2011.

Digital Signature Versus Other Forms of Electronic Signature: Which Is Better?

Digital signature has been increasingly considered as the most secure and robust form of electronic signature.[127] The use of digital signatures is regarded as the best method to secure electronic payments and thus an appropriate response to online forgery.[128] Digital signatures can also protect credit card numbers, credit and bank information and other sensitive information from hackers.[129] Anderson and Closen found that '[a]mong the many Internet security issues facing lawmakers, a partial solution that has come to the forefront is the use of digital signature to authenticate documents'.[130] Digital signatures may not be the final solution to authentication technologies but certainly have 'no serious contender'.[131]

Koger claimed that under E-Sign, the exchanges of e-mail or faxes can be inferred as an e-contract.[132] According to her, 'what is to prevent a person from pointing to an e-mail message that you may have sent and then claiming that you signed it because your name appeared as the sender of the e-mail message?'[133] She further argued that without the use of digital signatures for securing data integrity, it would be very difficult for businesses to safeguard themselves against fraud.[134] The neutral technologies cannot guarantee data integrity, and such drawback may actually discourage rather than encourage the use of electronic contracts.[135]

According to Hays, legal formalities serve three important functions in a contract: *evidentiary*, *channelling* and *cautionary* functions, and for all three functions, the digital signature is superior as compared to other forms of electronic signature.[136] For instance, with regard to the *evidentiary* function, an encrypted electronic

---

[127] Henry H Perritt Jr., 'Legal and Technological Infrastructures for Electronic Payment Systems' (1996) 22(1) *Rutgers Computer and Technology Law Journal* 1; K H Pun, et al., 'Review of the Electronic Transactions Ordinance: Can the Personal Identification Number Replace the Digital Signature?' (2002) 32 *Hong Kong Law Journal* 241; Christopher P Keefe, 'A Law student's Guide to the Future of Transactions over the Internet: A Review of the Digital Signature Guidelines' (1997) 1 *Virginia Journal of Law and Technology*. http://www.vjolt.net/vol1/issue/vol1_art6.html at 28 January 2011.

[128] Perritt Jr., above n 126, 43.

[129] Keefe, above n 126.

[130] John C Anderson and Michael L Closen, 'Document Authentication in Electronic Commerce: The Misleading Notary Public Analog for the Digital Signature Certification Authority' (1999) 17(3) *The John Marshall Journal of Computer & Information Law* 833, 838.

[131] James Backhouse, 'Assessing the Certification Authorities: Guarding the Guardians of Secure E-Commerce' (2002) 9(3) *Journal of Financial Crime* 217, 217.

[132] Koger, above n 55, 511.

[133] Ibid 511.

[134] Ibid 512.

[135] Ibid.

[136] Michael J Hays, 'The E-Sign Act of 2000: The Triumph of Function over Form in American Contract Law' (2001) 76(4) *Notre Dame Law Review* 1183, 1202 (citations omitted).

document using digital signature verified by a third party (e.g. a CA) is easier to provide as evidence of contract as compared to a typed name at the end of an e-mail.[137] The *channelling* function of a digital signature makes it a more effective tool to distinguish between legal and non-legal contracts relative to other forms of electronic signature which consider any electronic transaction as a legally valid contract.[138] Finally, with regard to the *cautionary* function, a digital signature is considered more secure because the user is required to use his/her private key that he/she needs to keep as confidential.[139] Also, investing in key-pair encryption technology is expensive which is likely to remind the user of the legal seriousness associated with its use, every time he/she uses his/her digital signature.[140] On the other hand, with the electronic signature approach when one clicks the mouse on the *I-Agree* button, that act probably amounts to signing an agreement without being aware that he/she is entering into a legally binding contract.[141]

Pun et al. claimed that digital signature 'is the most secure and practical solution to signing electronic documents'.[142] They argued that the three basic requirements of a handwritten signature, namely, *authorisation*, *approval* and *no fraud,* can only be satisfied by the digital signature technology and not other forms of electronic signature such as personal identification number (PIN) and biometrics. PIN and biometrics can only satisfy the *authorisation* requirement and not the *approval* and *no fraud* requirements. Since digital signatures can *freeze*[143] the document, they can satisfy the *approval* and the *no fraud* requirements.[144] Not always is it possible for an electronic signature technology to satisfy all the functions of a traditional signature such as *cautionary* and *originality* and perhaps that is why the EU Electronic Signatures Directive has given special evidentiary status to *advanced electronic signatures*, in other words, digital signatures.[145]

Security Issues with Electronic Signatures

The security aspect of electronic signatures especially digital signatures has been widely debated particularly with regard to the storage of a private key. Angel, Davis and Perry argued that a digital signature, unlike a handwritten signature, is not an

---

137 Ibid.

138 Ibid.

139 Ibid 1208.

140 Ibid.

141 Ibid.

142 Pun et al., above n 126, 257.

143 By freeze the authors imply that any changes made to the document after the digital signature has been attached are apparent. In other words, they refer to retaining the integrity of the document.

144 Pun et al., above n 126, 252.

145 M H M Schellekens, *Electronic Signatures: Authentication Technology from a Legal Perspective* (2004) 91. For Electronic Signatures Directive, see above n 52.

inherent characteristic of the signatory and can be performed by anyone who has access to the private key.[146] Clarke pointed out another weakness of the digital signature technology. He believed that the availability of various software and hardware in the market has made it easy to break into a subscriber's computer and access his/her private key.[147] Software and hardware are also available in the market that can hack into someone else's computer systems. Such software and hardware can be purchased by anyone and used maliciously to access another person's key-strokes including passwords that are secretly e-mailed to the hacker.[148] Internet also makes computers susceptible to risk without the subscriber of the private key being aware of it.[149] For instance, he/she may unknowingly install a software from the Internet which allows a remote computer to secretly take control of his/her computer.[150] McCullagh, Little and Caelli raised alarms regarding some technological weaknesses associated with the use of electronic documents.[151] They claimed that what the signer of a digital signature sees on his/her computer monitor may not necessarily be the same in the computer's memory.[152]

The use of passwords as a means to secure a digital signature, in particular, the private key, has also been examined by a few authors. It is often argued that passwords or passphrases are not an adequate method of protecting a private key.[153] People often choose passwords that are easy to guess[154] or omit to change password at regular intervals unless forced to do so, making a private key secured behind such passwords prone to attack.[155]

A few studies have also looked into the use of smart cards for storing a private key. However, there has been mixed opinions in favour of smart card usage. Many believe that the use of portable information storage devices (PISDs) such as smart

[146] John Angel, 'Why use Digital Signatures for Electronic Commerce?' (1999) 2 *Journal of Information, Law and Technology*. http://www2.warwick.ac.uk/fac/soc/law/elj/jilt/1999_2/angel/ at 28 January 2012; Don Davis, 'Compliance Defects in Public-key Cryptography' (Paper presented at the 6th Conference on USENIX Security Symposium, Focusing on Applications of Cryptography, San Jose, California, 22–25 July 1996) 17; Perry, above n 112, 215.

[147] Roger Clarke, 'The Fundamental Inadequacies of Public Key Infrastructure' (Paper presented at the 9th International Conference on Information Systems, Bled, Slovenia, 27–29 June 2001).

[148] Stephen Mason and Nicholas Bohm, 'The Signature in Electronic Conveyancing: An Unresolved Issue?' (2003) *The Conveyancer and Property Lawyer* 460, 465.

[149] Clarke, above n 146.

[150] Clarke, above n 146.

[151] Adrian McCullagh, Peter Little and William J Caelli, 'Electronic Signatures: Understand the Past to Develop the Future' (1998) 21(2) *University of New South Wales Law Journal* 452.

[152] Ibid 464.

[153] See Stephen G Myers, 'Potential Liability under the Illinois Electronic Commerce Security Act: Is it a Risk Worth Taking?' (1999) 17(3) *The John Marshall Journal of Computer & Information Law* 909, 941; Davis, above n 145.

[154] Mason and Bohm, above n 147, 465–466; Davis, above n 145.

[155] Mason and Bohm, above n 147, 465–466.

card is a secure option for the storage of a private key.[156] Myers noted that with the usage of smart cards or cryptographic tokens, the private key never resides in the computer's memory, and therefore, an unauthorised user will not be able to retrieve it even if he/she gains access to the subscriber's computer.[157] Others argue that storing a private key on a smart card is insecure because the latter can easily be stolen.[158] Although the storage of a private key on a smart card may not be a foolproof option, it is believed that a private key stored on a secure/tamper-resistant smart card or hardware token such as a flash disk will substantially reduce the threat to key compromise.[159]

Biometrics has also been considered as another desirable option for securing a private key.[160] Bharvada argued that although smart cards can be lost or stolen and passwords and PINs can be forgotten or tampered with, biometrics is not susceptible to such problems.[161] She remarked that as biometrics becomes cheaper, powerful and more convenient to use, the way ahead could be a combination of biometrics and a private key.[162] Julia-Barceló and Vinje considered smart cards plus biometrics as a more desirable option for reducing risk associated with the loss and theft of key pairs.[163] However, Biddle remarked that the usage of smart cards particularly smart cards with biometrics to protect a private key is only a wishful thinking as these technologies are neither commercially deployed currently nor will they be in the foreseeable future.[164]

Conversely, some studies have pointed out that none of the above-mentioned methods used to protect a private key – password, smart card or biometrics – could be secure enough. Bohm, Brown and Gladman argued that 'neither PCs [personal computers], nor smart cards, biometrics or any methods currently available or likely to be available in the near future can enable a user to keep his signature key secure'.[165]

---

[156] R Julia-Barceló and T Vinje, 'Towards a European Framework for Digital Signatures and Encryption' (1998) 14(2) *Computer Law & Security Report* 79, 82; William Kuechler and Fritz H Grupe, 'Digital Signatures: A Business View' (2003) 20(1) *Information Systems Management* 19, 28; Myers, above n 152, 941.

[157] Myers, above n 152, 941.

[158] R R Jueneman and R J Robertson Jr., 'Biometrics and Digital Signatures in Electronic Commerce' (1998) 38(3) *Jurimetrics* 427, 428; Davis, above n 145.

[159] Jueneman and Robertson Jr., above n 157, 443; Davis, above n 145.

[160] Kamini Bharvada, 'Electronic Signatures, Biometrics and PKI in the UK' (2002) 16(3) *International Review of Law, Computers & Technology* 265; Julia-Barceló and Vinje, above n 155, 82; Myers, above n 152, 941.

[161] Bharvada, above n 159, 269.

[162] Bharvada, above n 159, 274.

[163] Julia-Barceló and Vinje, above n 155, 82.

[164] Bradford C Biddle, 'Legislating Market Winners: Digital Signature Laws and the Electronic Commerce Market Place' (1997) 34 *San Diego Law Review* 1225, 1235.

[165] Nicholas Bohm, Ian Brown and Brian Gladman, 'Electronic Commerce: Who Carries the Risk of Fraud' (2000) 3 *Journal of Information, Law and Technology* [13]. http://www2.warwick.ac.uk/fac/soc/law/elj/jilt/2000_3/bohm at 29 January 2012.

A few other studies have discussed the human and institutional risks associated with the use of digital signatures.[166] Technologies such as digital signature can only provide computer-to-computer security, but 'there will still be human security problems of people using someone else's computer or computer account improperly'.[167] There is also human frailty involved in the sense that many people know how to avoid losing credit cards and door keys but they still lose them.[168]

Legal Issues with Electronic Signatures

Legal issues in the context of electronic signatures have also been a subject of much discussion. Evidentiary issues such as proving electronic signatures in the court and complexities associated with the burden of proof have been debated by several scholars.

Jueneman and Robertson expressed concerns with regard to the issue of burden of proof.[169] Referring to some US ETLs which were later superseded by UETA and E-Sign, they argued that in the court of law, the burden of proof is on the plaintiff to prove that the defendant signed the document.[170] However, there are two instances in which this is altered: for a notarised signature and where a statute provides that a signature is presumed genuine in a certain circumstance, for instance, where it is made on a negotiable instrument.[171] In such cases, the burden shifts to the defendant to prove that he/she is more likely not to have signed the document.[172] They believed that the use of a security procedure such as a digital signature greatly reduces the risk of impersonation, and therefore, some electronic signature legislation (not all) create special evidentiary rule with regard to proving the originator and the content of the document. According to them, there are two schools of thought.[173] The first school is either silent on this issue or leaves it to the trier of the fact to take into consideration relevant evidence and circumstances; the second school is that if a security procedure is used, there is a rebuttable presumption that the electronic document was signed and sent by the sender and has not been altered.[174]

---

[166] See William A Hodkowski, 'The Future of Internet Security: How New Technologies Will Shape the Internet and Affect the Law' (1997) 13(1) *Computer and High Technology Law Journal* 217; Mason and Bohm, above n 147; Jueneman and Robertson Jr., above n 157.

[167] Hodkowski, above n 165, 273.

[168] Mason and Bohm, above n 147, 465.

[169] See Jueneman and Robertson Jr., above n 157.

[170] Ibid 431.

[171] Ibid 432–433.

[172] Ibid.

[173] Ibid 434–437.

[174] Ibid.

In Australia, although the law of evidence makes provisions for electronic communication including electronic signatures,[175] scholars question the efficacy of such law. McCullagh, Little and Caelli remarked that the law of evidence 'will require revision to recognise electronic transactions and signatures'.[176] On the other hand, McCullagh and Caelli looked into the issue of proving a digital signature in the court, in particular, the complexities arising with burden of proof.[177] They noted that where the public key used by a recipient verifies a digital signature in question, the burden of proof shifts from the recipient to the owner of the private key to prove that it is not his/her signature.[178] They argued that such reversal of burden of proof in the electronic environment is incorrect because the verification of the digital signature by the recipient only proves that the private key of the owner has been used to create the digital signature but not whether the owner of the private key is the actual signatory.[179] McCullagh and Caelli described three different approaches with regard to a forged signature: (a) in a paper-based environment, the burden of proof is on the relying party (or recipient) to prove that the manuscript signature is not a forgery; (b) under s 15 of the ETA, the burden of proof is on the relying party to prove that the electronic communication (electronic signature) was in fact sent by the originator (signatory); and (c) under Art 13 of the MLEC, the burden of proof is on the owner of the private key to prove that the digital signature is a forgery.[180] While in paper-based environment the signatory has personal control over the signing mechanisms, in the electronic environment the signatory has to rely on his/her private key to create a digital signature. Also, since there are various potential technical problems with transactions in the electronic environment, for example, the private key can be stolen or misused without the owner of the private key being aware, 'neither party – the signer or the recipient – is in a position to produce the necessary evidence to prove their respective case',[181] in case of fraud.[182]

Mason concurred with McCullagh and Caelli that Art 13 of the MLEC places the burden of proof on the owner of a private key to prove that the disputed signature does not belong to him. [183] Article 13(1) of the MLEC in fact originates from Art 5 of the *UNCITRAL Model Law on International Credit Transfers* which defines the

---

[175] Note the ETA and the *Evidence Act 1995* (Cth) make provisions for evidentiary issues associated with electronic signatures. A thorough discussion regarding this issue is provided in Chap. 6.

[176] McCullagh, Little and Caelli, above n 150, 465.

[177] Adrian McCullagh and William J Caelli, 'Non-repudiation in the Digital Environment' (2000) 5(8) *First Monday* http://firstmonday.org/issues/issue5_8/mccullagh/index.html at 28 January 2012.

[178] Ibid.

[179] Ibid.

[180] Ibid.

[181] Ibid.

[182] Ibid.

[183] Stephen Mason, 'The Evidential Issues Relating to Electronic Signatures-Part II' (2002) 18(4) *Computer Law & Security Report* 241.

obligation of the sender of a payment order.[184] Since a credit transfer requires a contractual agreement between the parties featuring the agreed technical procedures to be used, credit transfer provisions cannot be made applicable to digital signatures because PKI uses the open network of the Internet.[185] Mason argued that in case of a dispute with regard to an electronic signature, 'it will be for the judge to examine the evidence to determine whether it can be shown that the electronic signature in question was actually used by the owning party'.[186]

Provisions relating to legal liability have also been found to be quite complex and at times evasive. They vary across different countries and jurisdictions. While the US E-Sign does not explicitly cover the issue of liability,[187] under the Electronic Signatures Directive,[188] recognised CAs issuing a qualified digital signature certificate[189] can be liable to anyone who suffers a loss as a result of relying on his/her digital signature (advanced electronic signature) certificate.[190]

Biddle pointed out that the technology-specific ETLs such as the *Utah Digital Signature Act 1995* – which was later superseded by the UETA[191] – impose an unlimited and absolute liability on the subscriber of a digital signature where a private key is misappropriated.[192] This is so even though the subscriber exercises due care in keeping his/her private key secure. Comparing the loss of a private key in those circumstances with that of a credit card, he noted that a person whose credit card is lost is liable only to an extent of A$50 but that a subscriber of a digital signature has unlimited liability.[193] In his opinion, no rational consumer would like to bear the liability for misappropriation of his/her private key where he or she is not at fault.[194]

---

[184] Ibid 241.

[185] Ibid.

[186] Ibid.

[187] Josh Bell et al., 'Electronic Signature Regulation' (2001) 17(6) *Computer Law & Security Report* 399, 400. Koger claimed that the evidentiary issue associated with the technology-neutral legislation such as E-Sign law is a major problem given that this legislation neither creates any presumption of validity nor provides any litmus test to ascertain the intent of the signer of an electronic signature and the authenticity of the document; the burden is on the recipient to determine the authenticity of the document. See Koger, above n 55, 508.

[188] The European Union Electronic Signatures Directive has been discussed in above n 49.

[189] As mentioned above, a qualified digital signature certificate is a certificate that meets specific security standards and is issued by a recognised CA. See above n 53.

[190] The burden of proof in such circumstances is on CAs to satisfy the court that they did not act negligently. Note that because the legislation fails to make provisions for CA's financial liability, a CA can cap his liability by adding a liability ceiling limit clause to the digital signature certificate. See Michael J Osty and Michael Pulcanio, 'The Liability of Certification Authorities to Relying Third Parties' (1999) 17(3) *The John Marshall Journal of Computer & Information Law* 961; Bell et al., above n 186, 400. However, in the case of digital signatures issued by CAs that are not recognised, the liability issue will be determined in accordance with the national liability rules of the respective country within the EU. See Bell et al., above n 186, 400.

[191] UETA has been discussed in above n 58.

[192] Biddle, above n 163, 1236.

[193] Ibid.

[194] Biddle, above n 163, 1237.

Since CAs cannot prevent the misuse of a private key and also as they are unaware as for what amount of transaction with relying party has a digital signature been used, they cannot 'insure against such indeterminate losses via pricing mechanisms'.[195] While there are strong arguments for a subscriber not to use his/her digital signature, there are equally strong arguments for the recipient of a digital signature not to rely on such a signature. Consequently, a recipient may refuse to accept a digital signature because that would expose him to financial risks in the event that the subscriber has colluded with criminals or persons with vested interest. Biddle was of the view that such *liability trilemma* can only be solved by having a closed loop PKI where through contracts the rights and responsibilities of each party can be defined.[196]

Human frailty has also featured in some electronic signature legislation. Myer noted that legislation such as the *Illinois Electronic Commerce Security Act* which was also later overridden by the UETA[197] require the subscriber of a digital signature to observe a *reasonable standard of care* to protect the secrecy of a private key.[198] However, he argued that such legislation are inadequate and instead the subscriber should have the liability to take *absolute care* to protect his/her private key.[199] He believed that where a duty of *absolute care* is imposed, the subscriber will take extra preventative efforts to protect his/her private key.[200]

The Cost of Obtaining an Electronic Signature

The cost aspect of electronic signatures has also been raised by a few scholars. However, most of these studies focused on establishment cost related to PKI and CAs, and very few considered the effect of cost at the subscriber's level. Clarke remarked that obtaining of a digital signature certificate was very expensive.[201] According to Ackerman and Davis, due to high costs, only a few end users own digital signature certificates.[202] As a result, the cost factor has largely contributed to the low acceptance rate of digital signatures.[203] Perry claimed that there are other electronic signature technologies that are less expensive and which can be considered as an alternative to the digital signature technology although he did not particularly specify those alternative technologies.[204]

---

[195] Ibid.

[196] Ibid.

[197] See above n 58.

[198] Myers, above n 152, 931.

[199] Ibid 939.

[200] Ibid 924.

[201] Clarke, above n 146.

[202] Ackerman, and Davis, above n 112, 922.

[203] Ibid.

[204] Perry, above n 112, 220. However, Koger argued that there has been a decline in the cost of digital signatures. See Koger, above n 55, 512.

Is the Electronic Signature Technology Complex?

Scholars have also expressed concerns with regard to the complexity aspect of the electronic signature technology. Clarke claimed that there are a few shortcomings in PKI-based digital signatures and that the process of obtaining a digital signature certificate is extremely complex and intrusive.[205] Bell et al. advocated that a 'reliable PKI still needs to be developed by commercial enterprises'.[206] Schultz noted that the encryption technology underlying digital signatures is not user friendly and this has resulted in a reluctance to use the technology and at times its outright rejection.[207] On the other hand, Roßnagel argued that an average user does not need to know the basics of encryptions to use digital signatures just as a user uses an automated teller machine (ATM) without any understanding of the underlying processes and security measures.[208] All that is essential is that the technology is easy to use and understand.

Comparison of Various ETLs

Several scholars have examined national and international ETLs, in particular, the US E-Sign. According to Hartley and Watson, E-Sign has achieved the goal of providing a consistent legal framework with regard to the use, acceptance and legality of electronic transactions but has left many practical details for businesses to sort out.[209] The interplay between E-Sign, UETA and other state-level ETLs in the USA has also been examined by scholars.[210] Ramage claimed that US businesses are reluctant to go for any particular type of electronic signature technology since none has been recommended by these ETLs. She observed that 'perhaps businesses would be more inclined to use electronic signatures if there were a specific technology'[211] proposed by legislation.

Various cross comparisons of ETLs have been conducted by scholars. Berman, Bell et al. and Koger compared E-Sign with the EU Electronic Signatures Directive

---

[205] Clarke, above n 146.

[206] Bell et al., above n 186, 402.

[207] Schultz, above n 122, 675.

[208] Roßnagel, above n 108, 77.

[209] Jennifer A Hartley, 'Electronic Signatures and Electronic Records in Cyber-Contracting' (2003) 49(1) *The Practical Lawyer* 51, 51. See also Mike Watson, 'E-Commerce and E-Law; Is Everything E-okay? Analysis of the Electronic Signature in Global and National Commerce Act' (2001) 53(4) *Baylor Law Review* 803.

[210] Jeanne R Ramage, 'Slow to Sign Online' (2001) 23 *Pennsylvania Lawyer* 32; Donald C Lampe, 'The Uniform Electronic Transactions Act and Federal ESIGN Law: An Overview' (2001) 55 *Consumer Finance Law Quarterly Report* 255; Adam R Smart, 'E-Sign Versus State Electronic Signature Laws: The Electronic Statutory Battleground' (2001) 5 *North Carolina Banking Institute* 485; Steven Domanowski, 'E-Sign: Paperless Transactions in the New Millennium' (2001) 51(2) *DePaul Law Review* 619.

[211] Ramage, above n 209, 34.

and ETLs of some other jurisdictions.[212] Bell et al. noted that the E-Sign is both narrow and broad in its scope. It is narrow in the sense that it mandates the usage of electronic signatures but leaves it to the market to decide other issues such as the type of technology. It is broad in the sense that it is not only confined to electronic signatures but also validates the usage of electronic records. In contrast, the Electronic Signatures Directive is more comprehensive as it does not only deal with electronic signatures but also provides regulatory and organisational structure for advanced electronic signatures, that is, digital signature.[213] Koger claimed that the Electronic Signatures Directive gives presumption of legal validity to electronic signatures and extra legal certainty to advanced electronic signatures. By failing to provide legal certainty to users of digital signatures, E-Sign is likely to hamper e-commerce between the US and EU countries. She noted that E-Sign was adopted mainly as a result of businesses lobbying the US legislature for a technology-neutral legislation. However, in doing so, they failed to anticipate that the 'minimalist legislation could end up being detrimental to their cause'.[214] In a cross comparison of a few ETLs,[215] Blythe noted that the UK and the US ETLs are too minimalist in nature and require some kind of stringency as with the Electronic Signatures Directive.[216] Visoiu discussed some of the ETLs passed by EU countries such as Romania, Hungary, Poland, Czech Republic and Bulgaria and noted that most of these laws are more or less in conformity with the Electronic Signatures Directive.[217]

Prescribing a Global Regulatory Framework for Electronic Signatures

Koger argued that the three different types of legislative approaches worldwide (i.e. technology specific, minimalist and two-prong) complicate rather than facilitate the growth of international trade.[218] Berman emphasised that there is a need to

---

[212] Andrew B Berman, 'International Divergence: The 'Keys' to Signing on the Digital Line – The Cross-Border Recognition of Electronic Contracts and Digital Signatures' (2001) 28 *Syracuse Journal of International Law and Commerce* 125; Christina Spyrelli, 'Electronic Signatures: A Transatlantic Bridge? An EU and US Legal Approach Towards Electronic Authentication' (2002) 2 *Journal of Information, Law and Technology*. http://www2.warwick.ac.uk/fac/soc/law/elj/jilt/2002_2 at 29 January, 2012. Bell et al., above n 186; Koger, above n 55.

[213] Bell et al., above n 186, 400.

[214] Koger, above n 55, 515.

[215] In particular, the MLEC, the MLES, the *Electronic Communications Act 2000* (UK), the Electronic Signatures Directive, the E-Sign and the UETA were compared.

[216] Stephen E Blythe, 'Digital Signature Law of the United Nations, European Union, United Kingdom and United States: Promotion of Growth in E-Commerce with Enhanced Security' (2005) 11(2) *Richmond Journal of Law and Technology* 6, 18.

[217] Daniel F Visoiu, 'Digital Signature Legislation in Central Europe' (2002) 30(3) *International Business Lawyer* 109, 111. For ETLs in Belgium and Dutch jurisdictions, see J Dumortier and Eecke, above n 119; Schellekens, above n 144.

[218] Koger, above n 55, 493.

harmonise ETLs through a global regulatory framework.[219] On the other hand, Braley claimed that a global regulatory framework for electronic signatures is not viable. She believed that one global model law is probably impracticable. Her suggestion was that countries should individually make efforts by rendering their laws as easy and harmonious as possible so that e-commerce succeeds across international boundaries.[220] Carr remarked that although UNCITRAL has played a major role in the harmonisation of electronic signature laws, the provisions regarding the procedural and liability rules in the MLES are not comprehensive enough to attain the desired harmonisation.[221]

Conclusion

This chapter comprised two main segments. The first segment provided an outline of the historical development of electronic signatures and some key legislation that were enacted nationally and internationally. In particular, it described the origin of electronic signature, notably digital signature, and how it had gradually been enhanced and recognised as a more acceptable form of signature. It also provided an overview of the development in the mid-1990s of the first legislation in the USA to regulate the use of electronic signatures and the successive plethora of legislation, model laws, directive and convention that have been enacted across countries in order to further facilitate their use.

The second part of this chapter focused on the key issues that have been raised by scholars with regard to the use of electronic signatures. In particular, a wide spectrum of concerns have been expressed both from technical and legal perspectives of the technology such as the following: the technology involves confusing terminologies, it is expensive, it is complex, it is fraught with security and legal risks, and there is a lack of harmony in the legislation governing electronic signatures across jurisdictions. These concerns can be considered as potential factors that contribute to the slow take-up of electronic signatures.

---

[219] Berman, above n 211, 155. Swire and Litan, however, suggest a supranational agreement on digital signature technology. See generally Peter P Swire and Robert E Litan, *None of your Business: World Data Flows, Electronic Commerce, and the European Privacy Directive* (1998) 206.

[220] Sarah Wood Braley, 'Why Electronic Signatures can Increase Electronic Transactions and the Need for Laws Governing Electronic Signatures' (2001) 4(2) *Law and Business Review of the Americas* 417, 443.

[221] Indira Carr, 'UNCITRAL & Electronic Signatures: A Light Touch at Harmonisation' (2003) 1(1) *Hertfordshire Law Journal*, 14, 25.

Chapter 4
The Electronic Signature Technology: Potential Issues with Regard to Its Usage

One obvious question that arises is as follows: do businesses feel the need to change from the use of manuscript signatures to electronic signatures? And therefore, does the low usage result from a lack of need to change to the new technology? The answer to this question could have shed important insights on the issue of low usage. However, as shown later in this chapter, there exists a general ignorance or lack of knowledge about the electronic signature technology in the business community. With such a high level of ignorance and misunderstanding about the technology, and its risks and benefits, it is difficult to conclude whether businesses' low usage of the technology has arisen from a lack of need for it.

The main purpose of this chapter is to examine the factors that could potentially contribute to a low usage of the electronic signature technology among Australian businesses. Participants' views from the interviews indicated six potential factors that have led or are likely to lead to a low usage of the electronic signature technology among Australian businesses. These are ignorance or lack of understanding of the technology, culture and customs, cost, complexity, security and legal obstacles. Note that most participants knew about the existence of the term electronic signature but did not have an adequate understanding of the technology. Based on this basic knowledge, they commented about the potential factors contributing or likely to contribute to the low usage of electronic signatures. However, in some instances, this basic knowledge was not adequate to comment on factors such as the complex nature of the technology. In those circumstances, their comments were mostly speculative in nature.

A. Srivastava, *Electronic Signatures for B2B Contracts: Evidence from Australia*,
DOI 10.1007/978-81-322-0743-6_4, © Springer India 2013

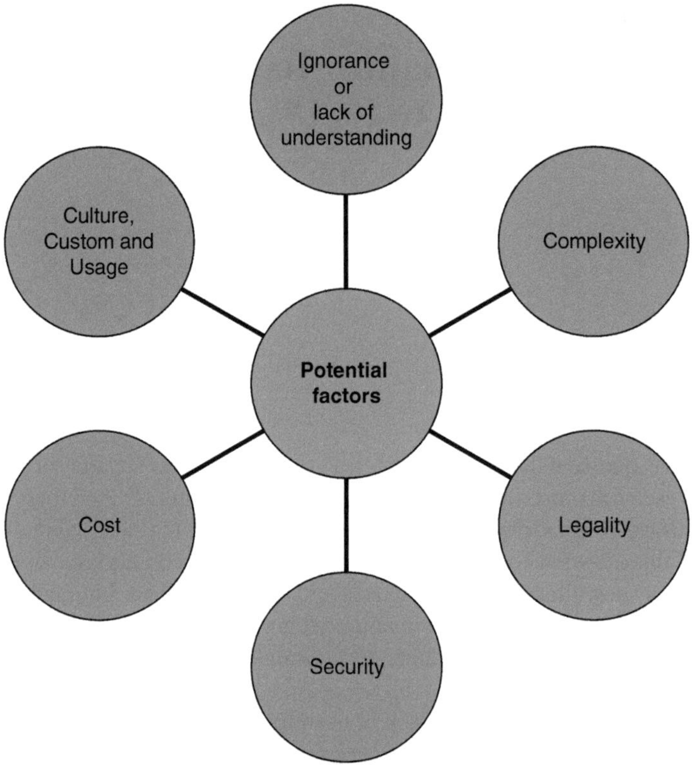

Fig. 4.1 Potential factors for the low usage of electronic signatures

Factors that May Potentially Affect the Usage of Electronic Signatures

Factors such as security, legality, cost and complexity have been identified in the literature as important issues with the use of electronic signatures, and they can potentially impede the use of the technology. During the data coding process, six main themes emerged that are likely to contribute to a low usage of the electronic signature technology among Australian businesses. Figure 4.1 gives a snapshot of these six factors. Out of these various factors, security and legal concerns appear to be the most dominant and are therefore discussed separately in Chaps. 5 and 6.

Ignorance or Lack of Understanding of the Technology

Australian businesses' knowledge about electronic signatures, which was revealed through participants, was found to be overwhelmingly poor. Before examining participants' understanding of electronic signatures, it is necessary to remind the reader

Fig. 4.2 Digital signature

that electronic signatures are not defined in the ETA.[1] However, other legislation based on the *Model Law on Electronic Commerce 1996* (MLEC), such as the New Zealand's *Electronic Transactions Act 2002,* does provide a definition for the technology. In particular, s 5 states that an electronic signature in relation to information in electronic form means 'a method used to identify a person and to indicate that person's approval of that information'.[2]

The digital signature technology is one of the various forms of electronic signature (see Fig. 4.2). The special characteristic of a digital signature is that it is a technology-specific mechanism based on public-key cryptography (PKC).[3] Note that at the time of conducting this study/interview, the use of digital signatures was mandatory for Australian companies with a turnover of A$20 million or more, for filing tax returns with the Australian Taxation Office (ATO).[4] All interviewees were staff of participating companies that had a turnover of more than A$20 million.

Although their organisation was using digital signatures with the ATO, many participants had little or no knowledge of what a digital signature represented and how it worked. During the interviews, the author explicitly enquired of participants whether they were aware that their organisation was making tax lodgements with the ATO through the use of digital signature certificates. 'No I am afraid I have not

---

[1] This issue has been discussed in detail in Chap. 3.

[2] *Electronic Transactions Act 2002* (NZ) s 5.

[3] As discussed in Chap. 2, in public-key cryptography (PKC), a digital signature subscriber has two keys, a private key and a public key. Both keys are unique to the subscriber and work as a functioning key pair. The private key is only known to the user, just like a password or PIN, whereas the public key is known to the public. The sender of the message uses a hash algorithm and his private key to create a digital signature and uses the recipient's public key to encrypt and send the message. The recipient of the message uses his private key to decrypt the message and the sender's public key for confirming the integrity of the message. See Appendix A for a technical explanation as how PKC works.

[4] From 5 April 2010, instead of digital certificates, ATO have adopted a new Australian government online security system called the AUSkey. While organisations can continue using their digital certificates to login to their online services, they need to upgrade their digital certificate to an AUSkey before it expires to ensure any permissions stored in online access manager are carried across to the new AUSkey. See www.ato.gov.au

heard about it'[5] was their typical answer.[6] Others who had heard of it were unsure what a digital signature meant or what was the underlying technology.[7]

Ignorance or Lack of Proper Understanding of the Term Electronic Signature

> I have heard that the president of the USA has a little machine that runs across the page and signs his name. At times I feel like I should have one of those when I sign … I can sign hundreds of documents in a row by hand.[8]

This was the perception that a participant had about the electronic signature technology. There appeared to be a general lack of understanding of the term electronic signature among participants. Most participants knew about the existence of electronic signatures, but they did not have adequate understanding of the technology. Their answers varied from 'I don't really know'[9] what the electronic signature technology is about; electronic signatures raise 'quite a difficult question'[10]; to 'I don't know enough about the electronic signature technology'.[11] About a quarter of them[12] had never heard of the term electronic signature and were completely ignorant of the existence of the technology. Such ignorance was not anticipated given most of the participating organisations were using digital signatures with the ATO.[13]

Diverse descriptions of electronic signatures were obtained from participants who were aware of the technology.[14] Although they knew about the existence of electronic signatures, their understanding of the technology was quite limited. Figure 4.3 depicts the various ways electronic signature was described by participants who said that they were aware of the technology. Less than a third of them[15] could give a proper definition of the term electronic signature. One IT participant who correctly described an electronic signature stated that:

---

[5] P24_Co15_Legal, Paragraph 13.

[6] Interestingly, a couple of participants grasped the concept perfectly, explaining digital signature technology that involved encryption and key pairs (P22_Co13_Legal, Paragraph 5; P27_Co17_Legal, Paragraph 8).

[7] 'I think I might have heard it but I haven't really explored any further at this point of time' (P14_Co9_Paragraph 35).

[8] P15_Co10_Legal, Paragraph 31.

[9] P2_Co2_Legal, Paragraph 5.

[10] P2_Co2_Legal, Paragraph 5.

[11] P18_Co11_Legal, Paragraph 187.

[12] 7 out of 27 participants.

[13] The author had expected participants to be aware of their organisations' use of electronic signatures when dealing with the ATO given that electronic signatures may have required their involvement. For example, the IT people might have helped with the setting-up of the technology and senior managers might have provided approval to a particular staff to act as an authorised representative on behalf of their organisation when dealing with the ATO using digital signatures.

[14] 20 out of 27 participants.

[15] 6 out of 20 participants.

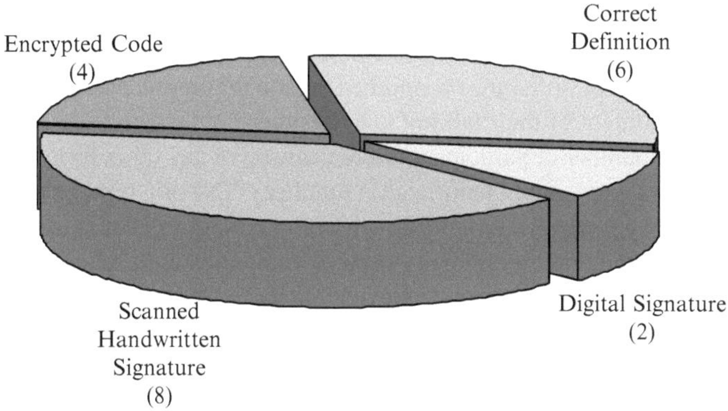

Fig. 4.3 Definition of electronic signature

> There are different types of electronic signatures ranging from a scanned or copy handwritten signature stored in electronic form, to a proven secured digital signature using public key encryption technologies.[16]

A significant number of participants[17] believed that an electronic signature is a scanned copy of a handwritten signature. One typical definition of an electronic signature was 'a replication of a person's [manuscript] signature which is in the electronic format – being on e-mails – and anything transmitted via the Internet'.[18] Another participant described it as a 'scanned signature of a person electronically transferred to a document rather than by putting their pen to a piece of paper'.[19] 'It actually gets put on electronically',[20] he added. Note that it is quite common for a scanned image of a manuscript signature to be wrongly considered as the only form of electronic signature.[21]

One out of five interviewees[22] believed that an electronic signature is 'an encrypted code' (Fig. 4.3).[23] A legal participant described an electronic signature as: 'You encrypt messages and ensure that only certain people can actually access and read the message sent across the net. People cannot intercept that message'.[24]

[16] P20_Co11_IT, Paragraph 4.

[17] 8 out of 20 participants.

[18] For example, P6_Co4_Legal, Paragraph 6.

[19] P24_Co15_Legal, Paragraph 5. Other descriptions of electronic signatures were 'electronic signature is as scanned image' (P14_Co9_SM, Paragraph 27); 'It is the cutting and pasting of a JPEG image' (P21_Co12_Legal, Paragraph 67).

[20] P24_Co15_Legal, Paragraph 5.

[21] See Vince Tuesday, *User Indifference Thwarts Electronic Signature effort* (2002) Computerworld. http://www.computerworld.com/securitytopics/security/story/0,10801,67303,00.html at 28 January 2011; *Shark Tank: Not exactly what the doctor ordered* (2003) Computerworld. http://blogs.computerworld.com/sharky/20030129 at 22 March 2011.

[22] 4 out of 20 participants.

[23] For example, P19_Co11_SM, Paragraph 6; P20_Co11_IT, Paragraph 4; P5_Co3_IT, Paragraph 7.

[24] P22_Co13_Legal, Paragraph 21.

A senior management (SM) participant, on the other hand, described an electronic signature as 'a small piece of software that is stored on a computer, and it interacts with another piece of software on another person's computer and allows the two parties to be confident of their talking to each other'.[25]

A significant number of participants were unaware of any other forms of electronic signature such as a personal identification number (PIN) or a typed name at the end of an e-mail. They were also unfamiliar with biometric devices that use fingerprints, retina scans or some other technology used to authenticate the identity of a person.

Finally, a couple of participants believed that there was no difference between an electronic signature and a digital signature. For instance, an electronic signature was described as a mechanism involving encryption and a digital certificate.[26] 'I obviously felt that both are the same',[27] remarked another participant.

Confusion Between the Term Electronic Signature and Digital Signature

Anecdotal evidence has often pointed out the general confusion that prevails between the electronic and digital signature terminologies and how these two terms are used interchangeably.[28] Such confusion may have some significant implications on the use of electronic signatures. Foremost, since digital signature is recognised as the most superior and secure form of electronic signature, referring to it as an electronic signature may hamper its legal seriousness. Also, such confusion increases the risks of relying on less secure forms of electronic signature. For example, an ignorant party may wrongfully consider a contract with an electronic signature in the form of a typed name on an e-mail – without any security features of a digital signature such as encryption – to be legally valid, particularly in countries which differentiate the legal validity of a digital signature from other forms of electronic signature.[29]

A few participants referred to an electronic signature as a digital signature and vice versa. One company had demonstrated quite some enthusiasm to participate in this study when it was first contacted by the author saying that it had been conducting banking transactions using digital signatures for the last couple of years.[30] However, while interviewing an IT participant[31] from the company, the author realised that what the company meant by *digital* signature was simply a scanned image of a manuscript signature, which was being used to endorse cheques. In addition, the continuous use of the terms electronic signature and digital signature interchangeably

[25] P12_Co7_SM, Paragraph 7.

[26] P7_Co4_IT, Paragraph 5.

[27] P6_Co4_Legal, Paragraph 30.

[28] See above, n 21.

[29] See Chap. 3 for the legal status of digital signatures.

[30] Co3.

[31] P5_Co3_IT, Paragraph 17.

during the entire interview process, when referring to the scanned image of a manuscript signature, clearly reflected the participant's[32] lack of understanding of the term electronic signature. He was certainly very surprised when the interviewer pointed out to him the difference between the two terminologies at the end of the interview. Overall, however, IT participants showed a higher level of understanding and knowledge about digital signatures and other forms of electronic signature relative to legal and SM participants.

As with any new technology, its usage rests on its awareness and understanding. If businesses are ignorant or have a lack of understanding of about any new technology in the market, they would be hesitant to adopt it. In the same vein, if they are ignorant and have inadequate understanding of electronic signatures, they would be hesitant to adopt them. More than half of the participants[33] identified ignorance or lack of knowledge of the electronic signature technology as the main reason for its non-usage in the Australian business community. They believed that a lack of understanding of electronic signatures and how they functioned were largely responsible for businesses' lack of interest in the technology for their electronic dealings. In particular, one interviewee remarked that 'a lack of understanding of the technology itself was the cause for not using electronic signatures'.[34] Another participant remarked:

> [E]verybody knows how a physical signature works so it's so easy to say we have got to sign a physical document whereas if you are not sure how the electronic signature works then you are never going to say it is okay'.[35]

Note that most businesses that were interviewed had put in place the digital signature technology in their system for dealing electronically with the ATO,[36] and this was sufficient to get the ball rolling. Yet, none of them showed any drive or enthusiasm to use it for executing contracts and conducting their day-to-day commercial transactions.

Blame Game

One purpose of having a mix of participants from legal, IT and management arenas was that electronic signatures integrate all three spheres. Businesses require the collaboration of the three parties to implement the technology and ensure its smooth functioning. However, views expressed by participants suggested that very often the responsibility of initiating the technology was shifted from one department to the other. In most instances, the IT department was held responsible for implementing

---

[32] P5_Co3_IT, Paragraph 17.

[33] 14 out of 27 participants.

[34] P22_Co1_Legal, Paragraph 62.

[35] P24_Co15_Legal, Paragraph 136.

[36] At this junction, readers are again reminded that participating companies were conducting electronic dealings with regulatory bodies such as the ATO with the use of digital signatures.

such technology. On a few occasions, the legal team was also held accountable for the failure of the electronic signature technology to penetrate the business sector. Such a blame game seemed to result from a general ignorance or lack of understanding of the technology.

'It is really to IT to say, look here is a better way of improving the process and this is the technology that exists',[37] remarked a legal participant. Two other legal participants shared similar views saying that:

> It's more of an IT issue than I suppose a legal issue I would imagine because legal issues are not large … It is up to the IT. If we get a new system, a new way of doing it, it is up to the IT who might be responsible, being given the responsibility to communicate it to the business so that it is implemented smoothly. So I think what is going to happen is that either IT would have to initiate or someone will have to tap IT on their shoulder and say guys this is what I would like you to do.[38]
>
> The lawyers would want the comfort from the IT people. When the IT people think they can confidently put the systems and security in place they can talk to the legal people and if the legal people feel that they are not leaving their company exposed in anyway like you know executing documents that are going to be questioned, later then it would be done.[39]

A few SM participants, on the other hand, were of the view that IT and legal staff should both take the initiative to encourage the usage of electronic signatures. One SM participant remarked, 'Someone like our IT security manager who should perhaps present the various business areas with the assistance of the legal and the communications team and they could sort of make everyone aware of the issue'.[40]

Some participants suggested that government authorities or other bodies such as the Australian Corporate Lawyers Association (ACLA) or the Australian Computer Society (ACS) should shoulder the responsibilities of introducing the technology to the Australian business community.[41] Participants believed that such bodies should take the responsibility of creating awareness and educating the business community about electronic signatures. An IT participant noted that instead of the drive coming from the IT department, it requires 'the government to be speaking to the legal counsel … and saying look … this is the law, this applies to companies. … really, the technology is there'.[42] A small number of participants were also of the view that government authorities should make the use of electronic signatures mandatory for businesses.[43] 'If push comes from the right area of the government or whatever to make this happen …, I don't think there would be any problem in accepting it', [44] noted a SM participant.

---

[37] P22_Co13_Legal, Paragraph 191.

[38] P18_Co11_Legal, Paragraph 260.

[39] P15_Co10_Legal, Paragraph 137.

[40] P19_Co11_SM, Paragraph 252.

[41] For example, P6_Co4_Legal, Paragraph 180; P26_Co16_SM, Paragraph 105; P27_Co17_Legal, Paragraph 125; P7_Co4_IT, Paragraph 100.

[42] P25_Co15_IT, Paragraph 112.

[43] For example, P7_Co4_IT, Paragraph 125; P14_Co9_SM, Paragraph 150; P13_Co8_SM, Paragraph 134.

[44] P14_Co9_SM, Paragraph 150.

Culture, Custom and Usage

Another issue raised by a few participants that has led or is likely to lead to a low usage of electronic signatures is the culture and custom associated with manuscript signatures. 'The concept of a written signature is deeply embedded in our culture',[45] said Gelbord, 'and even if a technology offers added value, it can often take years to be adopted by the public'.[46]

'The epitome of a signature is the act of an individual writing his name in his own hand on a document, usually in the form of a manuscript signature'.[47] A manuscript signature has been a tried and trusted method of signing documents for hundreds of years for executing contracts and commercial transactions by the business community. For instance, authorised company representatives sit across the table to sign sale agreements and joint ventures using their manuscript signature. Before affixing the signature, they usually read or flip through the document to see whether everything is in order. The documents are then signed and securely locked in a filing cabinet or safe. Such ceremonious activities of signing a document appear to be deeply rooted in the business culture and psyche. The following statement put forward by a participant is worthy of note:

> The person who is signing the document will often flip through the physical document … well, if they get an electronic one, it's just a very unfamiliar concept for someone to browse through on the screen. I don't think people are comfortable doing that.[48]

Moreover, it was common for the party signing the document on behalf of the organisation to personally view the other party affixing its manuscript signature on the document.[49] 'When you see someone doing it and you see the ink and you watch it happen you know that it has been done. There is an element of confidence because you have seen it being done',[50] remarked a participant. This is, of course, not possible with electronic signatures. '[The parties involved in a transaction] do not feel confident in doing it electronically sitting miles away'[51] was a typical remark.

Participants raised several issues related to the ceremonial act of signing and securing contracts. First and foremost, they believed that contracts and commercial dealings are traditionally executed using handwritten signatures. One participant remarked that 'things have always been done via pen and paper'.[52] 'I have never seen in my experience as a lawyer, contracts being executed any other way than a

---

[45] Boaz Gelbord, 'Signing Your 011001010: The Problems of Digital Signatures' (2000) 43(12) *Communications of the ACM* 27, 27.

[46] Ibid.

[47] Stephen Mason, *Electronic Signatures in Law* (2nd ed, 2007) 8.

[48] P24_Co15_Legal, Paragraph 152.

[49] P8_Co5_Legal, Paragraph 34.

[50] P2_Co2_Legal, Paragraph 27.

[51] P8_Co5_Legal, Paragraph 34.

[52] P18_Co11_Legal, Paragraph 133.

manuscript signature on a page',[53] he added. Another participant claimed that electronic signatures are void of all the rituals usually associated with manuscript signatures 'so using electronic signatures really comes down to changing the culture and habit of people'.[54]

Culturally, paper documents with manuscript signatures once completed are held in secure repositories. Participants believed that storing electronic files on a computer was not as safe as storing paper files in a safe.[55] One participant who had experienced a computer crash remarked, 'There wasn't another back up around so I lost the whole lot of stuff … so electronic signatures are fine … but where is it stored and how safe is the storage?'[56]

In the corporate context, a company's seal is culturally the common way of executing documents even though legally since 2001, the company's seal is no longer a requirement if the document is signed by two directors or a director and the company's secretary.[57] Participants believed that the use of company seals to effect transactions is an integral part of the business culture in Australia. One participant made the following remark:

> A company still uses an old stamp/seal even though there is no legal requirement to use it. They still want to use the seal because it's part of their culture. It is all part of the ceremony. The seal goes chop like having rubber stamp bang on the document otherwise it is not considered legally executed. It is all part of ceremony and tradition and part of the business process.[58]

Since manuscript signatures have established themselves as the only method of executing documents in business, participants claimed to be quite contented with their use and were sceptical to replace them with electronic signatures. One participant expressed his contentment that businesses execute documents using manuscript signatures by saying, 'people signing on a piece of paper doesn't seem to be a problem. … It just doesn't seem to be in my mind some sort of problem that we need to address'.[59] Note that the use of manuscript signature is not a problem and electronic signature has never been advocated as a solution to any problem. It simply represents a convenient tool especially for sealing commercial transactions, saving significant amount of time and money, in particular with overseas transactions.

Age factor is also likely to contribute to a low usage of electronic signatures. Mature persons holding executive or managerial positions in the organisation might not feel the need to change the prevailing business culture of manuscript signatures. It is quite common for the young age group to be technology savvy, whereas mature age individuals are generally more conservative. Where such people have been

[53] P18_Co11_Legal, Paragraph 133.

[54] P8_Co5_Legal, Paragraph 106.

[55] P18_Co11_Legal, Paragraph 64; P4_Co3_Legal, Paragraph 90; P1_Co1_Legal, Paragraph 69.

[56] P1_Co1_Legal, Paragraph 69.

[57] *Corporations Act 2001* (Cth) s 127.

[58] P2_Co2_Legal, Paragraph 27.

[59] P18_Co11_Legal, Paragraph 129.

accustomed to using manuscript signatures for a long time, they would hesitate to embark into the use of a new technology such as electronic signature. For instance, staff who execute commercial contracts and documents at the managerial level generally belong to the mature age group. These people are likely to demonstrate more averseness to the risks involved with any new process or technology including electronic signatures and would therefore be sceptical to adopt any such change. For instance, one participation remarked that 'it may be a generation thing that young guys like you [the interviewer] come through and are perhaps a bit more accepting it [electronic signature] and old blokes like me do not necessarily want to accept it'. [60] Another participant emphatically stated that 'it is a big hurdle for mature staff to get over the established culture of manuscript signatures and shift to electronic signatures'.[61]

Complexities in Using Electronic Signatures

An electronic signature has been defined as a technologically neutral term which focuses on the purpose of the signature as a mechanism of assent and identification of the signatory.[62] An electronic signature has been described to be as simple or as complex as the circumstances require, but as far as digital signatures are concerned, the procedural techniques involved in their usage have often been argued to have a negative effect on their intended users.[63] 'Those who are not successful with technology use a strategy of avoidance. When confronted by a technological problem, they walk away'.[64]

On the issue of complexity, a few participants' comments were directed particularly towards digital signatures. Three main arguments were raised with regard to the complexity of the digital signature technology: the difficulty involved in using the technology, the complexity associated with the setting-up of the technology and the requirement for the recipient organisation to be equipped with the same technology at its end.

[60] P4_Co3_Legal, Paragraph 15.

[61] P3_Co2_IT, Paragraph 33.

[62] See UNCITRAL *Model law on Electronic Signatures 2001*. The text of the model law can be found on the UNCITRAL website at http://www.uncitral.org/uncitral/en/uncitral_texts/electronic_commerce/2001Model_signatures.html at 15 January 2012.

[63] The complexity of electronic signatures has been discussed in Chap. 3.

[64] Michelle M Weil and Larry D Rosen, *TechnoStress: Coping with Technology@ work@ home@ play* (1997) 46. Further, according to Weil and Rosen, up to 85 % of the population experiences some discomfort with technology.

The Difficulty Involved in Using the Digital Signature Technology

A few studies have found the digital signature technology to be rather complex.[65] Schultz claimed that the encryption technology underlying digital signatures involves 'usability hurdles [that have resulted] in a reluctance to use the technology or in many cases, outright rejection of the technology'.[66] Gelbord remarked that 'a major disadvantage of digital signatures is that people are reluctant to place their trust in a system that requires a high level of mathematical knowledge to understand'.[67]

The above arguments were substantiated by a few participants who believed that digital signatures were based on programmes that were too technical and cumbersome.[68] These participants claimed that the technology will be more readily accepted if it is implemented with a simpler interface and is easy to use. They believed that once it is well understood how the digital signature technology functions, it would be more readily accepted. An SM participant noted, 'Once you get it and understand it, you pick it up very quickly and generally it is fairly widely accepted straight away'.[69]

A legal participant remarked that 'using digital signatures as a form of identification represented a troublesome and complex ceremonious process'.[70] Another participant described the use of digital signatures as mind-boggling.[71] He pointed out some technical difficulties encountered with the technology when lodging documents electronically to the ATO, such as the password would fail to work on occasions or the username and/or password would get messed up by the user, and such issues often carried the risk of delays.[72]

The Setting-Up of the Digital Signature Technology

The second complexity associated with digital signatures was raised by a few participants related to the setting-up of the technology and the elaborate digital signature certificate application procedure.[73] Participants claimed that the process of receiving both the key pairs and the digital signature certificate from the certification

---

[65] Roger Clarke, 'The Fundamental Inadequacies of Public Key Infrastructure' (Paper presented at the 9th International Conference on Information Systems, Bled, Slovenia, 27–29 June 2001); J Bell et al., 'Electronic Signature Regulation' (2001) 17(6) *Computer Law & Security Report* 399; Eugene Schultz, 'The Gap Between Cryptography and Information Security' (2002) 21(8) *Computers & Security* 674.

[66] See Schultz, above n 65, 675.

[67] Gelbord, above n 46, 27.

[68] 7 participants held this view.

[69] P14_Co9_SM, Paragraph 115.

[70] P11_Co6_Legal, Paragraph 16.

[71] P1_Co1_Legal, Paragraph 77.

[72] P1_Co1_Legal, Paragraph 11.

[73] Note that the application procedure and setting-up process of the digital signature technology have been described in Chap. 2.

authority (CA) was complex, inconvenient and intrusive.[74] 'The big issue is that it [digital signature] is a pain in the ass to set up',[75] remarked a participant. The use of digital signatures can thus result into an unnecessary complexity for both the organisation wishing to use the technology and the partner organisation with which it enters into an online contract or commercial transaction. Such complexities represented a significant barrier to the use of digital signatures. This is reflected in following comment made by an IT participant:

> If we would be sending you a [digitally signed] document, it means we would have to share the key pairs. You then have to set up a process which involves the CA, isn't it? So I think there is another step in it that might just be a little bit … complex is not the right word … but there is another step in that process that might be a bit of a stumbling block.[76]

A small number of participants also considered the setting-up process for digital signatures as time consuming given that it involves a change.[77] 'To implement a change is very difficult and very time consuming',[78] remarked an IT participant.

Requirements of the Recipient Organisation

The final source of complexity raised by a few participants related to the compatibility of the technology between two parties dealing with each other.[79] Digital signature technology requires that two parties entering into a contract or conducting an electronic transaction be equipped with the same technology at both ends for its operability. Thus, if an organisation would like to use digital signature with its business partner, it would need to convince the latter to use the same technology at its end. A participant remarked, 'you can't use and communicate with that technology until you establish that the other party has that technology'.[80] 'It adds another level of complication',[81] he added. The following was noted by another participant:

> Very few, if any, of the companies we deal with here and particularly overseas favour electronic signatures because of the authentication problems. Unless and until both parties to a contract agree on the same authentication system, we will always prefer non-electronic signatures.[82]

---

[74] For example, P1_Co1_Legal, Paragraph 19; P11_Co6_Legal, Paragraph 16; P7_Co4_IT, Paragraph 53.

[75] P1_Co1_Legal, Paragraph 19.

[76] P9_Co5_IT, Paragraph 73.

[77] For example, P3_Co2_IT, Paragraph 56; P4_Co3_Legal, Paragraph 63; P9_Co5_IT, Paragraph 73.

[78] P3_Co2_IT, Paragraph 56.

[79] For example, P1_Co1_Legal, Paragraph 36; P11_Co6_Legal, Paragraph 34; P13_Co8_SM, Paragraph 96; P22_Co13_Legal, Paragraph 82; and P23_Co14_SM, Paragraph 124.

[80] P22_Co13_Legal, Paragraph 82.

[81] P22_Co13_Legal, Paragraph 82.

[82] P11_Co6_Legal, Paragraph 34.

In addition, the two companies would be required to give similar training to their staff. 'That obviously can be a pretty severe impediment because obviously you have to educate the other party who are not really educated',[83] said a participant. Such stringent requirements were considered to be a significant impediment to the acceptance of digital signatures.

The Cost Aspect of Electronic Signatures

The cost aspect of electronic signatures particularly digital signatures has been a subject of debate among a few scholars.[84] They have argued that the high expenses associated with the use of the technology represent a major disincentive to users. Cost has therefore been identified as an important barrier to the use of digital signatures.[85]

According to several participants,[86] the cost of obtaining a digital signature certificate from a *Gatekeeper* accredited CA[87] was trivial for Australian businesses.[88] They claimed that their organisation could easily afford to use the digital signature technology. 'I wouldn't imagine that cost would be prohibitive because big companies would spend a lot more on IT systems',[89] or 'I don't think cost would be an issue you know, if it make things speedier … I can't imagine it would be costly',[90] were typical remarks made by participants. One IT participant remarked that:

> [s]pending 10 to 30 grands on software is nothing where we can prove its benefits straight off … it's budgeted for within our software development. Security is high risk; we spend on security for our hardware and internet on our data networks across the world … so that's a small expense in that regard.[91]

While such views were shared by several IT and legal participants as well, a majority of senior management representatives of participating companies found digital signatures to be inexpensive and affordable. This is suggestive of the potential support that businesses are likely to obtain from their management from the

---

[83] P4_Co3_Legal, Paragraph 63.

[84] M S Ackerman and D T Davis, 'Privacy and Security Issues in E-Commerce', in D C Jones (ed) *New Economy Handbook* (2003), 911–930; Raymond Perry, 'E-Conveyancing: Problems Ahead?' (2003) 67 *The Conveyancer and Property Lawyer* 215; Clarke, above n 65.

[85] Ackerman and Davis, above n 84, 922.

[86] 16 out of 27 participants.

[87] A digital signature certificate costs A$130–200 in Australia. See below n 119.

[88] For example, P13_Co8_SM, Paragraph 71; P14_Co9_SM, Paragraph 119; P3_Co2_IT, Paragraph 69.

[89] P2_Co2_Legal, Paragraph 48.

[90] P15_Co10_Legal, Paragraph 141.

[91] P3_Co2_IT, Paragraph 69.

cost aspect. 'That's quite inexpensive. I don't think there will be a drama',[92] said one SM participant. Another remarked, 'we wouldn't hesitate to invest in that kind of technology'.[93]

However, while the setting-up cost was not considered a major issue for these large organisations, participants expressed concerns about the cost incurred in the education and training of end users of digital signatures.[94] To make matter worse, often such expenses also encompassed the cost of training staff of the partner organisations if electronic signatures were to be used. One participant remarked, 'Unfortunately, at the moment the majority of our customers are not ready to receive digital signatures so there is the cost of educating them as well, and we are not interested in doing that'.[95]

Overall, cost was found to be a prohibitive factor in the use of electronic signatures by less than half of the participants.[96] 'Cost might be prohibitive because the technology hasn't been fully accepted so the cost is probably still high as well. So that's a potential factor',[97] commented a participant.

Many participants[98] also raised the issue that businesses would only want to invest in the digital signature technology and/or any other form of electronic signature if they are cost-effective. However, there were also some concerns raised whether the benefits could be measured. 'I'm really interested in the benefit of incurring that cost in terms of understanding the cost impact of the efficiencies that are achieved from doing that',[99] remarked one participant. A couple of others said:

> It's really going to be what's the initial upfront cost and what benefits do we get from it ... Spending a lot of money on application and what benefit you get from it, that's what will drive a lot of people's decisions in whether they use it or not.[100]
>
> I would like to be able to get the digital signature sorted out internally ... saves time signing holiday forms, lease forms, changes to salary, employment forms you name it ... all require signatures and if we can get somebody to just key in ... then we basically get rid of lot of paper work but you have got to get out a measurable return and that's the challenge ... I can see lots of savings but I can't actually put a hard number on them.[101]

A legal participant expressed uncertainty whether the use of the electronic signature technology would save time and money or increase security.[102] In his opinion, there was no urgency to take up the technology unless it would generate such benefits.

---

[92] P14_Co9_SM, Paragraph 119.

[93] P13_Co8_SM, Paragraph 71.

[94] For example, P5_Co3_IT, Paragraph 110; P5_Co3_IT, Paragraph 66.

[95] P5_Co3_IT, Paragraph 66. Note that very few participants considered the cost of obtaining a digital signature certificate to be a prohibitive factor.

[96] 11 out of 27 participants.

[97] P4_Co3_Legal, Paragraph 117.

[98] 10 out of 27 participants.

[99] P13_Co8_SM, Paragraph 96.

[100] P14_Co9_SM, Paragraph 119.

[101] P5_Co3_IT, Paragraph 114.

[102] P4_Co3_Legal, Paragraph 63.

'How it is going to save time or save money or increase security? And if that isn't being done then there is no imperative to take up the technology',[103] he commented.

Consequently, several participants[104] highlighted the importance of a cost-benefit assessment of using electronic signatures. They believed that the risks factors in terms of the cost of implementing the technology should be examined as against how often it would be used. The following argument was raised by a participant:

> We need to examine the cost benefit of moving towards such a solution [electronic signatures] and whether or not we can mitigate the risk with other solutions that might be cheaper to implement, more cost effective and/or can address multiple risks.[105]

An IT participant claimed that his job could be at stake if he lobbied for electronic signatures to his chief executive officer (CEO) without conducting a cost-benefit analysis. His comment was as follows:

> I have to put up a case where I could show that we would make a return or would save cost or would meet a legal regulation, and put it in front of the CEO. If I can't prove it in any of those three areas then I'm wasting my time and probably risking my job.[106]

Security and Legal Concerns

Other than the lack of knowledge on the electronic signature technology, the cost and complexities associated with its usage and the prevailing culture of using manuscript signature strongly embedded in organisations, security and legal concerns were also speculated as factors that can potentially contribute to businesses' low usage of electronic signatures and, as mentioned above, were in fact identified as major obstacles to their acceptance.

An electronic signature, unlike a handwritten signature, does not partake of any natural characteristics of the signatory. It involves the usage of the computer and the Internet, which are believed to be insecure. There is fear and anxiety that a hacker will access someone else' computer or break through the systems' security via the Internet and use the person's electronic signature maliciously.

An electronic signature can be secured through three principle methods: the use of passwords (where the electronic signature is stored on the hard disk of a computer), through the use of portable information storage devices (PISDs) and through the use of biometric devices.[107] However, there have been issues associated

---

[103] P4_Co3_Legal, Paragraph 63.

[104] 10 out of 27 participants.

[105] P20_Co11_IT, Paragraph 32.

[106] P5_Co3_IT, Paragraph 35.

[107] See Steven Furnell, 'An Assessment of Website Password Practices' (2007) 26(7) *Computers & Security* 445, 445; Bruce Schneier, *Beyond Fear: Thinking sensibly about security in an uncertain world* (2003) 186.

with all three security methods. Many participants claimed that there can indeed be a reluctance towards the use of the electronic signature technology because of security concerns. Given the significance of the concerns raised by participants, Chap. 5 has been devoted to an extensive and in-depth analysis of the security issues associated with electronic signatures.

Similarly, Chap. 6 deals with participants' concerns about the legal issues arising with the use of electronic signatures. In particular, complexities arising with evidentiary matters when proving authenticity of electronic signatures in the court of law were raised. Participants also expressed concerns with regard to the development of contracts with international partners because of a lack of harmony in legislation across countries. Another important issue that was examined in this chapter was businesses' ignorance with regard to the legislation governing electronic signatures.

An Analysis of Participants' Views

The above data analysis identified various factors that have led or are likely to lead to a low adoption of the electronic signature technology in the Australian business community. These factors comprised lack of understanding of the electronic signature technology, prevailing culture and custom associated with manuscript signatures, cost and complexities related to the technology and legal and security concerns with the use of electronic signatures. While some of the issues raised by participants are justified, several of them appeared to be unfounded and based on misconceptions.

First, many participants revealed an ignorance or lack of understanding of the electronic signature technology and a confusion between the terms *electronic* and *digital* signature. Academic writings on the issue of ignorance or understanding of the electronic signature technology are scarce[108] although views expressed in some press clippings and anecdotes reveal that there exists a misunderstanding about the difference between the two terminologies, *electronic* and *digital* signature.[109] An expert in the field who was contacted by the author seemed to hold a similar view.[110] Another scholar said that whoever coined the term *electronic signature* has a lot to answer for. 'If the expression "electronic identity" or "electronic identification" had

[108] Very few scholars are of the view that ignorance is the main factor behind the lack of acceptance of electronic signatures. See Heiko Roßnagel 'On Diffusion and Confusion-Why Electronic Signatures Have Failed,' in S. Fischer-Hübner et al. (eds) *Trust and Privacy in Digital Business* (2006) 71, 77.

[109] Vince Tuesday, *User Indifference Thwarts Electronic Signature effort* (2002) Computerworld. http://www.computerworld.com/securitytopics/security/story/0,10801,67303,00.html at 28 January 2011; *Shark Tank: Not exactly what the doctor ordered* (2003) Computerworld. http://blogs.computerworld.com/sharky/20030129 at 22 March 2011.

[110] This expert expressed his views to the author through an e-mail correspondence.

prevailed, the world would be a simpler place',[111] he further remarked. He believed that the expression electronic signature has created unnecessary complexities with regard to the laws governing the technology.[112]

Second, a few participants believed that the use of manuscript signatures has become a part of the Australian business culture and custom which they would be unwilling to give up. Such culture and customs strongly embedded in businesses may act as a significant deterrent to the use of electronic signatures. However, it is believed that the old order will give way to the new as business managers and leaders become more aware of the technology and its benefits.

Third, a few participants claimed that mature age individuals would be reticent to replace manuscript signatures by the new technology.[113] Note that many of the electronic innovations in communication, including computers, that are available today have only been realised in the recent past. Among the current cohort of mature age individuals, a large number of them are unlikely to have had much exposure to such electronic technologies. In some instances, mature age individuals have not had any opportunity to learn how to utilise many of these new technologies. In other instances, where opportunities have been available, time constraints or reduced cognitive abilities have prohibited acquisition of new skills. However, research in the area of ageing and technical adoption shows that older people are able to adopt new technologies provided they get the necessary support for the switch.[114]

Fourth, a few participants were of the view that the use of electronic signatures is complex and confusing. However, these issues were raised mostly in the context of digital signature, while other forms of electronic signature such as e-mail and scanned image of a manuscript signature were not necessarily perceived as complex to use. In particular, the digital signature technology was found to involve complicated application programmes that would render it non-user friendly, a complex setting-up process and a stringent requirement for the recipient organisation to be equipped with a similar technology.

---

[111] John Huntley, 'Book Review of Electronic Signatures, Law and Regulation by Lorna Brazell, (Thomson, Sweet & Maxwell, 2004)' (2007) 15(2) *International Journal of Law and Information Technology* 227, 227.

[112] Ibid 228. Another scholar, Tom Worthington, is of the view that the confusion between the two terms electronic signature and digital signature can be overcome by dropping the term electronic and simply calling it signature. See Tom Worthington, *Digital Evidence for Lawyers and IT Professional* (2006) Tom W Communications Pty Ltd. http://blog.tomw.net.au/2006/08/digital-evidence-for-lawyers-and-it.html at 27 February 2012.

[113] Some studies have also revealed that mature age individuals develop a fear that they would be unable to learn new technical skills that a new technological solution (i.e. electronic signature) demands. See Janou Vos, *The Role of Personality and Emotions in Employee Resistance to Change* (Master Thesis, Erasmus University, 2006) 16; Brenda Kearns, *Technology and Change Management* (2004). http://www.comp.dit.ie/rfitzpatrick/MSc_Publications/2004_Brenda_Kearns.pdf at 25 January 2012.

[114] Wayne Fisher and Slawo Wesolkowski, 'The Social and Economic Costs of Technology Resistance' (1999) Winter *IEEE Canadian Review* 14, 15. See also Arthur D Fisk, Wendy A Rogers and Neff Walker, *Aging and Skilled Performance: Advances in Theory and Applications* (1996).

A few participants' were of the view that digital signatures are fraught with complexities. The author concurs with such views but believes that such complexities can also act as an attribute as they would make it difficult for an average individual to use a digital signature. Thus, due to its complex nature, the use of digital signatures would only be confined to selective people in an organisation who have acquired an expertise or training in this respect. From a security standpoint, the complex nature of the technology can therefore be regarded as its strength since it enhances digital signatures' security by restricting its usage by the general staff.

The author also concurs with some participants who claimed that the requirement of an identical technology by the recipient organisation is troublesome and can be perceived as a drawback of the digital signature technology. It appears that because of this *chicken and egg* problem, a company will not take up the technology until its main trading partners implement it. On the other hand, the partners will also refrain from taking up the technology until the company does. However, such complexities would easily be traded for the security that digital signatures provide.[115] Note that digital signatures are the most secure form of electronic signature because each time the digital signature is used, it makes a unique document that can only be decrypted with the appropriate public key.[116] A final note on the issue of complexity worth noting is that much of the confusion with electronic signatures arises from an ignorance or lack of understanding of the technology. The electronic signature technology, in particular, digital signature, is not necessarily as complex as it is perceived.[117] This perceived complexity is often an outcome of their lack of understanding of the technology.

Fifth, a few participants considered the financial cost of educating and training staff as one potential deterrent factor for the adoption of the new technology. Of course if a company cannot afford the luxury to introduce the digital signature technology, it will resist its adoption.[118] However, expenses such as the cost of obtaining digital signature certificates should certainly not be a disincentive to

---

[115] As discussed in Chap. 3, renowned scholars in the field of electronic signatures argue in favour of the digital signature technology. In their opinion, it is the most secure form of electronic signature and has no serious contender. See, for example, John C Anderson and Michael L Closen, 'Document Authentication in Electronic Commerce: The Misleading Notary Public Analog for the Digital Signature Certification Authority' (1999) 17(3) *The John Marshall Journal of Computer & Information Law* 833, 838; James Backhouse, 'Assessing the Certification Authorities: Guarding the Guardians of Secure E-Commerce' (2002) 9(3) *Journal of Financial Crime* 217, 217.

[116] Pun et al. refer to it as the *freezing* of the document. See K H Pun et al., 'Review of the Electronic Transactions Ordinance: Can the Personal Identification Number Replace the Digital Signatures' (2002) 32 *Hong Kong Law Journal* 241, 252.

[117] It is to be noted that a comprehensive description of the digital signature technology and its functioning has been discussed in Chap. 2.

[118] Note that some scholars have considered financial constraints as one of the factors that lead to a resistance to change in organisations. See Richard P Rumelt, 'Inertia and Transformation', in C A Montgomery (ed), *Resource-based and Evolutionary Theories of the Firm* (1993) 101.

implement the technology. A digital signature certificate costs A$130–200 in Australia.[119] Such expenses appear trivial in terms of implementation cost for participating companies, which were large public listed companies.

A few participants also expressed concerns that using electronic signatures might not be cost-effective. However, the author disagrees with this view and believes that such expenses may simply represent short-run hiccups. In the long run, the benefits derived from the use of electronic signatures can be enormous, and thus, any money directed towards the technology and its implementation may be well spent.

Concluding Observations

This chapter identified several factors that have led or can potentially contribute to a low usage of the electronic signature technology in the Australian business community. It appears that much of the reluctance towards the technology can be overcome, and electronic signatures particularly digital signatures can be promoted at the level of the Australian business community. In this regard, the following observations are made.

First, businesses may be ignorant or have little understanding of the technology. They need to be made aware of the technology and its benefits. They would only be willing to change the deep-rooted culture of manuscript signatures to electronic signatures if they recognise the need for the change and appreciate the relative benefits of using the new technology.[120] 'In order for people to respond positively to change, they must feel change will bring them benefits'.[121] Therefore, businesses need to realise that electronic signatures would enhance their performance and capabilities and provide them the ease of signing contracts, joint ventures and conduct electronic dealings sitting in front of their computer anywhere in the world. Electronic signatures can save them the trouble of getting their document signed at

---

[119] VeriSign, *VeriSign Gatekeeper: Gatekeeper Pricing*. http://www.verisign.com.au/gatekeeper/pricing.shtml. 23 March 2011.

[120] The author would like to point out at this stage that in the information systems literature, there is a well-known theory called the *Technology Acceptance Model* (TAM). See F D Davis, 'Perceived Usefulness, Perceived Ease of Use, and User Acceptance of Information Technology' (1989) 13(3) *MIS Quarterly* 319. The TAM aims at identifying factors that facilitate the acceptance of a new technology. It focuses on two major characteristics one of which is *perceived usefulness*. Perceived usefulness can be defined as the degree to which an individual or organisation believes that using a particular information system would enhance its performance. See, especially, F D Davis, 'User Acceptance of Information Technology: System Characteristics, User Perceptions and Behavioral Impacts' (1993) 38(3) *International Journal of Man–machine Studies* 475; Vishwanthan Venkatesh et al., 'User Acceptance of Information Technology: Toward a Unified View' (2003) 27(3) *MIS Quarterly* 425. Note that, however, a thorough analysis of the TAM in the context of electronic signatures is beyond the scope of this book.

[121] R Hirshheim and M Newman, 'Information Systems and User Resistance: Theory and Practice' (1988) 31 (5) *The Computer Journal* 398, 399.

one end and then faxed through or couriered over to another country and signed by the other party. Only if businesses recognise the need for a change will the existing belief be dispelled that electronic signatures are troublesome and cumbersome.[122]

Furthermore, businesses need to recognise that an electronic signature can be an extremely convenient tool especially for busy senior executives who are often on official tours. They would save significant amount of time and money with added convenience and flexibility, hitherto unknown. The following comment made by a participant is apposite:

> I mean it would really free up business because you know the CEO is a very busy person and he is also in transit in places and needs to sign stacks and stacks of documents. Now he will get final versions on his computer – his hand held PDA– he will be very happy with them. But with normal signatures he will have to come into the office to sign … I mean everyone is stuck [with manual signatures].[123]

Second, businesses need to realise that the convenience that electronic signatures provide amply justifies the expenses involved in their use. Although in the short run they may incur certain expenses in terms of training and educating their staff, the long run gains would most likely outweigh the expenses.

Third, if the prevailing ignorance, lack of understanding and confusion about the new technology can be addressed, businesses will realise that electronic signatures, in particular, digital signatures are one step forward from electronic banking and making purchases via the Internet. This can be achieved through training and education programmes for staff who will be directly or indirectly involved in the use of the electronic signature technology.

Fourth, there is a lack of definition of electronic signature in the ETA. If the act and corresponding state laws are amended to provide a comprehensive definition of electronic signature as well as digital signature, much of the confusion that businesses have will be cleared. A proper understanding of the technology will in turn lend more confidence to its usage.[124]

This chapter examined four of the six factors identified can act as important impediments to the use of electronic signatures: ignorance or lack of understanding of the electronic signature technology, prevailing culture and custom associated with manuscript signatures, complexities with the use of electronic signature and the cost of the technology. The following chapter examines security concerns with regard to electronic signatures.

---

[122] Note that *perceived ease of use* is the second major characteristic of the TAM. It can be defined as the degree to which a person believes that using a particular system would be free of any physical and mental effort. See Davis, 'Perceived Usefulness, Perceived Ease of Use, and User Acceptance of Information Technology' above n 120; Davis, 'User acceptance of information technology: system characteristics, user perceptions and behavioral impacts' above n 120; Venkatesh et al., above n 120.

[123] P15_Co10_Legal, Paragraph 103.

[124] In this regard, reference can be made to the *Electronic Transactions (Amendment) Ordinance 2004* (HK) which was amended in 2004. The new ordinance provides the definition of both electronic signature and digital signature. Note that this issue has been dealt in detail in Chap. 6.

Chapter 5
Security Issues Driving the Non-acceptance of Electronic Signatures

What Is Security?

Merriam-Webster online dictionary defines security as the quality or state of being secure, freedom from danger and freedom from fear or anxiety.[1] In the context of electronic signatures, there is always a danger, fear or anxiety regarding their unauthorised or malicious use. The protection from such unauthorised and malicious usage requires some process, device or mechanism that ensures the confidentiality of electronic signatures. Note that there are three basic ways to secure electronic signatures: through the use of passwords where an electronic signature is stored on the hard disk of a computer, using portable information storage devices (PISDs) and using biometric devices. The underlying theoretical underpinning for these three methods of securing electronic signatures relates to the three ways of authenticating a user: by something he/she knows, by something he/she has and by something he/she is.[2] Security is also achieved through a secure transmission process including the Internet such that a document signed through an electronic signature is not tampered with by a third person and reaches the recipient in the form in which it left the signatory.

Although legal, information technology (IT) and management disciplines have different perceptions of security, their definitions of the term *security* broadly underpin the dictionary meaning of the word security (Fig. 5.1). For the legal fraternity, the

---

[1] *Merriam-Webster's Online Dictionary* (2011) Merriam-Webster. http://www.merriamwebster.com/dictionary/security at 2 March 2012. Schneier, a well renowned security expert, is of the view that security is about preventing adverse consequences from the intentional and unwarranted actions of others. See Bruce Schneier, *Beyond Fear: Thinking Sensibly About Security in an Uncertain World* (2003) 11.

[2] Steven Furnell, 'An Assessment of Website Password Practices' (2007) 26(7) *Computers & Security* 445, 445.

A. Srivastava, *Electronic Signatures for B2B Contracts: Evidence from Australia*, DOI 10.1007/978-81-322-0743-6_5, © Springer India 2013

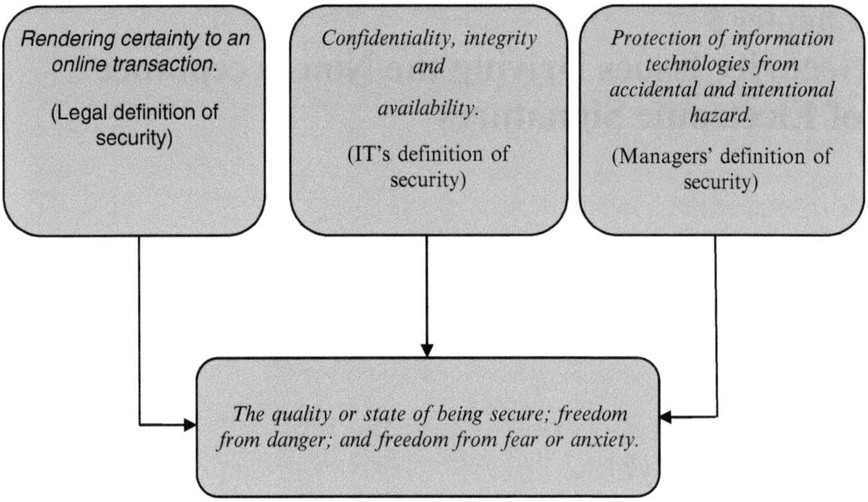

Fig. 5.1 Definition of security (This diagram is based on the definition of security from the three respective disciplines. See below n 3, n 4 and n 5)

term security means that which renders a matter sure.[3] In the information technology realm, security is associated with confidentiality, integrity and availability.[4] In the field of management, security means the 'protection of information technologies from accidental and intentional hazards'.[5] From the point of view of electronic signatures, the definition of security appears to be closer to those used in the IT and management spheres. Participants' views of security will be better understood if terminologies such as *confidentiality*, *integrity, availability*[6] and *protection of information technologies from accidental and intentional hazard* are borrowed from these disciplines and explained in the context of electronic signatures.

Confidentiality refers to the concealment of an electronic signature through mechanisms such as passwords, PISDs and biometrics. *Integrity* means ensuring no changes are made to the contents of a document signed through an electronic signature; *integrity* also extends to detecting and reporting if there has been any unauthorised attempt to change the contents of a document signed electronically. *Availability* refers

[3] For example, in the context of contract, providing security means rendering certain the performance of the contract. See *The Lectric Law Library's Lexicon* (2008) Lectric Law Library. http://www.lectlaw.com/def2/s140.htm at 10 March 2012.

[4] See Matt Bishop, *Computer Security: Art and Science* (2003) 3–6.

[5] A Grandori and M Warner, *International Encyclopaedia of Business and Management* (1996) Vol 5, 4419.

[6] *Confidentiality* is the concealment of information or data through the use of an access control mechanism like password, *integrity* refers to the trustworthiness of data or resources and *availability* refers to the ability to use data at any time and the prevention of any outside interference. See Bishop above n 4.

to the ability of the owner of an electronic signature to use it whenever he/she desires. Lastly, *accidental and intentional hazard* refers to the risk of a technical failure leading to (say) the accidental crashing of a computer on which an electronic signature was stored or where there is an intentional unauthorised access to someone's electronic signature.

Electronic Signatures and Security Fears

Prior studies and anecdotal evidence indicate that security is a potential factor contributing to the non-acceptance of electronic signatures.[7] To get some insights on this issue, the first question set to participants was whether their organisation had concerns about the security aspect of electronic signatures. A small proportion of participants in each group considered electronic signatures as a safe alternative to manuscript signatures for effecting commercial transactions, including the execution of online contracts. They believed that security was not the reason for their non-usage. One such participant who claimed that the use of electronic signatures was secure said, 'No, I would not be concerned about the security aspect of it. If we can conduct our banking online I would imagine that there is no problem with using electronic signatures'.[8] Some participants, however, thought that businesses' security fears reflected their lack of understanding of the nature, function and use of electronic signatures. As remarked by one participant, 'there is not enough comfort in it [an electronic signature] at the moment and it's pretty much from the lack of understanding of the technology behind it'.[9] Another participant noted that 'people don't know how safe it [an electronic signature] is and how it should be used'.[10] 'That leads to insecurity and that is why people don't want to use it', he added.[11]

On the other hand, the majority of participants believed that businesses have not embraced the idea of integrating electronic signatures into their work environment for a number of security reasons. There were concerns that the technology that currently exists does not provide sufficient safeguards to users. As a result, it would be well nigh impossible for electronic signatures to be used as a secure form of authentication.

---

[7] See, for example, Adrian McCullagh, Peter Little and William J Caelli, 'Electronic Signatures: Understand the Past to Develop the Future' (1998) 21(2) *University of New South Wales Law Journal* 452; Stephen Mason and Nicholas Bohm, 'The Signature in Electronic Conveyancing: An Unresolved Issue?' (2003) 67 *The Conveyancer and Property Lawyer* 460; Roger Clarke, 'The Fundamental Inadequacies of Public Key Infrastructure' (Paper presented at the 9th International Conference on Information Systems, Bled, Slovenia, 27–29 June 2001); John Angel, 'Why use Digital Signatures for Electronic Commerce?' (1999) 2 *Journal of Information, Law and Technology*. http://www2.warwick.ac.uk/fac/soc/law/elj/jilt/1999_2/angel/ at 28 February 2012. Note that views of these eminent scholars and other experts have been discussed in Chap. 3.

[8] P13_Co8_SM, Paragraph 54.

[9] P8_Co5_Legal, Paragraph 63.

[10] P2_Co2_Legal, Paragraph 57.

[11] P2_Co2_Legal, Paragraph 57.

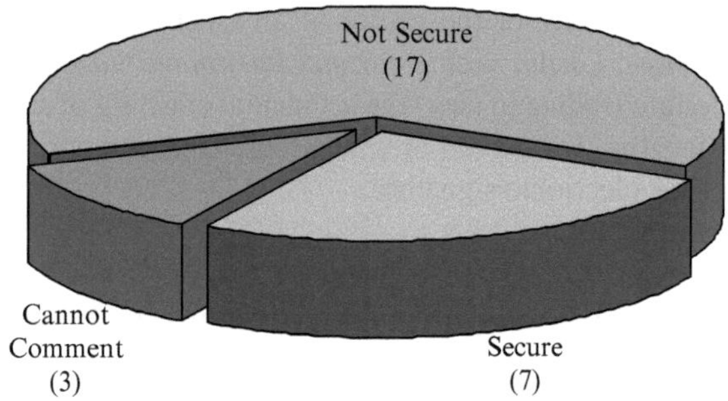

Fig. 5.2 Are electronic signatures secure?

Close to two-third of all participants implicitly or explicitly considered the issue of security as an important impediment to the acceptance of electronic signatures (Fig. 5.2).[12] 'It's very much the insecurity of the whole thing that is why it hasn't been widely accepted',[13] claimed one participant. Participants were concerned that someone could hack into another person's computer system and maliciously use his/her electronic signature without the person's knowledge.[14] [T]he last thing you want for the other party [to the contract] to say is that hang on I didn't sign it, that wasn't me, I didn't do it',[15] said a participant. Another participant remarked:

> [I]f we are referring to the scanned handwritten signature as an electronic signature then given they are still used for authentication purposes, then storing them anywhere in an insecure storage area presents a risk ... somebody can access your signature and pretend to be you.[16]

The fears expressed by participants were both of technical and legal nature. From a technical standpoint, participants feared that a person could fraudulently use someone else's electronic signature and pass it as his/her own. '[O]nce it's on the computer anyone can access it. ... it's pretty easy to get hold of it if you want to get it', remarked a legal participant.[17] On the other hand, from a legal stance, participants feared that a plaintiff would not be able to satisfy the court that a forger has forged or affixed his/her electronic signature. As remarked by one of the participants, 'when it comes down to proving, you don't know if this was actually executed by the named person'.[18]

[12] Seventeen participants considered security to be an issue; Seven claimed that security is not an issue while the remaining three were unable to comment.

[13] P8_Co5_Legal, Paragraph 114.

[14] For example, P15_Co10_Legal, Paragraph 63.

[15] P2_Co2_Legal, Paragraph 88.

[16] P20_Co11_IT, Paragraph 24.

[17] P24_Co15_Legal, Paragraph 55.

[18] P6_Co4_Legal, Paragraph 76. Note that legal issues with regard to electronic signatures are dealt in the following chapter.

Having said that, the issue of trust was also evoked by a few participants. They recognised the importance of trust relationships within an organisation. They believed that when it comes to security, it is more an issue of developing trust in their staff that the latter would not indulge in unethical activities.

> Unless people lock their computer when they are away from it and things like that, that could happen but I guess I don't feel uneasy. I guess I am sitting here and I am talking to you and my computer is on and I haven't locked it. But you know I wouldn't be too concerned somebody would go and do something that they shouldn't and that's really more I guess of having trust on the people around you and so on.[19]

Electronic Signatures and Secure Storage

As mentioned above, there are different ways of securing electronic signatures: through the use of passwords where an electronic signature is stored on the hard disk of a computer, using PISDs and using biometric devices. The next subsections discuss these three security methods in light of participants' views.

Password as a Security Measure

In recent times, computers have become the norm for conducting business. A computer workstation is used either exclusively by a particular user or by more than one users based on an organisation's policy and financial constraints. Where a workstation is used by multiple users, separate login IDs and passwords are usually provided to each user.

The most common form of storage of an electronic signature is on the hard disk of a computer.[20] A user wishing to affix his/her electronic signature will use a keyboard and/or a mouse for its activation,[21] and the signature will then be attached to a particular data message.[22] However, the risk is that the same command can be given by an unauthorised user who also has access to that computer because technically it is the computer that 'signs' rather than the actual owner of the electronic signature. Participants resolutely believed that unattended workstations are insecure, and anybody could use them for malicious purposes.

---

[19] P13_Co9_SM, Paragraph 145.

[20] Especially for non-individual digital signature certificates or organisation digital signature certificates.

[21] In the case of digital signature, it is the private key that the subscriber activates to create a digital signature.

[22] Data message means '... information generated, sent, received or stored by electronic, optical or similar means including ... electronic mail, telegram, telex or telecopy ...:' art 2(c) of the UNCITRAL *Model Law on Electronic signatures 2001.*

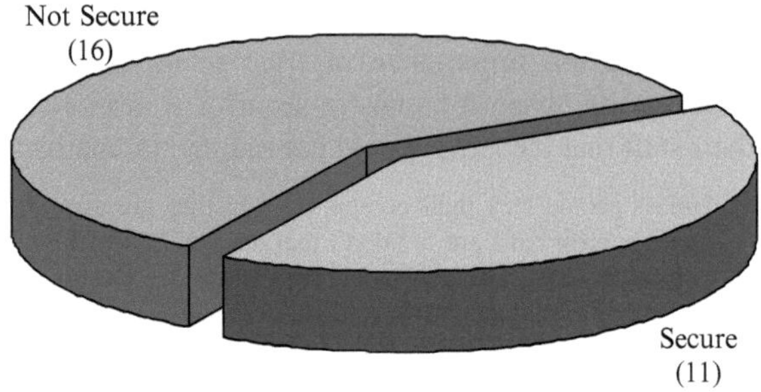

Fig. 5.3 Is the hard disk secure?

> When you are off then you do have to log in with a username and password so it's pretty rudimentary but still we recognise that you have a PC sitting there all day and anybody can walk up and do what they want.[23]

Some SM participants complained that confidentiality could never be guaranteed because IT staff could always have access to information stored on computers. Thus, they considered anything stored on computers to be unsafe. The following comment reflects a SM participant's concern about how confidentiality could be violated by someone from the IT team.

> Generally there's always somebody in the IT department that has access to your computer and that's when somebody leaves, his computer is handed over and all the information is there and can be retrieved. So I think probably, I think there is still a bit of feeling there that maybe IT will ... somebody could be looking at what I am doing and how do I protect myself from that and I don't know what you can do to that.[24]

In such circumstances the question arises: how secure a user would feel whose electronic signature is residing on his/her computer? This question was directly addressed to participants. The majority of them[25] believed that the hard disk was not a secure method of storage (Fig. 5.3).

In general, participants were of the view that electronic signatures need to be password-protected.[26] In their opinion, there would be much less concern that an unauthorised person would use someone else's electronic signature if it is secured by a password. A legal participant said that:

> Well, I personally would feel uncomfortable with everyone having access to my electronic signature ... so therefore I would want that on my PC which does have a password so I only have access to it.[27]

---

[23] P25_Co15_IT, Paragraph 51.

[24] P13_Co9_SM, Paragraph 87.

[25] 16 out of 27 participants.

[26] For example, P26_Co16_SM, Paragraph 37; P24_Co15_Legal, Paragraph 104. Another participant remarked, 'I would be quite happy with password protected electronic signatures. I have a whole range of information in my computer that is password protected and I'm happy with that ... no one has hacked in yet so it's reasonably safe' (P26_Co16_SM, Paragraph 37).

[27] P6_Co4_Legal, Paragraph 110.

Some participants suggested that an electronic signature needs to be secured with not only one but a couple of passwords – one to log onto the computer and another one to access the electronic signature.

> You have got to get your password for the computer then you get your own sort of password that you don't need to in emergencies give to your PA so I think that that would definitely be a more secure way.[28]

On the other hand, a few participants identified problems with the use of passwords. It was pointed out that in spite of an information security policy set up by IT departments/team,[29] a large number of staff would fail to abide by guidelines on the change of passwords at regular intervals.

> When you log into a system you are given a default password. My experience is that fifty percent of the people still have that password so ... anywhere down the track ... I am not sure what we really have to do ... I think if we have to move on to that ... take steps to really follow through on forcing people to change their passwords ... we do have a policy called information security policy and that essentially talks about changing the password regularly.[30]

PISD as a Security Measure

General considerations

Electronic signatures can also be stored on PISDs such as a smart card[31] or a Universal Standard Bus (USB) token (i.e. flash disk).[32] A smart card is similar in shape and size to a credit card. It is activated using a smart card reader which is attached to the computer. However, unlike a credit card which uses a magnetic stripe

[28] P18_Co11_Legal, Paragraph 141.

[29] As remarked by one IT participant, 'I am very strict on it. ... logon passwords are not to be written down ... not to be repetitive ... like just changing the number at the end. ... they are not to be written down anywhere, not to be stored on the computer system. They are meant to be stored in people's head and rotated every three months' (P3_Co2_IT, Paragraph 78).

[30] P18_Co11_Legal, Paragraph 124.

[31] The earliest research into smart cards was carried out by two German inventors, Jürgen Dethloff and Helmut Grötrupp. In 1968, they patented their idea of using plastic cards to carry microchips. See Katherine M Shelfer et al., 'Smart Cards' (2004) 60 *Advances in Computers* 149. However, the concept of smart card that we know today was patented by Roland Mareno in 1974. See R Mareno, Methods of Data Storage and Data Storage Systems, United States Patent 3, 971,916, July 1976, filed as French patent application FR 7410191 on 25 May 1974. See also Dirk Husemann, 'Standards in the Smart Card World' (2001) 36(4) *Computer Networks* 473.

[32] USB tokens such as flash disk are similar in shape and size to a house key and can be plugged into USB ports which come attached with most computers and laptops these days.

for storing data,[33] a smart card has a microprocessor chip not larger than 25 mm^2 fixed to it.[34] A smart card can store a larger amount of data as compared to a magnetic stripe card and in addition, has a powerful processing capability. It is amenable to cryptographic implementation and thus enables the subscriber to sign and encrypt[35] a document using his/her digital signature. On the other hand, a USB token such as a flash disk is different in shape and size. A flash disk can be plugged into the USB port which is available on most computers and laptops nowadays.

The advantage of using a PISD device for storing electronic signatures is that it remains under the physical possession of the authorised user. In that sense, it is like a credit card which a person can easily store in his/her wallet or pocket. Because of PISDs' almost total infallibility, a few scholars consider them a secure option for the storage of electronic signatures.[36] With PISDs, the electronic signature does not reside on the computer's hard disk. This relieves the owner from the fear that his/her unattended computer containing his/her electronic signature would be maliciously used by someone else.[37] The use of a PISD device also ensures security since it blocks undesirable access to any IT staff.[38] Against this background, participants' responses are next examined.

Security Perceptions

Although a PISD is generally considered a safer method of securing electronic signatures by scholars, only less than half of the participants[39] shared such views.

---

[33] The standardised magnetic stripe card is by far the most commonly used card in payment systems across the world although recently a few financial companies particularly in Europe have started issuing credit cards embedded with the smart card technology. See BT Today, 'Fingerprint Cards Announces Biometric Payment Card' (2008) 16(2) *Biometric Technology Today* 3, 3. Similarly, in Australia, the *Commonwealth Bank of Australia* issues credit cards to its customers that have both a magnetic stripe as well as a microprocessor chip.

[34] Hong Qian Karen Lu, 'Network Smart Card Review and Analysis (2007) 51(9) *Computer Networks* 2234, 2234.

[35] Johan Borst, Bart Preneel and Rijmen Vincent, 'Cryptography on Smart Cards' (2001) 36(4) *Computer Networks* 423, 423.

[36] Note that these authors were referring to the private key of a digital signature. David M'Raïhi and Moti Yung, 'E-Commerce Applications of Smart Cards' (2001) 36(4) *Computer Networks* 453, 457; R Julia-Barceló and T Vinje, 'Towards a European Framework for Digital Signatures and Encryption' (1998) 14(2) *Computer Law & Security Report* 79, 82; Stephen G Myers, 'Potential Liability Under the Illinois Electronic Commerce Security Act: Is it a Risk Worth Taking?' (1999) 17(3) *The John Marshall Journal of Computer & Information Law* 909. Scholars' views on this matter have been discussed in Chap. 3.

[37] Myers, above n 36, 941.

[38] As mentioned above in n 24, a SM participant pointed out that IT people generally have access to staff's computers, and thus, anything stored on hard disks can be considered unsafe. In those circumstances, storing electronic signatures on PISDs is likely to provide more security.

[39] 11 out of 27 participants.

These participants extolled the virtues of PISDs claiming that unlike a hard disk, a PISD stays in the physical possession of its owner as is the case with credit cards. They believed that a PISD was a safer option as it considerably reduces the threat of any external interference.[40] One participant remarked that PISDs were the only secure way of storing electronic signatures because if stored on the hard disk, anybody could walk up to a computer and pretend to be the authorised user.[41] He remarked that:

> [y]ou cannot be an authorised user unless you have a device or dongle or card reader or whatever that you walk around in person and identify yourself to the computer that that is your digital certificate and that is the only most secure and only real secure digital certificate that you can have ... or otherwise anybody can walk up to my computer and pretend they are me.[42]

The participant suggested that a USB key (flash disk) or a smart card was the best form of PISD for storing an electronic signature as long as it had another layer of protection in the form of a PIN or password for access.[43] Another participant believed that PISDs such as smart cards would be the next practicable solution for businesses to store electronic signatures.[44]

Despite the clear advantage that PISDs have over the use of passwords as an alternative method of storing electronic signatures on a computer's hard disk, the use of PISDs is not a foolproof method. Naturally, therefore, concerns were expressed by participants about its efficacy. The majority of them[45] considered the use of PISDs to be unsafe. Fear was expressed that as with a key or a wallet, a PISD can be lost or stolen and can get into wrong hands. It can thus be read or/and used by the author of the malicious act.[46] A participant remarked that one could accidentally drop his/her PISD in the lift and someone else could easily pick it up and use it. 'People do lose their wallets ... thus it [a PISD] doesn't sound really secure', he added.[47] Another participant noted that:

> I guess you could have a chance to lose your card. I am not sure, I am not familiar with the smart card technology that much. If you can steal someone else's card, then can you access information on the card or not?[48]

---

[40] As one participant remarked, 'Well I mean physically this is safer as a person keeps his mobile key or disk with him' (P8_Co5_Legal, Paragraph 71).

[41] P7_Co4_IT, Paragraph 37.

[42] P7_Co4_IT, Paragraph 37.

[43] 'I would say either the USB key or a smart card would be better than having it on a hard disk but I would also suggest that the device itself needs a protection of its own, sign on or some sort' (P7_Co4_IT, Paragraph 85).

[44] 'I think smart card will be the next logical step for businesses' (P25_Co15_IT, Paragraph 59).

[45] 16 out of 27 participants.

[46] 'If you lose a smart card, who is to decide that someone else can't read that smart card or use that smart card?'(P2_Co2_Legal, Paragraph 64).

[47] P18_Co11_Legal, Paragraph 147.

[48] P4_Co3_Legal, Paragraph 105.

IT participants expressed concerns that there was a very large chance of PISDs being lost and the electronic signature being used maliciously by its finder. They believed that the storage of electronic signatures on the hard disk of a computer was a better option than a PISD. Two such comments made by IT participants were:

> Look, my opinion would be it is safer to put electronic signatures on a hard disk [rather than use PISDs]. All our corporate data is valuable and only people with the right security access can get to it ... so long as the security is set up properly so that only people with the right authorisation get to the digital signature certificates, I have no problem. I think that I would be more comfortable having it on a hard disk as distinct from say a USB key that people are walking around with.[49]
>
> No, it's exactly the same position with the PC with the added thing that it is more likely to be used fraudulently because somebody could look for a smart card. If it is on a PC they have got to know which PC is it on where the file is hidden on the PC. If it's on a smart card they will just pinch the card ... to me that's less secure than the other way. It's also open to people losing them and all that sort of thing ... I wouldn't see that a better solution at all.[50]

SM participants were also generally of the same view. One of them said, 'I reckon it's safer on the hard disk ... I think that's safer than having something portable like a USB device'.[51] Of course, PISDs could be made safer through the use of a password/PIN. A number of legal participants canvassed this view. They believed that by restricting access to a PISD through a PIN/password, the PISD technology could be improved to retain the integrity of electronic signatures.[52]

Some participants were not well aware of this new technology.[53] They claimed that they did not have much faith in it.[54] One participant was under the impression that a smart card uses the magnetic stripe technology commonly embedded in credit cards.[55] He remarked that since he had earlier been a victim of a credit card fraud, he would prefer not to use a smart card.

> Look, I am not a great fan of smart cards, only because I had my American Express card and Master card reproduced and built through someone locally getting the magnetic imprint somehow. So I don't think magnetic tapes are secure.[56]

---

[49] P9_Co5_IT, Paragraphs 106.

[50] P5_Co3_IT, Paragraph 90.

[51] P23_Co14_SM, Paragraph 78.

[52] As one participant remarked, 'Perhaps you can combine with a password that might be like a PIN card' (P18_Co11_Legal, Paragraph 151).

[53] A SM participant noted, 'I think that the USB technology is fairly new and is not much known in our organisation' (P13_Co9_SM, Paragraph 101). A few legal participants were also unaware of the PISD technology.

[54] They were as yet talking about it as an option that must be explored.

[55] As mentioned in above n 33, the smart card is different from a credit card. Most credit cards make use of a magnetic stripe for storing data, whereas a smart card has a microprocessor affixed to the card that uses cryptographic authentication protocol for processing data. For technical details on the cryptography and protocols used in smart cards, see L C Guillou, M Ugon and J-J Quisquater, 'Cryptographic Authentication Protocols for Smart Cards' (2001) 36(4) *Computer Networks* 437. See also Borst, Preneel and Rijmen, above n 35.

[56] P26_Co16_SM, Paragraph 41.

However, he was also of the opinion that if smart cards were embedded with some form of chip in order to ensure their security, they could be accepted as a reliable method for storing electronic signatures.

> If there is a more secure way of using smart card like a chip in it or something, then I think that's probably a better technology and I have no problem of adopting that at all ... but just the strikable magnetic reader, I think is a highly reproducible mechanism.[57]

The above concerns raised by participants regarding smart cards largely reflected their lack of understanding of the underlying technology. This often resulted in a fear to use smart cards. Mostly, SM and legal participants revealed such ignorance, while IT participants who most likely had a sound knowledge in the area did not raise any issue about smart cards from a technical standpoint.

Biometrics as a Security Measure

Apart from passwords and PISDs, another method of securing electronic signatures is through the use of biometrics.[58] In this case, instead of using a password or a PISD to access his/her electronic signature, a subscriber uses biometrics such as fingerprint and retina scan. Various studies have considered biometrics as a secure and viable option for the storage of electronic signatures, in particular, the private key of a digital signature.[59] While smart cards could be lost or stolen, and passwords and PINs could be forgotten or tampered with, biometric devices are difficult to penetrate.[60] To have a better appreciation of participants' views, the nature and general functions of biometric devices are first outlined.

As mentioned in Chap. 2, there are various kinds of biometrics. The level of security that various biometric devices provide will depend on the device that is being used. Some types of biometrics are highly secure while others are not as secure. There is often a trade-off between cost and the level of security that biometric devices provide. For example, biometrics such as iris recognition and DNA matching are highly secure[61] with an error rate as low as 1 in 1.1 million and 1 in 5 million, respectively.[62]

---

[57] P26_Co16_SM, Paragraph 41.

[58] As mentioned in Chap. 2, these biometrics can also be considered as a form of electronic signature.

[59] Stephen G Myers, 'Potential Liability under the Illinois Electronic Commerce Security Act: Is it a Risk Worth Taking?' (1999) 17(3) *The John Marshall Journal of Computer & Information Law* 909, 941; R Julia-Barceló and T Vinje, 'Towards a European Framework for Digital Signatures and Encryption' (1998) 14(2) *Computer Law & Security Report* 79, 82; Kamini Bharvada, 'Electronic Signatures, Biometrics and PKI in the UK' (2002) 16(3) *International Review of Law, Computers & Technology* 265, 269.

[60] Bharvada, above n 35, 269.

[61] Other forms of secure biometrics are retina recognition and vein patterns.

[62] Harold F Tipton and Micki Krause, *Information Security Management Handbook* (5th ed, 2004) 14.

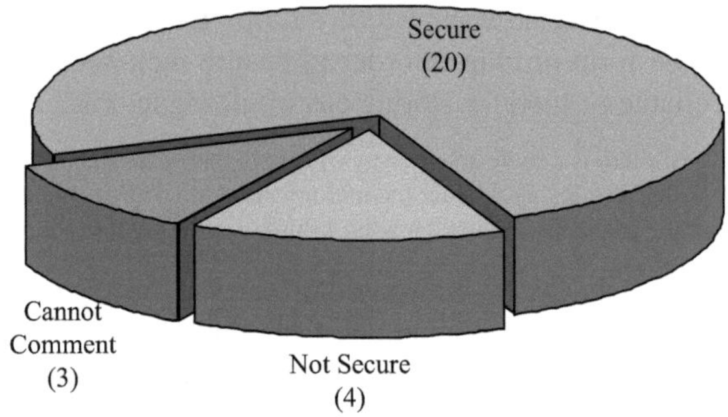

Fig. 5.4 Are biometric devices secure?

However, such biometric security devices are extremely expensive, and their high cost is unlikely to be borne by small or even medium-size businesses in Australia. Other biometric devices such as keystrokes and signature dynamics are less expensive but only moderately secure.[63]

Most participants[64] believed that the use of such technology was a secure method of authentication (Fig. 5.4). On the other hand, a small number of interviewees[65] considered biometrics to be unsafe. There was an equal number who had very little or no knowledge of biometric devices and were therefore unable to comment.[66]

The general view among legal and SM participants with regard to biometrics was that they were more secure and harder to crack than any security mechanisms such as passwords and PISDs. They found biometrics to be fail-safe[67] and more trustworthy because they individualised and personalised one's physical attributes such as fingerprint and retina scan. One participant was convinced that 'to crack biometrics such as fingerprints or retina scan or whatever was not accessible to most people, [was] harder'.[68]

IT participants also felt that the use of biometrics was a very safe and secure process to provide security to electronic signatures[69] and that it could be described as 'the ultimate form of protection'.[70] As expected they were relatively more familiar with biometrics than other participants and quite a few remarked that the technology was already in use in their organisation for purposes other than electronic signatures.[71]

[63] Ibid.

[64] 20 out of 27 participants.

[65] 4 out of 27 participants.

[66] For example, a couple of participants remarked: '[My] technical knowledge is lacking' (P6_Co4_Legal, Paragraph, 138); 'I don't know how effective it is' (P24_Co15_Legal, Paragraph, 119).

[67] For example, P18_Co11_Legal, Paragraph 155; P2_Co2_Legal, Paragraph 64.

[68] P4_Co3_Legal, Paragraph 113.

[69] For example, a few remarks made were 'That's a clever thought having some sort of biometric that authenticates the person. If it was to that level, ya, that would be very acceptable definitely' (P9_Co5_IT, Paragraph 110); 'Oh better than just a password … it's another form of security' (P3_Co2_IT, Paragraph 85); 'I think that's a lot safer than smart cards' (P3_Co2_IT, Paragraph 86).

[70] P7_Co4_IT, Paragraph 97.

[71] An IT participant pointed out that his organisation was issuing new laptops that were equipped with biometric scanners to its staff. According to another participant, his company was using a thumb print device on USBs for staff to access the organisation's network with a view to providing a double layer of security and confidentiality.

On the other hand, there were a small number of participants who believed that there exist security threats even with biometrics. According to them, 'someone could decrypt the [biometric] code so the risk [was] still there'.[72] However, more than security, participants claimed to have issues with the usability aspect of the biometric devices. Those who had personal experience with using biometrics, in particular, the fingerprint technology, claimed that they were troublesome to use. According to one IT participant, his organisation had tried using the fingerprint access technology on its office computers but had to face a host of problems. If a user's 'finger was greasy or blurry, dirty or had a cut or ink stain, the computer denied him access'.[73] Thus, the organisation had no other choice but to reject it. Another IT participant shared a similar experience. He had received a portable digital assistant (PDA) from his organisation that was embedded with a fingerprint reader instead of a password; that would take him 'three or four goes'[74] every time he would use the PDA before he would gain access to it. According to these participants, biometric technology such as fingerprint was still in its infancy, and it still had a long way to go before it could be readily accepted.[75]

> Look, what they are thinking I think, it's a bit futuristic ... movie stuff like ... people putting thumb print and retina scan and all that type of things. I think smart card will be the next logical step for business but I think it will happen someday, ultimately it will happen ... am I against it personally? no no ... because I think it will happen.[76]

The Internet

So far, this chapter has examined the three methods that are commonly used to provide security to electronic signatures. However, electronic signatures are transmitted via the Internet, and therefore, it is also important to consider problems that are likely to arise because of the use of the Internet.

The Internet is commonly believed to be insecure. Even the most widely used computer operating systems in the world cannot guarantee security of messages sent through the Internet.[77] The use of the Internet can make a computer susceptible to risk without a user of an electronic signature being aware of it.[78] A user may unknowingly install a malicious software from the Internet which secretly allows a

---

[72] P23_Co14_SM, Paragraph 83.

[73] P5_Co3_IT, Paragraph 98.

[74] P7_Co4_IT, Paragraph 59.

[75] For example, P5_Co3_IT, Paragraph 98; P7_Co4_IT, Paragraph 59.

[76] P25_Co15_IT, Paragraph 59.

[77] See 'Hi-tech Giant Microsoft has Acknowledged that a Security Flaw in its Popular Internet Passport Service left 200 Million Consumer Accounts Vulnerable to Hackers and Thieves': Editorial, 'Online Flaw a Visa to Thieves', *World, Herald Sun* (Melbourne), 10 May 2003, 19.

[78] Clarke, above n 7.

remote computer to surreptitiously take control of the user's computer.[79] Computers connected to the Internet are also vulnerable to attacks where the software is remotely installed on a distant computer to capture and transmit a user's keyboard data to that location.[80] According to a business e-fraud survey of senior executives from 92 large public and private Australian companies, '[s]eventy-nine percent of the respondents indicated that a security breach to their electronic commerce system would most likely occur via the Internet or other external access'.[81] Such concerns are likely to create reluctance on the part of businesses to use the Internet[82] and therefore to use electronic signatures, an Internet-based technology.

A high proportion of participants[83] considered the Internet to be unsafe. In their opinion, any document traversing through the Internet, including documents signed through electronic signatures, is prone to security threat. Nearly two-third of legal and SM participants considered the Internet to be insecure, while all IT participants were of the view that the Internet was indeed unsafe.

Although IT participants believed that the Internet was insecure, they were mostly of the view that such insecurity was unlikely to deter them from using electronic signatures. They believed that the Internet could be a safe vehicle to transmit electronic signatures particularly digital signatures provided that the encryption technology was properly used for sending documents via the Internet.[84] To ensure the safety of an electronic signature during transmission via the Internet, a participant made the following suggestion:

> If you have got like some of the new wireless standards, ... if that was used more on electronic signatures where the pass keys are 1024 bits and keep adjusting themselves every 10 minutes ... that's going to be pretty hard to crack at the moment and that sort of stuff if it's kept up-to-date ... sorts of standards of encryption similar to what wireless is ... if that was used ... [it] would be a lot safer.[85]

---

[79] Clarke, above n 7.

[80] Steve Burnett, and Stephen Paine, *RSA Security's Official Guide to Cryptography* (2001) 7.

[81] Drugs and Crime Prevention Committee, Parliament of Victoria, *Inquiry into Fraud and Electronic Commerce* (2004) 75. http://www.parliament.vic.gov.au/dcpc/Reports/DCPC_FraudElectronicCommerce_05-01-2004.pdf at 21 March 2012.

[82] Paul Markillie, 'A Survey of E-Commerce: Unlimited Opportunities?', *The Economist*, 15 May 2004, 14.

[83] 20 out of 27 participants.

[84] The reason why these IT participants felt secure with regard to transactions over the Internet was because they were doing their personal banking online and were satisfied with the Internet from a security perspective. 'I do my own banking on the Internet and as far as security is there and is encrypted correctly there is no problem. The only problem with the Internet is that things are delayed due to its nature, but security I don't think is an issue' (P5_Co3_IT, Paragraph 102). Another IT participant stated that security of any document traversing through the Internet 'depends upon the encryption level, how hard it is to crack' (P3_Co2_IT, Paragraph 103). He believed that security was not an issue where encryption technology is used to the highest level. Note that as discussed in Chap. 2, the encryption technologies underlying digital signatures can ensure confidentiality of information. See also Margaret Jackson, 'Internet Privacy' (2003) 53(2) *Telecommunications Journal of Australia* 21, 29.

[85] P3_Co2_IT, Paragraph 103.

With regard to legal participants, while a small number of them considered the Internet to be secure, the majority feared that it was not a safe medium of communication and transaction despite advancement in technology in the form of firewall software and secure socket layer (SSL). The following remarks made by a couple of participants reflected their views:

> We are always aware that when dealing with any transaction over the telecommunication network there is always that risk of it being accessed from external sources ... you might have your firewall and various defence mechanisms but having come from an IT company in the past, having actually met very clever programmers and computer experts ... nothing is safe if they are determined enough.[86]
>
> I think even if there is a padlock down the bottom of the internet page [SSL] or whatever ... there is always some whiz kid out there who can hack into anything. I mean they can hack into NASA and CIA then why couldn't they hack into our company?[87]

Among SM participants, less than a third of them believed that the Internet was a secure method of transmitting electronic signatures. One participant claimed that Internet communications are more secure than transactions made on paper. 'A formal handwritten signature is easier to forge than an electronic signature',[88] he remarked. Another participant who also believed that the Internet was a safe medium of communication said that he never had any problem with his banking transactions effected via the Internet and therefore would not expect any safety concern with the use of electronic signatures.[89]

Some SM participants were of the view that frauds within an organisation were more common than those via the Internet because most malicious activities are committed internally. Thus, with electronic signatures, it is more likely that a user's signature will be forged by his/her own colleagues within an organisation rather than externally via the Internet.

> The fraud normally is an internal fraud than transmission fraud and so I think the euphoria of people collecting thousands of cards through syphoning and data out of pay pal and things like that ... yes, a fairly strong imagination.[90]

A Critique of Participants' Views

The usefulness and effectiveness of electronic signatures have been more misunderstood than understood. The above discussion of participants' views regarding the safety of electronic signatures often featured unnecessary concerns. As recently put

---

[86] P8_Co5_Legal, Paragraph 26.

[87] P2_Co2_Legal, Paragraph 44.

[88] P12_Co7_SM, Paragraph 39.

[89] 'Personally, I use banking facilities over the Internet and things like that. I don't have any concerns with it'. (P13_Co9_SM, Paragraph 83).

[90] P26_Co16_SM, Paragraph 57.

forward by a guru in the field of security, 'security is really two different things. It's a feeling and it's a reality. And they're very different. You can feel secure even though you're not, and you can be secure even though you don't feel it'.[91] He believed that 'if the feeling [of security] is greater than the reality, one has a false sense of security; if the reality is greater than the fear, then one has a false sense of insecurity which in extreme cases could be called paranoia … or irrational fear'.[92]

Unnecessary concerns and occasionally irrational fear have unfortunately translated into reluctance in the business community to integrate electronic signatures into their systems. This section provides a critical analysis of participants' views, disputing some of their unfounded fears and concerns.

Several security issues were raised by participants. Note that there are always risks involved when valuables or assets are not adequately secured. The same applies to electronic signatures. They can also be forged if adequate security is not provided. Certainly, if computers are left unattended and employees can easily access colleagues' electronic signature, malicious acts are likely to be committed.

First, the use of strong passwords is indispensable for securing electronic signatures. It provides protection to an electronic signature stored on a computer against malicious access by an unauthorised person.[93] However, from participants' views, it appears that despite password security policies implemented by their organisation's IT team, staff would hardly abide by them. This characterises some kind of carelessness towards passwords. Such lackadaisical attitudes towards the use of passwords are in conformity with various studies and surveys that have investigated password security.[94] Studies have found that people often choose passwords that are easily revealed.[95] In particular, one in every five users chooses his/her name as a password, while one in every ten uses his/her birthday as a password.[96] Such weak passwords

---

[91] Bruce Schneier, 'Art and Science: Bruce Schneier Shares Security Ideas at Museum', *Network World,* 28 March 2008. http://www.networkworld.com/news/2008/032808-schneier.html?page=1 at 20 March 2012.

[92] Ibid.

[93] An IT participant showed his concern when he said that without strong passwords 'it is always risky for your PC to be sitting there all day. Anybody can walk up to it and do whatever he or she likes' (P25_Co15_IT, Paragraph 51).

[94] See Ernst & Young, *Global Information Security Survey 2006-Achieving Success in a Globalized World: Is Your Way Secure?* (2006). http://www.naider.com/upload/ernst%20young.pdf at 21 March 2012; Steven Furnell, 'Authenticating Ourselves: Will We Ever Escape the Password?' (2005) 3 *Network Security* 8, 9; John Leyden, *Office Workers Give Away Password for a Cheap Pen* (2003) The Register. http://www.theregister.co.uk/2003/04/18/office_workers_give_away_passwords/ at 21 March 2012.

[95] 'Lazy workers beware! Study reveals the most popular computer password (and, yes, it's 'Password1')', *Daily Mail,* 6 March 2012. http://www.dailymail.co.uk/news/article-2110924/Lazy-workers-beware-Study-reveals-popular-password-yes-Password1.html at 20 March 2012.

[96] International Chamber of Commerce, *Being Coy about your Age makes Good E-Security Sense* (2000). http://www.iccwbo.org/search/query.asp at 25 April 2011. In another study, 80 % of the people surveyed had passwords related to golf. See Wayne C Summers and Edward Bosworth, 'Password Policy: The Good, the Bad, and the Ugly (Paper presented at the Winter International Symposium on Information and Communication Technologies (WISICT'04), Cancum, Mexico, 5–8 January 2004).

can be effortlessly obtained either through the help of social engineering[97] or cracked through the help of some software.[98]

Why are passwords so vulnerable to security threats? This is because individuals tend to choose passwords that are easy to guess. If lengthy and complex passwords are chosen instead, they would not be easily cracked.[99] In addition, if passwords are changed at regular intervals, as usually advised, they are very likely to remain secure. However, failing to implement such precautionary measures makes electronic signatures behind such passwords prone to attack.[100]

Thus, despite the common belief among participants that the storage of electronic signatures on a computer's hard disk could be secured through the use of passwords, this is not necessarily true. The primary factor that makes passwords unsafe for securing electronic signatures is users' sloppy usage and management of their passwords.[101]

Second, in regard to PISDs, the majority of participants considered such devices to be unsafe. Concerns were raised that PISDs could be easily lost or stolen and used for malicious purposes. Such fears and concerns towards the use of PISDs have

---

[97] For more details on social engineering and password security, see Michael E Whitman, Herbert J Mattord, *Management of Information Security* (2004).

[98] Joseph A Cazier and B Dawn Medlin (2006) 'Password Security: An Empirical Investigation into E-Commerce Passwords and their Crack Times' (2006) 15(6) *Information Systems Security* 45, 47. Social engineering involves social skills to convince an individual to disclose either directly personal details such as a password or those details that will help identify the individual's password. For example, in a European trade show, using social engineering skills, its organisers asked unsuspecting office workers travelling through the London tube for their office computer passwords. More than 70 % of the respondents disclosed such details without hesitation. See Kerry Murphy, 'Psst: a candy Bar for Your Password?,' *IT Business, The Australian* (Melbourne), 27 April 2004, 6. Also 'study after study shows that [people] will give up passwords if asked in the right way'. See Keith Regan, *The Fine Art of Password Protection* (2003) E-Commerce Times. http://www.ecommercetimes.com/story/21776.html at 20 March 2012. In those cases where social engineering is unsuccessful or not applicable, passwords can be cracked through a range of software which is readily available in the marketplace. For example, *L0phtCrack* is a widely available software that can be used to crack open a password. In a recent study, it was found that more than 99 % of passwords used in e-commerce can be effortlessly cracked using the *L0phtCrack 5* software. An astounding 90 % of the passwords were found to be cracked within a minute. See Cazier and Medlin, above n 98. For a list of software available that can be used to crack or recover passwords, see Free Download Manager *Software Downloads Site*. http://www.freedownloadmanager.org/download.htm/ at 5 March 2012.

[99] Craig Donovan, *Strong Passwords* (2002) SANS Institute. http://www.giac.org/paper/gsec/43/strong-passwords/100348 at 15 March 2012.

[100] See Don Davis, 'Compliance Defects in Public-key Cryptography' (Paper presented at the 6th Conference on USENIX Security Symposium, Focusing on Applications of Cryptography, San Jose, CA, 22–25 July 1996).

[101] The researcher's findings are in conformity with scholars' views on this subject. Scholars believe that there is a high usability barrier to the proper handling of passwords and that they represent one of the most exploitable elements in the chain of security. See J Mulligan and A J Elbirt, 'Desktop Security and Usability Trade-offs: An Evaluation of Password Management Systems' (2005) 14(2) *Information Systems Security* 10, 10.

often been brought up in the literature.[102] The use of PISDs for storing electronic signatures has largely been associated with human frailty.[103] As with credit cards, in spite of recommended precautionary measures, users may potentially lose their PISD device such as a smart card and a flash disk.[104]

On the other hand, there was a common perception among participants that electronic signatures stored on a PISD and secured with a password/PIN could provide adequate security. However, the researcher argues that if users are careless towards their computer passwords, then there is an equally good chance that they would also be careless towards their PISD's password/PIN. In those cases where users lose their PISD with their electronic signature stored on it but the password/PIN is secure, the security of the electronic signature will depend on the type of PISD used. Note that not all types of PISD provide adequate security. Out of the various forms of PISD, smart cards have generally been found to be the most secure[105] (See Appendix B on how a document is signed through a digital signature with the help of a private key stored on to a smart card). On the other hand, PISDs such as USB keys (flash disks) are susceptible to a number of practical and theoretical attacks.[106]

In spite of smart cards being technologically the most secure form of PISD, businesses would only use them if they are well-informed of such security features. In the above discussion, a lack of understanding about the smart card technology has appeared to be one of the factors underlying businesses' reluctance to use the technology particularly among legal and SM participants. Smart cards were wrongly believed to be embedded with the magnetic stripe technology that features in most credit cards.

Third, as shown above, even though a large number of participants believed that the storage of an electronic signature on a computer secured through a password/ PIN is safe, it is not necessarily the case given end users' careless attitude towards

---

[102] R R Jueneman and R J Robertson Jr, 'Biometrics and Digital Signatures in Electronic Commerce' (1998) 38(3) *Jurimetrics* 427, 428; Davis, above n 100.

[103] Mason and Bohm, above n 7, 465.

[104] Ibid.

[105] In the past few years, smart cards have become more powerful and secure. See Bart Preneel, 'A Survey of Recent Developments in Cryptographic Algorithms for Smart Cards' (2007) 51(9) *Computer Networks* 2223, 2230; Josep Domingo-Ferrer, et al., 'Advances in Smart Cards' (2007) 51(9) *Computer Networks* 2219, 2219; Drugs and Crime Prevention Committee, above n 82, 97. Developments in the field of smart card technology are ongoing. The industry is coming up with a new type of card known as the *Network Smart Card.* Unlike the traditional smart card that uses the international standard ISO 7816 communication protocol to communicate to a host computer through a smart card reader, a *Network Smart Card* is not required to follow this protocol. It can communicate directly with local and remote computers using standard Internet protocols. This enables them to provide end-to-end security over the Internet and protect digital identities effectively. See Lu, above n 34, 2234. See also Joaquin Torres, Antonio Izquierdo and Jose Maria Sierra, 'Advances in Network Smart Cards Authentication' (2007) 51(9) *Computer Networks* 2249.

[106] J Kingpin, 'Attacks on and Countermeasures for USB Hardware Token Devices' (Paper presented at the 5th Nordic Workshop on Secure IT Systems Encouraging Co-operation, Reykjavik, Iceland, 12–13 October 2000) 35.

their passwords. In the same vein, users also risk being careless towards their PISDs' password/PIN. An alternate method of securing electronic signatures that was discussed above is through the use of biometrics. Other than some usability issues, biometrics seem to overcome most of the weaknesses associated with the use of passwords and PISDs.[107]

Most interviewees considered the use of biometrics as a safe method of storing electronic signatures. Those who had some experience with the fingerprint technology indeed found it to be secure except for a few operational limitations. Comparing four types of biometrics (finger, voice, face and iris of the eye), a recent study revealed that the fingerprint was generally the most suitable type of biometric technology to date, not only from usability aspect but also from a security point of view (See Appendix C for further details).[108] Among the various factors used to assess or rate the different types of biometrics, fingerprints were found to have a higher false acceptance rate (FAR). In other words, they hardly ever allow access to an illegitimate user. On the other hand, a relatively high false rejection rate (FRR) for fingerprints suggested that at times it may fail to recognise the fingerprint of the legitimate user. Therefore, it may be possible that a subscriber who would want to send an important agreement signed through his/her electronic signature may be unable to activate it as the system would fail to recognise his/her fingerprint. Such concerns were also raised by participants regarding the use of fingerprint biometrics.[109] However, ongoing developments[110] in biometric technology are likely to address such limitations in coming years.

Fourth, the majority of participants feared that the Internet was insecure although they believed that it would not necessarily deter businesses from using electronic signatures. Some extolled the virtues of the Internet considering it to be a safe platform for data transmission provided that it was equipped with the encryption technology as a security tool.

From the researcher's standpoint, although the encryption technology can secure documents signed through electronic signatures traversing through the Internet, there still exists a major risk to an electronic signature stored on the hard disk of a computer. This is because most computers connected through the Internet are prone to be attacked by hackers. 'Hackers keep track of Internet Protocol (IP) addresses assigned by Internet service providers, scanning addresses to find PCs that do not have current security patches in place'.[111] An individual's electronic signature is

---

[107] More recently, biometrics has also been combined with server centric PKI where the subscriber/user's private key is stored on a centralised server and access is granted through his biometrics. However, the technology is still at an immature stage and the cost is too high. See A Jancic and M J Warren, 'PKI-Advantages and Obstacles' (Paper presented at 2nd Australian Information Security Management Conference on Securing the Future, Perth, Australia, 26 November 2006).

[108] Paul Reid, *Biometrics for Network Security* (2004) 10.

[109] See above n 75.

[110] See Leigh Funston, 'Biometric Technology Shines' (2007) (June) *Australian National Security Magazine* 28.

[111] Andrea Klein, 'Building an Identity Management Infrastructure for Today … and Tomorrow' (2007) 16(2) *Information Systems Security* 74, 74.

susceptible to attack from a remote computer in the global network through the use of software such as the *Inspector Copier*.[112]

However, an electronic signature is not only susceptible to attack by hackers sitting some distance away on a remote computer but also by employees within the organisation. As mentioned by a few participants, the higher risk of forgery of a subscriber's electronic signature is not through the Internet but through colleagues who are in close vicinity to his/her computer. Finally, although the use of passwords and/or biometrics can minimise such fraudulent actions, an electronic signature may still be at risk from office colleagues because of the use of the Intranet,[113] as is the case with the Internet.

Concluding Observations

This chapter examined participants' *perceived* lack of security with regard to electronic signatures. It appears that participants' such perceived lack of security is largely driven by ignorance and misunderstandings. In some instances, unnecessary concerns and occasionally irrational fear have also translated into reluctance in the business community to integrate electronic signatures into their systems. Advising prospective users of electronic signatures about the kind of safeguards that could be put in place to minimise risks associated with their usage can be a useful step towards overcoming their fears and hesitance. In this regard, the following observations are made.

If electronic signatures are properly stored, their misuse can be minimised. Those who use this new technology and fail to follow the required safeguards cannot pass on the blame to the technology. Unattended computers indeed pose security risks for electronic signatures stored on the machines' hard disks, even if they are secured with passwords. More importantly, these passwords need to be kept confidential as *loose lips sink ships*.[114] They require proper usage and management.[115]

---

[112] Such software can remotely back up data from the individual's computer by bypassing the operating system protections such as passwords used to secure the contents on his computer. In addition, the *KeyLogging* software, which can record key strokes and capture passwords, can also be downloaded from the Internet. A hacker can use such software to perform attacks on password-protected files such as an electronic signature stored on a computer's hard disk. See especially Burnett and Paine, above n 80, 7. See generally Jeordan Legon, *Student Hacks School, Erases Class Files* (2003) CNN.com 11 June 2003. http://www.cnn.com/2003/TECH/internet/06/10/school.hacked/index.html at 12 March 2012.

[113] An intranet is a network of computers within an organisation. The Intranet may or may not be connected to the global Internet. Examples of Intranet are the local area network (LAN), the metropolitan area network (MAN) and the wide area network (WAN).

[114] The phrase *loose lips sink ships* comes from a US war propaganda slogan during World War II. It was an attempt of the *Office of War Information* to limit the possibility that people might inadvertently give useful information to enemy spies. This was one of several similar slogans which all came under the campaigns basic message – 'Careless Talk Costs Lives'. See *The Phrase Finder*. http://www.phrases.org.uk/meanings/237250.html at 14 March 2012.

[115] A good practice is to use a password which is a combination of symbols, numbers and letters. See Peter P Swire, 'A Model for when Disclosure Helps Security: What is Different about Computer and Network Security?' (2004) 3 *Journal on Telecommunication & High Technology Law,* 163, 190.

This can be achieved using lengthy and complex passwords which are not shared with others.[116] Strict password policies can be implemented by organisations and ensured that employees conform to them. For instance, it should be ensured that passwords are not written down anywhere or stored on the computer system and that they are changed every few months.

On the other hand, replacing passwords with biometrics can be a secure option but not necessarily be a foolproof alternative. A computer with an electronic signature stored on its hard disk would most likely be connected at some stage or the other to the Internet and/or an Intranet. With the use of either Intranet or the Internet, there are high risks of remote attacks within an organisation or from a hacker sitting thousands of miles away. Remote attacks can bypass operating systems security, thereby making any desktop security measures such as biometrics, not to mention passwords, redundant. In order to protect electronic signatures from risks associated with the Internet/Intranet, a possible option is to store them on secure PISDs.

As discussed above, the most secure form of PISD is a smart card.[117] However, there are two issues associated with the use of smart cards. First, it appears that people are either unaware or have very little understanding of smart cards particularly the technology associated with them. Smart cards are often wrongly believed to be embedded with the magnetic stripe technology as are most bank credit cards. Educating the business sector about the technology underlying smart cards is likely to overcome the prevailing ignorance and misunderstanding.[118]

---

[116] In reality, there should be two passwords. One password should be used to secure access to the computer and the other to secure access to the electronic signature. Also, the two passwords should be different to enhance security.

[117] Readers may argue that electronic signatures stored on a smart card may be susceptible to Internet risks. This would happen when during the process of signing a document the smart card is connected to the computer that is in turn connected to the Intranet/Internet. During that period, a remote attack is possible on the electronic signature. However, since the smart card is in contact with the Intranet/Internet for only a very short period, this threat is minimal as compared to when electronic signatures are stored on a computer's hard disk which is often connected permanently to the Internet/ Intranet. However, the *Network Smart Card* can overcome this problem to a considerable extent. See Hong Qian Karen Lu, 'Network Smart Card Review and Analysis (2007) 51(9) *Computer Networks* 2234, 2234. . See also Joaquin Torres, Antonio Izquierdo and Jose Maria Sierra, 'Advances in Network Smart Cards Authentication' (2007) 51(9) *Computer Networks* 2249.

[118] Note that the former federal government was planning to introduce the national identity card that would have used the smart card technology. The intention was to replace a number of existing cards, including the Medicare card and various benefit cards issued by Centrelink and the Department of Veterans' Affairs with the ID card. Had this project been implemented, it would have most likely familiarised users with the smart card technology given the broad-based use of Medicare and Centrelink cards. For issues related to such cards, see Graham Greenleaf, 'Function Creep – Defined and Still Dangerous in Australia's Revised ID Card Bill' (2008) 24(1) *Computer Law & Security Report* 56; Graham Greenleaf, 'Australia's Proposed ID Card: Still Quacking like a Duck' (2007) 23(2) *Computer Law & Security Report* 156; Margaret Jackson and Julian Ligertwood, 'Identity Management: Is an Identity Card the Solution for Australia?'(2006) 24 *Prometheus* 379; Margaret Jackson and Julian Ligertwood, 'The Health and Social Services Access Card: What will it mean for Australians?' (Paper presented at the Financial Literacy, Banking and Identity Conference, Melbourne, Australia, 25–26 October 2006).

However, if users are not careful towards their smart cards' password/PIN – which is quite likely to happen because of their sloppy attitude towards computer passwords – the security of the stored electronic signatures can easily be compromised. To address this issue, biometrics may be considered as an alternative to passwords for securing smart cards. While there exist several types of biometric, the use of fingerprint has proved itself to be the most suitable technology to date from a security and usability aspect.

It appears that storing electronic signatures on smart cards – where the card holder's identity is authenticated through his/her fingerprint – is the most secure and viable option. If such a comprehensive security infrastructure is adopted, electronic signatures are likely to be protected from malicious acts. Note that with recent advancement in the smart card technology, it is now possible to have a fingerprint sensor on the smart card itself.[119]

However, simply by having a strong security infrastructure for protecting electronic signatures from any malicious use is not adequate to implement the technology. As per an IT security expert, an information security program can only be effective if it is complemented with 'awareness and training programs that address policy, procedures and tools'.[120] Similar strategies may be considered for electronic signatures.

[119] The fingerprint sensor works as follows: The user places his finger on the sensor area of the smart card once it is inserted into the reader. The feedback on access or denial is given through a green or red light embedded within the card. Note that the cost of these cards currently varies from US$40–US$60. See BT Today, 'A Standards-based Biometric Smart Card – At What Cost?' (2008) 16(1) *Biometric Technology Today* 3, 3. See also Denis Praca and Claude Barral, 'From Smart Cards to Smart Objects: The Road to New Smart Technologies' (2001) 36(4) *Computer Networks* 381, 386.

[120] Thomas R Peltier, 'Implementing an Information Security Awareness Program' (2005) 14(2) *Information Systems Security* 37, 37.

Chapter 6
Legal Understanding and Issues with Electronic Signatures

Concerns regarding evidentiary issues and other legal aspects of electronic signatures can be important impediments to the use of electronic signatures in the business community. Three main legal concerns were identified as potential factors that contribute to a reluctance to use the electronic signature technology. Firstly, the analysis identified an ignorance of the law itself to be an important contributor to the non-acceptance of electronic signatures in the business community. The majority of participants said they were unaware of the laws governing electronic signatures in Australia, and the rest had only a superficial knowledge of the provisions.[1] Businesses' lack of awareness and understanding of the legislation appeared to be largely responsible for their lack of appreciation of the technology. In addition, a failure to understand the legislation could potentially weaken businesses' confidence in using the technology.

Secondly, interview participants expressed concerns about evidentiary issues with regard to the use of electronic signatures. Close to half the number of participants were uncertain how electronic signatures would be proved in the court of law because their features are different from those of manuscript signatures. Serious concerns were also raised about the requirement of originals, witnesses and handwriting experts in the electronic realm.

Thirdly, participants revealed some apprehensions with regard to the use of electronic signatures because of the existence of separate electronic signature legislation models across different countries. A lack of harmonisation of the different electronic transactions laws (ETLs) could potentially create inconsistencies and complexities in the development of contracts with international partners. Many participants advocated that unless there was a reasonable synergy between these models, the business community would not feel comfortable using electronic signatures. This chapter provides a thorough discussion of these three legal issues.

---

[1] Eighteen out of twenty-seven participants were unaware of the legislation governing electronic signatures in Australia.

A. Srivastava, *Electronic Signatures for B2B Contracts: Evidence from Australia*,

DOI 10.1007/978-81-322-0743-6_6,

Lack of Knowledge and Understanding of the ETA

There was a fairly low level of awareness among participants of the law governing electronic signatures in Australia. The majority of them were unaware of the existence of the ETA[2] while the rest demonstrated only a limited understanding of the Act with very superficial knowledge of its provisions and other details.[3] Unawareness of the existence of the law was clearly revealed by this participant's statement:

> I think the government should come out with some legislation. There should be some kind of legislation that should be out in Australia which says that electronic signatures are an acceptable form and can legally replace paper-based form of signature. Then only we businesses may be thinking of using it.[4]

When analysed by subgroups of participants, it was reassuring to note that a higher proportion among legal participants knew about the existence of such law although the numbers were not as high as expected. Certainly, legal professionals were expected to be more abreast of the law. On the other hand, a high level of unawareness was noted among IT and senior management (SM) participants. A couple of participants clearly revealed their ignorance of the electronic signature legislation through these remarks:

> I am not aware of any such law. It is very surprising because my solicitor has never told me about anything as such that this new law is in place and electronic signatures can be a replacement to paper-based signature. Thanks for telling it to me.[5]
>
> We haven't looked into that and we accept legal documents or fax documents with signatures on them but this is as far as we have taken it. We really haven't gone and explored the wider legal aspect of understanding or where the law sits with it.[6]

Businesses' lack of awareness and understanding of the Australian legislation governing electronic signatures appeared to be a major reason for their lack of appreciation of the technology. As claimed by a participant, 'I assume that [an electronic signature] is an appropriate method of executing a document but perhaps my lack of knowledge of the law on that point is part of my reluctance towards it'.[7]

---

[2] Note that such unawareness also extends to any of the state and territory level electronic signature and transaction legislation. The states and territories' legislation are *Electronic Transactions Act 2000* (NSW), *Electronic Transactions Act 2000* (SA), *Electronic Transactions Act 2000* (Tas), *Electronic Transactions Act 2000* (ACT), *Electronic Transactions Act 2003* (WA), *Electronic Transactions (Victoria) Act 2000* (Vic), *Electronic Transactions (Queensland) Act 2000* (Qld) and *Electronic Transactions (Northern Territory) Act 2000* (NT).

[3] The following responses were noted from participants: 'I am not aware of it being a recognised form' (P16_Co4_Legal, Paragraph 68), 'I know there are viable options and there are rules around it but I do not know in great detail' (P18_Co11_Legal, Paragraph 197), 'We really haven't gone and explored the wider legal aspect of understanding or where the law sits with it' (P14_Co9_SM, Paragraph 123) and 'There are some legislation in 2001, the *Electronic Transactions Act* or something like that. That is all I remember but I am not deeply familiar with it' (P21_Co12_Legal, Paragraph 10).

[4] P12_Co7_SM, Paragraph 72.

[5] P12_Co7_SM, Paragraph 76.

[6] P14_Co9_SM, Paragraph 123.

[7] P2_Co2_Legal, Paragraph 31.

While the legislation could have played an important role in promoting the growth of electronic signatures, it has certainly not achieved this purpose. Businesses need to understand the legislation, what technologies come within the ambit of electronic signatures, how they are regulated and what are the legal requirements. Such understanding would enhance the legal seriousness of electronic signatures and, in turn, encourage businesses to use the new technology more confidently for conducting contracts and commercial transactions with other businesses.

Some participants were of the view that businesses would willingly switch over from the practice of manuscript signature to electronic signature for endorsing contracts and documents if they receive adequate legal advice.[8] However, providing adequate legal advice can be quite challenging for legal advisors given some fundamental drawbacks in the electronic signature legislation.[9] Legal advisors' inability to provide advice was clearly reflected in this participant's comment:

> I think our legal counsel would say, 'why the hell are you signing it that way?' and then I will ask him why ... then he would come and talk to me and say, 'look it's not secure enough, there is no adequate legal back up. I would prefer that you delay the whole thing, sign it originally and airbag the document to America which is only going to take 24 hours anyway.[10]

Participants' lack of understanding about electronic signatures and their legislation did not allow the researcher to carry out a detailed examination of participants' perceptions about the ETA. However, their views were sought on other legal issues regarding evidentiary matters and the existence of different legislative models at international level. The following sections discuss these issues.

Evidentiary Issues and Electronic Signatures

The issue of admissibility of evidence with regard to electronic documents and signatures has in general been addressed in the laws of Australia.[11] Such legislation make provisions that electronic documents and signatures shall not be denied admissibility on the ground that they are in electronic form.[12] Such provisions, however, give a leeway to the court not to admit electronic evidence on grounds other than

---

[8] For example, one participant remarked, 'If it became an accepted format of doing business then we will obviously upon legal advice enter into electronic contracts'. (P6_Co4_Legal, Paragraph 68).

[9] This issue is discussed below in n 88 and n 89.

[10] P1_Co1_Legal, Paragraph 153.

[11] The ETA and the *Evidence Act 1995* (Cth) make provisions with regard to this issue. For further discussions, see below n 47.

[12] ETA s 8. See also Philip N Argy, 'Law of Evidence: Relevance and Admissibility', in Stephen Mason (ed), *Electronic Evidence: Disclosure, Discovery and Admissibility* (2007) 122–147; David Zimmerman, 'Evidence in the Digital Age' (2002) 76(2) *Law Institute Journal* 77.

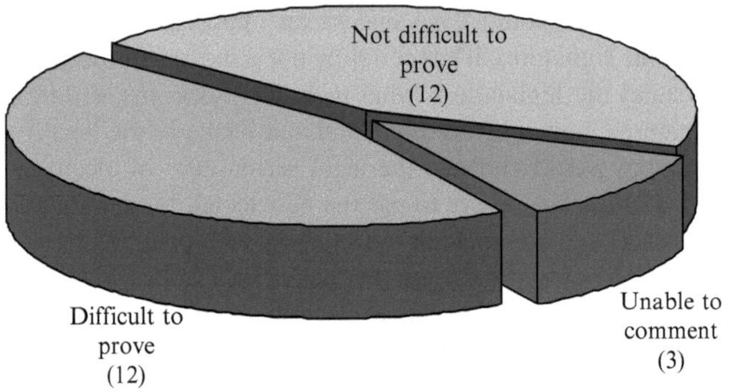

Fig. 6.1 Proving an electronic signature

their electronic form.[13] Because of this discretion, it is likely that the admissibility of electronic signatures will continue to be an issue. Proof of the authenticity of an electronic signature in case of dispute is also of concern.

Close to half the number of participants[14] believed that it would be quite simple to prove the authenticity of an electronic signature in the court of law (Fig. 6.1). Several statements such as: 'it is quite a simple task, especially if the services of IT experts are taken'[15]; proving electronic signatures in the court of law was 'possibly easier than … for example for a biologist to talk about DNA matching'[16]; and 'it would be easy to prove an electronic signature in the court of law because it is really the intent rather than the specifics on which evidence is based'[17] were suggestive that proving the authenticity of an electronic signature was not believed to be a major issue by businesses. One IT participant who was convinced that the authenticity of an electronic signature could be proved in the court but would certainly require a lot of documentary evidence said, 'I could prove that it will hold up in the court because we have lots of issues that go to the court and we have to produce room full of documents in fact. It could be proven that it could be held up in court'.[18] Another participant believed that the same legal procedure would be required in the court with electronic signatures as with manuscript signatures:

> I would imagine it's exactly the same … In court when they ask someone to verify a signature they often get a witness in who gives evidence that the signature is for that person. And

[13] A discussion regarding this issue is provided in n 89 below.

[14] 12 out of 27 participants.

[15] P4_Co3_Legal, Paragraph 137.

[16] P14_Co9_SM, Paragraph 163.

[17] P26_Co16_SM, Paragraph 65. The participant further remarked, 'I mean the case will revolve around: Are there other correspondences that led up to the negotiation of the price? Was there a date fixed to transfer of money? Were there negotiations about how the money will be transferred? … So if someone did forge my signature, then I think it would be pretty easy to identify from circumstantial evidence'.

[18] P3_Co2_IT, Paragraph 123.

> another thing comes down to authority, you still have to show who signed the document physically or electronically, who had the authority to do so. So I think all those issues [about evidence] would still be the same.[19]

One other participant claimed that the authenticity of a digital signature could be proved with the help of the IT department which can establish that appropriate security measures were in place when the signature was used. 'I think it wouldn't be as difficult [to prove] as if you simply have an e-mail from the other side saying that we accept the terms and conditions and we agree to be bound by that', he remarked.[20]

However, the above views were not necessarily shared by other participants. In fact, an equal number of them believed that there were inherent problems in proving electronic signatures in the court of law.[21] The main concern raised by participants was that electronic signatures, unlike manuscript signatures, are impersonal and it would therefore be a difficult task to determine whether or not an electronic signature belongs to the true signatory. Since no writing is involved in electronic signatures, 'how do we know that this is his [the signer's] signature',[22] questioned a participant. After all, one does not know who was the actual person who affixed the electronic signature. Where an electronic signature is affixed not by the signatory himself but someone else, it requires proving that the other person acted on the signer's authority. A participant described the difficulties of proving electronic signatures along the following words:

> When it comes down to proving you don't know if this was actually executed by the appropriate person. How do you prove that? Has it just been stuck on by a clerk or something like that, or has it been duly affixed or signed by an authorised officer?[23]

Certainly, a high proportion of the legal participants believed that proving the authenticity of electronic signatures would be a difficult task. Occasionally, legal advisors would discourage businesses to use electronic signatures, apprehensive of the complexities they involve when it comes down to proving their authenticity in the court of law. A couple of legal participants remarked:

> To the end 2001 I worked on Electronic Data Interchange (EDI) type of contracts. I worked for the IT department but I have to say that apart from the EDI type stuff which never took off no-one was particularly interested in electronic signatures and the lawyer wouldn't either. The lawyer would say, 'look I don't understand all these stuff or the law won't necessarily accept it as evidence or it's too difficult. Just rely on paper or fax or something like that'.[24]
>
> We are not ignorant of the fact that it could cause legal complications down the track so therefore we always conduct ourselves in best practice procedure so until using an electronic signature becomes a best practice we will continue with the best practice.[25]

---

[19] P18_Co11_Legal, Paragraph 201.

[20] P22_Co13_Legal, Paragraph 119.

[21] The remaining three participants were unable to comment on this matter.

[22] P2_Co2_Legal, Paragraph 80.

[23] P6_Co4_Legal, Paragraph 76.

[24] P1_Co1_Legal, Paragraph 61.

[25] P6_Co4_Legal, Paragraph 80.

A few scholars in the field were of the view that proving electronic signatures, in particular, digital signatures, is fraught of difficulty and evidential uncertainty. They believed that even if the holder of a private key would exercise due care to keep it secure, there is always a possibility that the private key could be misappropriated and misused.[26] This is because the electronic environment is riddled with technical vulnerabilities, such as a private key could be stolen or misused without its owner being aware of it.[27] Scholars also argued that with digital signatures, the holder of the private key can also lie that he/she did not affix his/her signature although in reality he/she did.[28] Thus, they believed that electronic signatures can never be a foolproof option.[29] In contrast, there are relatively less vulnerabilities in the paper-based environment where the signatory is argued to have more control over his/her signing mechanisms.[30]

Similar concerns were raised by participants. Some legal participants claimed that where an electronic signature is sought to be enforced in a court, it is likely that the other party may say he/she never signed it and that somebody else hacked into the system and maliciously affixed his/her electronic signature. Those who did not favour the use of electronic signature also argued that there was a potential scope for the opposing party to say that he/she had no control over the document containing his/her electronic signature or he/she did not actually attach it. The following are examples of typical concerns raised by participants:

> If something was on a computer for example, I imagine there might be issues such as showing evidence when the person actually logged onto their computer for the day and I know that's recorded ... and then there are the basic things like the person was in the building and actually signed it. But I think it would be rather difficult showing that or trying to prove that there is a probability that someone else could have logged on.[31]
>
> You've got a make sure that the contract is water tight and the last thing you want is the counter party to say that hang on I didn't sign it, it wasn't me. I didn't do it. I never thought about this. You want me to do what? Imagine selling a house and just getting an electronic signature. I wouldn't do that ... I would make sure that the transfer of land contract was signed in a blue carried pen from someone so that I know it was signed by him.[32]

---

[26] Adrian McCullagh and William J Caelli, 'Non-repudiation in the Digital Environment' (2000) 5(8) *First Monday*. http://firstmonday.org/issues/issue5_8/mccullagh/index.html at 28 January 2006; C Bradford Biddle, 'Legislating Market Winners: Digital Signature Laws and the Electronic Commerce Market Place' (1997) 34 *San Diego Law Review* 1225, 1235; Stephen G Myers, 'Potential Liability under the Illinois Electronic Commerce Security Act: Is it a Risk Worth Taking?' (1999) 17(3) *The John Marshall Journal of Computer & Information Law* 909, 941. Note that a detailed discussion regarding this issue has been provided in Chap. 3.

[27] McCullagh and Caelli, above n 26.

[28] For example, Chris Reed, 'Authenticating Electronic Mail Messages – Some Evidential Problems' (1989) 52(5) *The Modern Law Review* 649, 650.

[29] McCullagh and Caelli, above n 26.

[30] Ibid.

[31] P18_Co11_Legal, Paragraph 228.

[32] P2_Co2_Legal, Paragraph 88.

The other difficulty pointed out by a few participants was the absence of any documentary proof since with an electronic signature, there is no document containing the original signature. Thus, it was argued that electronic signatures cannot be proved in the same way as manuscript signatures where you are required to produce the original documents containing the signature. Concerns were also raised that the witnessing of contracts and other documents cannot be achieved in the case of electronic signatures. In addition, unlike with manuscript signatures, no handwriting test can be used with electronic signatures to determine who signed the document and when it was signed. The following subsections focus on these specific issues.

Absence of Originals

In the context of manuscript signature, traditionally, courts have relied on the question of whether a document presented to them is an original or not. However, in the case of electronic signature, it would not be clear what constitutes an original signature.[33] What a person sees on his/her computer's monitor is the representation of some electromagnetic signals.[34] There is no original or copy with electronic signatures. The principle of the admissibility of electronic signatures in evidence has therefore been a serious concern for businesses.

Several participants were of the view that it would be difficult to apply the law of evidence to electronic signatures. In the case of an electronic signature, one cannot distinguish between an original and a copy. As claimed a participant, 'there is only one document that is an original and that is the evidence, the primary evidence'.[35] But, because there is no distinction between the first, second or other copies of a signature generated electronically, the age-old legal concept of primary evidence and secondary evidence cannot be applied in the context of electronic signature.

Some participants resented the use of electronic signatures because they feared that an electronically signed document may be argued to be a photocopy and may therefore not necessarily be legally admissible. However, if the originality of an electronic signature could easily be proved in the court, they would be very willing to use the technology. As a legal participant remarked:

> If you could prove that all those copies are absolutely identical and there is no way that anyone could have tampered with them, and that they are all originals in a sense, and you can't get a better form of originality than the copies, then maybe we can think of using electronic signatures.[36]

---

[33] Lorna Brazell, *Electronic Signatures Law and Regulation* (2004) 199; Stephen Mason, *Electronic Signatures in Law* (2nd ed, 2007) 461.

[34] Brazell, above n 33, 201.

[35] P1_Co1_Legal, Paragraph 77.

[36] P1_Co1_Legal, Paragraph 77.

It was also believed that in the case of manuscript signatures, small nuances[37] or simply the colour of the ink used for the signature could demarcate an original from its photocopy. However, with electronic signatures, there is no distinction between an original and a photocopy:

> When I sign things in blue pen, you can tell the difference. With handwritten signatures, you can distinguish the original from the photocopy, for instance its little things like that. So yes, a court can have the same problem.[38]

Absence of Physical Presence of Witnesses

In most common law jurisdictions, signatures are required to be witnessed by a third party where additional assurance is required. This ensures that the signatory will have difficulty in repudiating his/her manuscript signature at a later stage. If a signature's authenticity is challenged at a later stage, oral testimony may be provided by the witness, which is likely to be admissible in court.

Some participants raised concerns that the witnessing of contracts and other documents cannot be achieved in the case of electronic signatures. They believed that there is no provision in the law that allows the witnessing of an electronic document, in particular, electronic signature:

> An authorised officer signing the document electronically through the use of electronic signatures will be doing so sitting at his computer in his office. If that signature is required to be witnessed how do you that? How do you know that that signature has been witnessed? There is no provision in law to witness a signature being made electronically.[39]

Another participant remarked that in the case of manuscript signature, the parties are physically present and one could confidently say, 'yes, it was he who signed it, I saw him doing it'.[40] That with electronic signatures one almost never witnesses the act of signing was a significant concern for businesses.

Absence of Handwriting Analysts

Where there is a dispute over a manuscript signature, evidence is adduced to show that the signature in question corresponds to that of the alleged signatory's normal signature. This often requires the help of a handwriting analyst who compares the signature in question with a sample of the signatory's signature signed naturally in

---

[37] Such nuances generally include slope, size, margins, spacing and construction of letters. See Mason, above n 33, 17.

[38] P2_Co2_Legal, Paragraph 92.

[39] P2_Co2_Legal, Paragraph 80.

[40] P15_Co10_Legal, Paragraph 103.

other circumstances. Generally two main aspects of a signature are considered: pictorial representation and the construction of letters. It is common for forgers to focus on pictorial details such as slope, size and spacing, but they often fail to copy the way the letters are constructed, that is, the direction of the letters. In addition, the signature is also verified on the basis of the attributes of the instrument used to affix the signature such as how smooth the signature has been signed and whether it is jagged or confident.[41]

Electronic signatures were subject to disapproval by a few participants who claimed that unlike manuscript signatures, the former cannot undergo the handwriting tests. In such circumstances, identifying the actual signatory becomes more difficult. This, they argued, made it difficult to catch a fraudster who used someone else's electronic signature. For example, if a fraudster hacks into someone else's computer and fraudulently uses his/her electronic signature to gain an unfair advantage, it will be quite hard to convince the court that neither the owner of the computer nor any authorised person used the owner's signature. In those circumstances, while it is possible to gather evidence when the computer was accessed, to prove that the fraudster accessed it at a particular time is a daunting task. In contrast, with manuscript signatures, a fraudulent signature can easily be identified with the help of handwriting experts:

> I think it would be rather difficult showing that or try to prove that there is a probability that someone else could have logged on [with electronic signatures] ... With a manuscript signature often you just need a proof. Someone can bring somebody who knows the signature or you can do handwriting tests.[42]

Internationalisation of Electronic Transactions Laws

The first chapter set out the differences across the three different law models that exist across the globe for the regulation of transactions made through electronic signatures.[43] Whether differences in the ETLs represent a deterrent factor towards the use of electronic signature for cross-border transactions was therefore sought.

The participating companies in this study were top public-listed Australian companies and have regular contractual dealings with business partners located throughout the world. Some participants were of the view that businesses were hesitant to use electronic signatures with their overseas business partners because of the differences in the prevailing electronic signature laws in the respective countries. In fact, a few participants did bring to the researcher's attention that their company had been approached by a few overseas business partners to conduct transactions through the medium of electronic signatures. Electronically signed contractual

---

[41] See Mason, above n 33, 17.

[42] P18_Co11_Legal, Paragraph 228.

[43] See Chap. 1 for further details.

documents had been sent out to them with a request to complete transactions using electronic signatures at their end. However, businesses were hesitant to use electronic signatures to seal international transactions, requesting manuscript signatures from these business partners. Part of this hesitation was associated with the difference in the legal structure underlying electronic signatures across the countries. Businesses were concerned that the electronic signature law in Australia would lack harmony with overseas legislation. The following is an example of such an incident:

> I received a contract from an overseas business partner which had an electronic signature attached to it. They wanted us to sign it electronically. ... I refused to do so ... I was not sure of the law ... I returned it to them for their handwritten signature.[44]

On the other hand, a few participants expressed their willingness to use electronic signature if the request would come from overseas partners. According to one participant, his company would not use electronic signatures 'unless there [was] an international push from someone'.[45] Another participant claimed that:

> [i]f we receive a document from America and they sign it and one of the requirements is that we sign it under the *Gatekeeper* or PKI system [digital signature] or something then we would look at it. We would go to our legal counsel ... and we would probably go ahead and do it but there has been no pressure on us to do anything.[46]

A Critique of Participants' Views

Since electronic signatures are convenient and economical and represent an easy method of conducting business, Australian legislators considered it necessary to give such signatures their imprimatur. However, by and large, the majority of businesses are reluctant to introduce this new method of effecting transactions. They prefer the age-old method of manuscript signatures to continue unless sufficient safeguards were built to protect the electronic signer against fraud. A number of issues were raised by participants in this respect. The researcher certainly acknowledges several of the concerns expressed by them on the legal front but also disagrees on a few issues.

Absence of Evidentiary Rules and Guidelines

Several participants revealed concerns with regard to proving electronic signatures in the court of law. Businesses feared that proving the authenticity of electronically signed documents would involve a serious challenge because they believed that the law does not make adequate provisions for proving such documents. The contention

[44] P6_Co4_Legal, Paragraph 150.

[45] P4_Co3_Legal, Paragraph 151.

[46] P10_Co6_Legal, Paragraph 43.

of the researcher is that participants' views reflected their lack of proper knowledge and understanding of the laws governing electronic signatures in Australia, in particular, the ETA and the *Evidence Act 1995* (Cth).[47] These Acts already accommodate most of the issues raised by participants. To shed light on evidentiary issues with regard to electronic signatures, the next section discusses the relevant sections of the ETA and the *Evidence Act 1995* (Cth).

The ETA

The ETA was introduced in Australia to remove legal impediments to the recognition of electronic documents and signatures. It postulates that an electronic transaction is not invalid because 'it took place wholly or partly by means of one or more electronic communications'.[48] According to the Act, legal requirements to give information in writing,[49] to produce a document,[50] to record information[51] or to retain a document[52] can be satisfied in electronic form. In particular, s 11 of the ETA states that the production of electronic records will be permitted provided the following requirements are met:

(a) Integrity of the information contained in the document is reliable.
(b) The electronic form of the document is readily accessible for subsequent reference.
(c) If the recipient is a Commonwealth entity, its information technology requirements are met.
(d) If the recipient is not a Commonwealth entity, the recipient consents to the receipt of an electronic communication.[53]

The *Evidence Act 1995* (Cth)

Section 48 of the *Evidence Act 1995* (Cth) permits production of electronic copies of documents.[54] Further, s 69 of the Act states that all documents that are part of *business records* are admissible in evidence unless they are bona fide impugned.

---

[47] Note that New South Wales, the Australian Capital Territory and Tasmania have adopted Evidence Acts that mirror the *Evidence Act 1995* (Cth). These Acts together are known as the *Uniform Evidence Acts*. The discussion in this chapter is confined to the Commonwealth Act.

[48] ETA s 8.

[49] ETA s 9.

[50] ETA s 10.

[51] ETA s 11.

[52] ETA s 12.

[53] ETA s 11.

[54] Note that electronic signatures can be treated as a document under the *Evidence Act 1995* (Cth) s 3. See below n 67.

Electronic signatures used to enter into business transactions should come within the definition of *business records* and consequently admissible in evidence. The most important section with regard to electronic signatures is s 146 which deals with *evidence produced by processes, machines and other devices*. It states:

(1) This section applies to a document or thing:

  (a) That is produced wholly or partly by a device or process
  (b) That is tendered by a party who asserts that, in producing the document or thing, the device or process has produced a particular outcome

(2) If it is reasonably open to find that the device or process is one that, or is of a kind that, if properly used, ordinarily produces that outcome, it is presumed (unless evidence sufficient to raise doubt about the presumption is adduced) that, in producing the document or thing on the occasion in question, the device or process produced that outcome.
Note:
Example: It would not be necessary to call evidence to prove that a photocopier normally produced complete copies of documents and that it was working properly when it was used to photocopy a particular document.[55]

Extending the above provisions to electronic signatures, the researcher argues that under s 146, in the absence of credible evidence to the contrary, an electronic signature particularly digital signature should be presumed authentic.[56] As with a document produced by a photocopier, in the case of a digital signature, it would therefore not be necessary to call evidence to prove that a private key has produced a digital signature and that it worked properly.[57] However, it can only be assumed that the digital signature attached to the document in question is that of its owner but it cannot guarantee that it was actually affixed by the owner/authorised person or

[55] *Evidence Act 1995* (Cth) s 146.

[56] See Philip Argy, 'Electronic Evidence, Document Retention and Privacy' (paper presented at the Australian Corporate Lawyers' Association (ACLA), Sydney, Australia, 30–31 March 2006).

[57] A holder of a private key may be able to adduce evidence to establish that an impostor misused his key while his computer was switched on and he was temporarily away in a staff meeting or that a malicious software code captured his private key from the computer and transferred it to a remote third party who maliciously used it to impersonate him. In such circumstances, the holder of the private key may still be held responsible under the law of agency or s 15 of the ETA (since the act of signing the document was performed by his employee whose act he is legally responsible of) or in negligence if the relying party can establish that the holder of the private key owed him a duty of care to take reasonable care of his private key and was careless towards it. However, note that the legal position in this regard is not very clear because of the nature of the common law and no precedents in the case law. See Mark Sneddon, *Legal Liability and E-Transactions: A Scoping Study for the National Electronic Authentication Council* (2000) [3.2]. http://unpan1.un.org/intradoc/groups/public/documents/APCITY/UNPAN014676.pdf at 5 December 2007.

someone else.[58] This impersonal aspect of electronic signatures causes an evidential uncertainty and was found to be a serious concern among participants.

The underlying reason for this evidential uncertainty appears to be the nature of the technology and not the law in Australia.[59] Although with an electronic signature, in particular, digital signature, it can be proved with a very high probability that a private key corresponding to a public key was used to sign a document it cannot be proved who signed the document – this is left to inference.[60] It is believed that the inference is weak in those cases where the holder of the private key keeps his/her key in a non-trusted computing platform such as an office or home computer.[61] However, the inference may be stronger in those cases where better evidence of the signer's identity is provided through biometrics and/or portable information storage devices (PISDs).[62]

The above provisions in both the ETA and the *Evidence Act 1995* (Cth) indicate the existence of rules and guidelines that can be used to prove an electronic signature. Participants' concerns regarding this issue are therefore not exactly tenable. They are mostly characterised by an ignorance of the law underlying electronic signatures. In this respect, the researcher believes that separate provisions on the admissibility of electronic signatures in evidence would provide more clarity on evidentiary matters related to electronic signatures. On this note, it is useful to point out that the UK's *Electronic Communications Act 2000* does make such provisions under s 7(1). The Act states that:

> 7(1) In any legal proceedings:
>
> (a) An electronic signature incorporated into or logically associated with a particular electronic communication or particular electronic data
> (b) The certification by any person of such a signature
>
> shall each be *admissible in evidence* in relation to any question as to the authenticity of the communication or data or as to the integrity of the communication or data.[63]

In the following sections, the researcher will focus on some specific issues related to proving electronic signatures.

[58] Note that s 15 of the ETA which provides for attribution of electronic communications is not of much help in this regard. It states that '… unless otherwise agreed between the purported originator and the addressee of an electronic communication, the purported originator of the electronic communication is bound by that communication only if the communication was sent by the purported originator or with the authority of the purported originator'.

[59] Sneddon, above n 57 [3.2].

[60] Ibid.

[61] Ibid.

[62] Ibid.

[63] *Electronic Communications Act 2000* (UK) s 7(1).

Lack of Primary Evidence

A few participants expressed concerns about the inconclusiveness of an electronic signature claiming that there is no actual or original document that is signed. In their contention, the law of evidence would struggle to deal with electronic signatures as there is an absence of primary evidence.[64] Such views appear to be based on a misunderstanding of the current law of evidence. Although the common law position enunciated over 250 years ago was that the *best evidence rule*[65] (which includes producing original documents containing signatures) should be followed to determine the existence of a signature, this law no longer prevails in the Australian federal and in several state jurisdictions.[66] Because s 51 of the *Evidence Act 1995* (Cth) has abolished the common law principles of the best evidence rule for proving a document's contents, the production of an original document is no longer a mandatory requirement to prove a fact. Section 51– original document rule abolished – states that the principles and rules of the common law that relate to the means of proving the contents of documents have been abolished. This implies that electronic signatures can be treated as a document under the *Evidence Act 1995* (Cth).[67] Thus, participants' concerns with regard to the absence of original documents with electronic signatures are unfounded and emanate from their lack of awareness of the current legal position in this regard.

Since no case law has dealt exclusively with the best evidence rule for electronic signatures, of significance is a decision of the High Court of Australia rendered before the passing of the *Evidence Act 1995* (Cth). In the *Butera v Director of Public Prosecutions for the State of Victoria*[68] case, it was held by the court that the

---

[64] For a discussion on primary and secondary evidence, see Mason, above n 33, 461.

[65] The *best evidence rule* can be traced back to more than 250 years to the case of *Omychund v Barker* (1745) 26 ER 15, 33. Lord Harwicke in the case stated that for evidence to be admissible, it must be 'the best that the nature of the case will allow'. In other words, the contents of a document are only admissible if the party attempting to adduce evidence of the contents is able to tender the original document. Traditionally, this rule has operated to eliminate evidence which has not been the best evidence, such as a copy of a document. This was basically the issue raised by participants when they expressed concerns about the original and copy of a signature. For a detailed understanding of the best evidence rule, see Edward W Cleary and John W Strong, 'The Best Evidence Rule: An Evaluation in Context' (1965) 51 *Iowa Law Review* 825.

[66] The states and territories in which the *best evidence rule* has been abolished are New South Wales, Australian Capital Territory and Tasmania. As mentioned above in n 47, these states and territories mirror the *Evidence Act 1995* (Cth). See ss 48 and 51 of the *Evidence Act 1995* (Cth). The states and territories in which *best evidence rule* are still active are South Australia, Western Australia, Northern Territory, Victoria and Queensland.

[67] Section 3 of the *Evidence Act 1995* (Cth) defines a *document* 'as any record of information, and includes: anything on which there is writing; anything on which there are marks, figures, symbols or perforations having a meaning for persons qualified to interpret them; anything from which sounds, images or writings can be reproduced with or without the aid of anything else; or a map, plan, drawing or photograph'.

[68] (1987) 164 CLR 180.

best evidence rule should not be applied to exclude evidence derived from tapes which are mechanically or electronically copied from an original tape. One could also argue that according to the precedent established in this case, there would be no issue of primary evidence or best evidence rule for electronic signatures either. Yet, for those states and territories in which the best evidence rule has not been abolished,[69] this High Court decision can act as a precedent.

Lack of Witnesses

Many participants showed concerns regarding the issue of witnessing. They feared that unlike with manuscript signatures, it was not possible to witness electronic signatures. Witnessing in the electronic realm has also been described as a complex issue by a few scholars.[70] However, they do not rule out the possibility of witnessing electronic signatures, in particular, digital signatures. Witnesses can use their digital signature to attest an electronically signed document. The witnessing of such documents would require that computers involved in signing the document be technically evaluated to trusted evaluation criteria.[71] In such an environment, the attester would verify the authenticity of the document through the signer's public key and would in turn witness the signatory's signature using his/her digital signature.[72]

Some jurisdictions require a process of attestation; for example, Ireland's *Electronic Commerce Act 2000* states that electronic signatures can be witnessed electronically provided certain requirements are satisfied. In particular, the main document must specify that it requires witnessing, and the signature of the signatory and the witness must be an advanced electronic signature (i.e. digital signature) based on a qualified certificate.[73]

The New Zealand's *Electronic Transactions Act 2002* also makes explicit provisions for the witnessing of electronic signatures. Section 23 specifically contains provisions for witnesses to witness a document using an electronic signature, if:

(a) Where a signature is being witnessed, that signature is also an electronic signature.
(b) The electronic signature of the witness meets requirements that correspond to those for a primary signature …, that is, the electronic signature adequately identifies the witness and adequately indicates that the signature or seal has

[69] As mentioned above in n 66, the states and territories in which the *best evidence rule* is still active are South Australia, Western Australia, Northern Territory, Victoria and Queensland.

[70] Adrian McCullagh, Peter Little, and William J Caelli, 'Electronic Signatures: Understand the Past to Develop the Future' (1998) 21(2) *University of New South Wales Law Journal* 452, 462.

[71] Ibid. Note that a lack of trusted systems may bring into question the legal validity and certainty of such actions.

[72] Ibid.

[73] *Electronic Commerce Act 2000* (Ireland) s 14.

been witnessed; is as reliable as is appropriate given the purpose for which, and the circumstances in which, the signature of the witness is required; and, in the case of a witness's signature on information required to be given to a person, the recipient of the information has consented to the use of an electronic signature rather than a traditional paper-based signature.[74]

Yet, in Australia, unlike other countries' legislation, no explicit provision on the issue of witnessing has been included in the ETA.

Absence of Handwriting Experts

Electronic signatures were subject to disapproval by some participants who claimed that unlike manuscript signatures, the former cannot undergo handwriting tests and therefore identifying the actual signatory becomes harder. However, this does not rule out the possibility of testing whether an electronic signature is genuine and authorised. The operations of the information system from which the signature originated at the time when the signature was created can be used to prove the genuineness of a signature.[75] Further, intrusion detection systems may be used to establish whether the document was signed maliciously by an intruder.[76] However, this may require a high standard of information security systems.

Having said that, the researcher believes that this may not necessarily be a foolproof means to identify the actual signatory. In the case of electronic signatures, the identity of the actual signatory will be a matter of inference. As noted above, inference may be weak in those cases where the holder of the private key keeps his/her key in a non-trusted computing platform such as an office or home computer.[77] However, the inference may be stronger in those cases where better evidence of a signer's identity has been provided through biometrics and/or PISDs.[78]

Lack of Harmonisation in International Laws

Some participants also showed reluctance towards the use of electronic signatures with their overseas business partners because of differences in the prevailing electronic signature law in the respective countries. As mentioned in Chap. 1, three different types of legislation (i.e. technology specific, minimalist and two-prong) prevail worldwide. Some scholars argued that these differences complicate rather

[74] *Electronic Transactions Act 2002* (NZ) s 23.

[75] Brazell, above n 33, 201.

[76] Ibid. Note intrusion detection systems can only detect intrusions but cannot prevent them.

[77] Sneddon, above n 57 [3.2].

[78] Ibid.

than facilitate the growth of international trade and emphasised the need for harmonisation through a global regulatory framework.[79] On the other hand, it has been claimed that a global regulatory framework is not exactly viable and practicable and that countries should individually take steps to make their laws as easy and harmonious as possible so that e-commerce succeeds across international boundaries.[80]

Note that the UNCITRAL has played a major role in the harmonisation of electronic signature laws through the creation of the *Model Law on Electronic Commerce 1996* (MLEC)[81] and later the *Model Law on Electronic Signatures 2001* (MLES).[82] The purpose of the model laws is to provide templates to its member countries to develop their national legislation that could give legal recognition to electronic transactions. It also serves as a tool for harmonising legislation across member countries.[83] However, despite such efforts by the UNCITRAL, there is still a lack of uniformity in ETLs across jurisdictions.

Recently, with a view 'to enhance legal certainty and commercial predictability where electronic communications are used in relation to international contracts',[84] the United Nations has passed the *United Nations Convention on the Use of Electronic Communications in International Contracts 2005* (the Convention).[85] This Convention was opened for signature from 16 January 2006 and the countries had to sign their acceptance by 16 January 2008.[86] In contrast to model laws where

---

[79] See Jennifer Koger, 'You Sign, E-sign, We All Fall Down: Why the United States Should Not Crown the Marketplace as Primary Legislator of Electronic Signatures' (2001) 11(2) *Transnational Law & Contemporary Problems* 491; Peter P Swire and Robert E Litan, *None of Your Business: World Data Flows, Electronic Commerce, and the European Privacy Directive* (1998), 206; Andrew B Berman, 'International Divergence: The "Keys" to Signing on the Digital Line – The Cross-border Recognition of Electronic Contracts and Digital Signatures' (2001) 28 *Syracuse Journal of International Law and Commerce* 125. Note these scholars' views have been dealt in detail in Chap. 3.

[80] Sarah Wood Braley, 'Why Electronic Signatures can Increase Electronic Transactions and the Need for Laws Governing Electronic Signatures' (2001) 4(2) *Law and Business Review of the Americas* 417.

[81] See UNCITRAL *Model law on Electronic Commerce 1996*. The text of the *Model Law on Electronic Commerce* can be found on the UNCITRAL website at http://www.uncitral.org/uncitral/en/uncitral_texts/electronic_commerce/1996Model.html 15 January 2008.

[82] See UNCITRAL *Model law on Electronic Signatures 2001*. The text of the MLES can be found on the UNCITRAL website at http://www.uncitral.org/uncitral/en/uncitral_texts/electronic_commerce/2001Model_signatures.html at 15 January 2008.

[83] *Guide to Enactment of the UNCITRAL Model Law on Electronic Signatures* (2001) UNCITRAL [26]. http://www.uncitral.org/pdf/english/texts/electcom/ml-elecsig-e.pdf at 5 January 2008.

[84] UNCITRAL, *2005 – United Nations Convention on the use of Electronic Communications in International Contracts* (2005). http://www.uncitral.org/uncitral/en/uncitral_texts/electronic_commerce/2005Convention.html at 10 June 2008.

[85] See UNCITRAL, *2005 – United Nations Convention on the use of Electronic Communications in International Contracts* (2005). http://www.uncitral.org/uncitral/en/uncitral_texts/electronic_commerce/2005Convention.html at 10 June 2008.

[86] Note that 18 member states have signed the treaty. The Convention is now closed for signature but remains open for ratification and accession before it becomes operational. For more details in this regard, see above n 84.

countries are allowed to modify or leave out some of their provisions, in the case of a convention, the possibility of changes is much more restricted.[87] Thus, the Convention is likely to provide more validity and certainty to international contracts and commercial transactions and, in turn, more confidence for Australian businesses to deal electronically with their business partners overseas.

Vagueness and Ambiguity in the ETA

Some participants claimed that businesses would willingly switch over from the practice of manuscript signature to electronic signature for endorsing contracts and documents if they would receive adequate legal advice. However, the author believes that providing adequate legal advice is quite challenging for legal advisors if there is drawbacks in the electronic signature legislation, including vagueness in the provisions relating to electronic signatures.

The major shortcoming of the Act is that it does not provide the definition of an electronic signature.[88] Section 10 of the ETA (based on Art 7 of the MLEC) that deals with the use of signatures in the electronic environment recognises the validity of electronic signatures under certain terms and conditions without describing what an electronic signature is. In particular, it states that where a Commonwealth law imposes completing a transaction through the means of a signature, the use of any method (presumably electronic signature) is valid provided the method satisfies the following four criteria:

(a) It identifies the person who made the signature.
(b) It indicates the person's approval to the contents of the document signed.
(c) It is as reliable as is appropriate for the purpose for which it is used.
(d) The recipient has agreed to the usage of that method.[89]

This section is clearly vague and ambiguous making it difficult to attribute a precise meaning to its provisions. Naturally, therefore, it undergoes criticism from scholars eminent in the field of electronic signatures. McCullagh and Caelli condemned the legislation on the ground that it does not provide 'any guidance as to what within the electronic commerce environment is or is not a valid electronic signature'.[90] According to Christensen and Low, that 'the method must be as reliable as is appropriate for the purpose for which the information was communicated'[91] is nothing but confusing.[92] What is considered appropriate in the circumstances, argued Christensen and Low, could be based on

---

[87] See above n 83 [26].

[88] Fitzerald et al. argued that ETA is a *light-touch* legislation because it does not define electronic signature. See Brian Fitzerald et al., *Internet and E-Commerce Law*, (2007) 552.

[89] See ETA s 10. Note the clause 'the recipient has agreed to the usage of that method' is an extra provision in the ETA as compared to the MLEC.

[90] McCullagh and Caelli, above n 26.

[91] ETA s 10.

[92] Sharon A Christensen, and Rouhshi Low, 'Moving the Statute of Frauds to the Digital Age' (2003) 77 *Australian Law Journal* 416, 422.

parties' personal preferences and a court's ex post facto rationalisation of individual approaches could vary greatly with no consistent pattern.[93] For example, the appropriateness of an electronic signature may not be the same for a day-to-day ordinary transaction as for complex business transactions involving large sums of money.

In the same vein, Mason argued that the *reliability* test is unrealistic.[94] According to him, if the parties to a contract have agreed in good faith on a particular technology and have acknowledged that the contract is authentic and valid, the court should not question its authenticity and validity on the grounds of reliability.[95] 'There should be no need for any court to take the matter any further', remarked Mason.[96]

Certainly, the above mentioned vagueness and ambiguity surrounding the use of signatures in the electronic environment is a major drawback of the ETA. It would indeed be hard for legal advisors to advise businesses to use electronic signatures with such loose, imprecise and ambiguous provisions in the laws. Most of the shortcomings in the Australian legislation on electronic signatures arise from the MLEC on which is underpinned the ETA. Post-MLEC, two other set of laws, the MLES and the Convention, have been drafted by the UNCITRAL that address the drawbacks in the initial model law. The following subsection gives an overview of these two legislations discussing their progressive developments and possible options for amendments in the ETA.

From MLEC to MLES and the Convention

After adopting the MLEC in 1996, the UNCITRAL decided to examine the issue of electronic signatures exclusively.[97] This led to the development of the MLES. Unlike the previous model, the MLES provides a definition of an electronic signature. Article 2(a) describes an electronic signature as:

> data in electronic form, affixed to or logically associated with a data message, which may be used to identify the signatory in relation to the data message and to indicate the signatory's approval of the information contained in the data message.[98]

Furthermore, Art 6 of the MLES, which is a replication of Art 7 of the MLEC[99] and on which is based s 10 of the ETA, provides guidance as to when an electronic signature

[93] Ibid.

[94] Mason's argument is in the context of Art 7 of the *Model Law on Electronic Commerce 1996,* which can also be applied to ETA because s 10 of the ETA is a replication of Art 7 of the model law. See Mason, above n 33, 136.

[95] Ibid.

[96] Ibid.

[97] *Guide to Enactment of the UNCITRAL Model Law on Electronic Signatures*, above n 83 [63].

[98] MLES Art 2(a).

[99] The MLEC was the first attempt by UNCITRAL to formulate a model legislation on electronic commerce for its member countries given that existing legislation governing communication and storage of information in most jurisdictions were inadequate or outdated and did not contemplate the use of electronic commerce: *Guide to Enactment of the UNCITRAL Model Law on Electronic Signatures*, above n 83 [3].

will be considered reliable and appropriate for the purpose of a specific document.[100] Article 6(3) states that an electronic signature is considered to be reliable if:

(a) The signature creation data are linked to the signatory.
(b) The signature creation data were, at the time of signing, under the control of the signatory.
(c) Any alteration to the electronic signature, made after the time of signing, is detectable.
(d) Where a purpose of the legal requirement for a signature is to provide assurance as to the integrity of the information to which it relates, any alteration made to that information after the time of signing is detectable.[101]

It is to be noted that although the MLES takes a stance as a technology-neutral model (Art 3), it was specifically drafted with public key infrastructure (PKI) in mind (i.e. digital signatures and certification authorities).[102] Thus, implicitly, the Act makes provision for digital signatures because no other form of electronic signature technology can presently satisfy the reliability test.[103]

The Convention is the latest development in the field of electronic transactions legislation models that focuses on issues arising in international contracts, including electronic signatures. Unlike the MLES, the Convention is strictly technology neutral (similar to the MLEC) and does not favour either implicitly or explicitly the use of digital signature or any other forms of electronic signature. Article 9(3) of the Convention establishes the minimum standards that electronic signatures require in order to fulfil the functions of a manuscript signature. It states that where the law requires that a communication or a contract should be signed by a party, or provides consequences for the absence of a signature, that requirement is met in relation to an electronic communication if:

(a) A method is used to identify the party and to indicate that party's intention in respect of the information contained in the electronic communication.
(b) The method used is either:

    (i) As reliable as appropriate for the purpose for which the electronic communication was generated or communicated, in the light of all the circumstances, including any relevant agreement; or
    (ii) Proven in fact to have fulfilled the functions described in subparagraph (a) above, by itself or together with further evidence.[104]

---

[100] MLES Art 6(3).

[101] MLES Art 6(3)(a)–(d). However, it is to be noted that Art 6(4) does not restrict any person to prove or to establish in any other way the appropriateness and reliability of the electronic signature in question.

[102] Although to keep it technology neutral, Art 6(4) states that it does not limit the liability of any person to establish the reliability of an electronic signature in any other way than Art 6(3), the MLES is tilted towards favouring the digital signature technology. See *Guide to Enactment of the UNCITRAL Model Law on Electronic Signatures*, above n 83 [12][28].

[103] For further discussion on MLES and this issue, see Chap. 3.

[104] *United Nations Convention on the Use of Electronic Communications in International Contracts* Art 9(3).

Clearly, Art 9(3) makes quite similar provisions to Art 7 of the MLEC and s 10 of the ETA.[105] However, it is important to note that this article has one extra provision, that is, Art 9(3)(b)(ii).

Under the MLEC and the ETA, the signature method that is electronic signature must satisfy the *reliability test*. This gives an opportunity to a party (including the court) to invoke the reliability test and invalidate the entire contract on the ground that the electronic signature was not appropriately reliable even if there is no dispute regarding the authenticity of the electronic signature.[106] However, this anomaly has been resolved in the Convention. With the extra provision in Art 9 (3)(b)(ii), no party is allowed to invoke the *reliability test* to repudiate its signature where the actual identity of the party and its actual intention could be proved (see Box 6.1).

Box 6.1 Explanatory Note by the UNCITRAL Secretariat on the United Nations Convention on the Use of Electronic Communications in International Contracts[108]

164. However, UNCITRAL considered that the Convention should not allow a party to invoke the 'reliability test' to repudiate its signature in cases where the actual identity of the party and its actual intention could be proved. The requirement that an electronic signature needs to be 'as reliable as appropriate' should not lead a court or trier of fact to invalidate the entire contract on the ground that the electronic signature was not appropriately reliable if there is no dispute about the identity of the person signing or the fact of signing, that is, no question as to authenticity of the electronic signature. Such a result would be particularly unfortunate, as it would allow a party to a transaction in which a signature was required to try to escape its obligations by denying that its signature (or the other party's signature) was valid – not on the ground that the purported signer did not sign, or that the document it signed had been altered, but only on the ground that the method of signature employed was not 'as reliable as appropriate' in the circumstances. In order to avoid these situations, paragraph 3 (b)(ii) validates a signature method – regardless of its reliability in principle – whenever the method used is proven in fact to have identified the signatory and indicated the signatory's intention in respect of the information contained in the electronic communication.

[105] The Convention also provides guidance as to when an electronic signature will be considered reliable and appropriate for the purpose of a specific document. This is similar to the MLEC. See UNCITRAL, *Explanatory note by the UNCITRAL secretariat on the United Nations Convention on the Use of Electronic Communications in International Contracts* (2005) [162]. http://www.uncitral.org/pdf/english/texts/electcom/06-57452_Ebook.pdf at 11 June 2008.

[106] See Mason, above n 33, 136.

Note that the above developments in the MLES and the Convention have recently been taken into consideration by Australia. Section 10 of the ETA (Cth) has recently been amended in accordance with Art 9(3) of the Convention.[107] All states and territories except Queensland have also revised their ETA. However, the amended legislation do not contain the definition of an electronic signature.

Concluding Observations

This chapter examined some prime legal issues associated with electronic signatures. On the one hand, participants revealed significant ignorance with respect to the law governing electronic signatures in Australia, in particular, the ETA and the law of evidence. Lawyers and legal advisors' knowledge in this area does not appear to be up to date. On the other hand, participants raised some valid arguments with regard to evidentiary matters. In this regard, the following observations are made.

First, it appears that the Australian business community is not properly informed and educated about the relevant legislation. Effective dissemination of information to businesses is a likely prerequisite to overcoming resistance to electronic signatures and can be achieved through mediums such as seminars and workshops organised by bodies such as the Law Council of Australia and the Australian Corporate Lawyers Association.

Second, legislative ambiguity prevails. This can be rectified if the ETA incorporates the definition of electronic signature and digital signature. Other countries such as Hong Kong have already implemented such changes in their legislation.[109] Enacting similar amendments will help the Australian business community as well as other stakeholders understand what an electronic signature represents. Clarity in the legislation is in turn likely to enhance businesses' confidence towards the use of the technology.

Third, the recent amendment of s 10 of the ETA in accordance with the Convention is a welcome change. The amended Act now deals with the issue of *appropriateness and reliability*. Other countries facing similar problem in their legislation should also consider amending their ETL in accordance with the Convention.[110]

Fourth, to address the issue of witnessing electronic signatures, a provision stating that witnessing can be done using electronic signatures (as with ETLs in

[107] UNCITRAL, above n 105 [164].

[108] See Electronic Transactions Amendment Act 2011. http://www.comlaw.gov.au/Details/C2011A00033 at 2 March 2012.

[109] See *Electronic Transactions (Amendment) Ordinance 2004* (HK).

[110] As mentioned earlier in above n 89, s10 of the ETA is similar to Art 7 of the MLEC. Thus, countries following the MLEC are facing the same problem faced by ETA and require an amendment to remove the vagueness in the provision relating to electronic signature.

other countries) can be inserted in the ETA.[111] Such a provision if included in the legislation will eliminate the concerns of the business community, in particular, their legal advisors who believe that electronic signatures and documents cannot be witnessed.

Fifth, the problem of admissibility of electronic signatures arises because neither the ETA nor the *Evidence Act 1995* (Cth) contains a separate section on electronic signatures. In this regard, the *Electronic Communications Act 2000* (UK) explicitly states that electronic signatures are admissible in evidence in any legal proceedings and this provides a useful model for Australia.

Finally, the author concurs with participants' views that with electronic signatures, identifying the actual signatory is a complex issue and that there is no foolproof means to achieve this. As discussed above, it usually comes down to inference – the inference being stronger in those cases where better evidence of a signer's identity is provided through biometrics and/or PISDs. Chapter 5 showed that biometrics embedded on PISDs is the safest option for securing electronic signatures. Thus, the author suggests that electronic signatures be stored on a PISD secured through biometrics as such security measures will provide a higher level of inference to identify the actual signatory.

---

[111] See *Electronic Transactions Act 2002* (NZ) s 23; *Electronic Commerce Act 2000* (Ireland) s 14.

Chapter 7
Conclusion

Introduction

Both on national and international fronts, legislative enactments representing various different models of providing for electronic signatures have been enacted. In addition, governments throughout the world have developed policies intended to promote the usage of electronic signatures, an important vehicle for advancing e-commerce. However, anecdotal evidence and reports in the media have pointed out that there has been a very slow take-up of the technology worldwide. A similar lack of willingness to adopt electronic signatures has prevailed in Australia despite the enactment of Australian legislation and the implementation of policies to encourage the use of the technology.

The aim of this book, as set out in Chap. 1, was to identify through empirical research the factors that have contributed or are likely to contribute to the low acceptance by the Australian business community of both electronic signatures generally and the more sophisticated digital signature, in particular, for entering into contracts and commercial transactions with each other. A number of subsidiary questions were initially posited as being relevant to this:

- Will businesses' hesitate to use electronic signatures because of security concerns underlying the technology?
- Is the business community concerned about the legal implications of using electronic signatures?
- Can cost be an impediment?
- Is the technology too complex to understand and use?
- Does the reluctance to use electronic signatures arise from a general ignorance or lack of understanding of the technology and/or the legislation governing the technology?

In order to identify the reasons for the hesitance of the Australian business community to use electronic signatures, a comprehensive empirical analysis was conducted through interviews of different stakeholders. These included legal

A. Srivastava, *Electronic Signatures for B2B Contracts: Evidence from Australia*,
DOI 10.1007/978-81-322-0743-6_7, © Springer India 2013

professionals, IT professionals and executives in senior management selected from a cross section of countrywide businesses.

In conformity with accepted interview methodology, data was collected from 27 participants through semi-structured interviews. Several broad themes and subthemes emerged from participants' views. Taking cue from the extant literature, these views were thoroughly analysed using *framework analysis* methodology to identify the potential impediments to the acceptance of the electronic signature technology by Australian businesses. In consequence of this research, empirical evidence has been developed which both confirms the anecdotal reports of the reluctance of businesses to employ electronic signature technology and indicates the reasons for this hesitance.

This chapter summarises the key findings of the research which underpin this book. In light of these findings, the author then provides a number of observations with regard to measures that might overcome businesses' low usage of electronic signatures.

Key Findings

A low adoption rate to a new technology or process is not unique to electronic signatures but also experienced in other fields such as management and marketing. It is a natural process and occurs among businesses for a variety of reasons. Several factors have been discussed in this book that have potentially led and are likely to lead to a low usage of electronic signatures in the Australian business community. The key findings arising from this research are reviewed below:

Ignorance or Lack of Understanding

A major finding in this research is the ignorance factor behind businesses' reluctance to use electronic signatures. There appears to be a general lack of understanding of the technology in the business community. A low adoption rate of electronic signatures has resulted overwhelmingly from such unawareness and lack of understanding about the technology and the legislation governing the technology.

Ignorance or Lack of Understanding of the Technology

A few participants admitted having never heard of electronic signatures. Others who were aware of its existence demonstrated very limited understanding of what the technology involves and in what various forms it exists. An electronic signature was generally believed to be a scanned image of a manuscript signature. In addition, a certain confusion was revealed between the term *electronic* and *digital* signature.

Businesses perceived their lack of understanding of the technology to be largely responsible for their reluctance to its usage.

Ignorance About the Legislation

A high ignorance also prevailed among businesses with regard to the legislation governing electronic signatures. More than two-third of the participants were unaware of the ETA legislating electronic signatures in Australia, and the rest revealed a superficial knowledge of the Act.

Businesses believed that electronic signatures were fraught with evidentiary problems. In their contention, unlike manuscript signatures, because no actual document is signed with electronic signatures, the law of evidence would struggle to deal with the absence of originals. Such views certainly appeared to be based on a misunderstanding of the current law of evidence which rules out the requirement of an original to prove a fact. Businesses' lack of awareness and understanding of the legislation appeared to be largely responsible for their lack of appreciation of the technology. In fact, the research revealed a high level of ignorance also at the level of lawyers' and legal advisors. A failure to understand the legislation appears to have potentially weakened businesses' confidence in using electronic signatures. In turn, such lack of appreciation and confidence in the technology has resulted in its low usage.

Security Concerns

There are three basic ways that electronic signatures can be secured, that is, through the use of passwords where an electronic signature is stored on the hard disk of a computer, using portable information storage devices (PISDs) and using biometric devices. Issues were found with all three methods of securing electronic signatures. Very often, participants' raised concerns and fears that were pointless and irrational.

Hard Disk Secured with Password

There was a general perception among participants that the storage of electronic signatures on the hard disk of a computer could be secured through the use of a password/PIN. However, it was also noted that despite password security policies implemented by organisations' IT department, staff would hardly ever abide by them. They would often choose passwords that would be easy to guess or fail to change them at regular intervals as recommended. A failure to implement precautionary measures has made electronic signatures behind such passwords prone to attack. Therefore, despite the common belief among a few participants that the storage of an electronic signature on a computer could be secured through the use of passwords, their careless attitude towards password usage and management made the hard disk an unsafe option for storing electronic signatures.

PISDs

The use of PISDs such as smart cards and flash disks to store electronic signatures was, in general, considered to be unsafe. Concerns were raised that PISDs could easily be lost or stolen and used for malicious purposes. On the other hand, electronic signatures stored on a PISD and secured with a password/PIN were believed to provide adequate security. However, participants did not seem to envisage that if a user is careless towards his/her computer password, then there is an equally good chance that he/she would also be careless towards his/her PISD's password/PIN. In the event that a user loses his/her PISD with his/her electronic signature stored on it but the password/PIN is secure, the security of the electronic signature largely depends on the type of PISD used. Smart cards have been found to be the most secure form of PISD. Latest developments in the field of smart cards have significantly enhanced their security and usability, thus increasing the safety of electronic signatures stored on such devices. However, businesses in general demonstrated very little understanding of the smart card technology and its security features. Quite a few were under the wrong impression that smart cards are embedded with the magnetic stripe technology featuring on most bank credit cards.

Biometrics

Except for a few operational limitations, participants generally considered biometrics to the most secure method of storing electronic signature. By individualising and personalising a person's physical attributes such as fingerprint and retina into computers or smart cards, it becomes harder to crack them than any other security mechanisms such as password/PIN. Relative to fraudulent acts with other storage mechanisms, there are only slim chances that biometric codes can ever be decrypted.

The Internet and the Intranet

The Internet, a prerequisite for the usage of the electronic signature technology, was mostly believed to be insecure although it was not considered to be a significant deterrent to the use of electronic signatures. However, participants believed that although a digital signature uses encryption technology and can therefore secure documents traversing through the Internet, it is still at risk from hackers as most office computers are nowadays connected to the Internet or an Intranet. According to participants, the real risk of forgery of an electronic signature arose not primarily from the use of the Internet but from fraudulent actions within an organisation. Although the use of passwords and/or biometrics can minimise malicious access to computers, electronic signatures are considered to still be at risks from office colleagues through the use of the Intranet.

Legal Concerns

Legal concerns associated with electronic signatures were also identified as one potential factor that can contribute to its low usage for contracts and commercial transactions. In particular, the following issues were raised: complexities arising with evidentiary matters when proving authenticity of electronic signatures in the court of law and inconsistencies and complexities in the development of contracts with international partners because of variation in international laws.

Evidentiary Matters

Concerns were expressed about the inconclusiveness of an electronic signature given there is no actual document that is signed. Participants' general view was that the law of evidence would struggle to deal with electronic signatures in the absence of originals/primary evidence. As noted earlier, participants' concerns have mainly resulted from their ignorance of the law of evidence in Australia and the ETA that already accommodates, in large part, for the potential evidentiary problems that arise with the use of electronic signatures. Participants also feared that, unlike with manuscript signatures, it was not possible to witness electronic signatures, thus adding another layer of complication. Finally, electronic signatures were subject to disapproval by participants who claimed that, unlike manuscript signatures, they cannot undergo handwriting tests and therefore identifying the actual signatory becomes harder in case of a dispute.

Variations in International Laws

On the international front, there was an apprehensiveness among participants to use electronic signatures because of variation in international laws governing electronic signatures. Participants believed that a lack of harmonisation of the three different types of legislation prevailing worldwide could potentially complicate the execution of contracts and commercial transactions with their overseas partners.

Complexity and Confusion

The general perception among participants was that the use of electronic signatures was complex and confusing. However, these issues were raised mostly in the context of digital signature while other forms of electronic signatures were not necessarily perceived as complex to use. In particular, the digital signature technology was found to involve complicated application programs that would render it non-user-friendly, a complex setting-up process and a stringent requirement for the recipient organisation to be equipped with a similar technology. However, participants failed to recognise that the complexity of the technology could also be regarded as an attribute. Seen from a different perspective, due to its complex nature, digital signatures can only be used by authorised people who have acquired an expertise/training in this respect. Thus, the complexity of the technology can potentially enhance its security by restricting its usage. In addition, digital signatures are considered as the most secure form of electronic signature because each time the digital signature is used, it makes a unique document in an encrypted form. It appeared that much of businesses' confusion with electronic signatures arises from an ignorance or lack of understanding of the technology. The electronic signature technology, in particular, digital signature, is not necessarily as complex as it is perceived. This perceived complexity is often an outcome of poor understanding and lack of information.

Cost

On the economic front, the expenses involved in educating and training staff was identified as an important factor that could deter the use of electronic signatures. On the other hand, expenses in terms of the cost of obtaining digital signature certificates were not considered to be a disincentive with regard to the use of the technology. Such cost could be trivial for participating companies because they represented large businesses in Australia.

Culture and Customs

Participants believed that the use of manuscript signatures has become a part of the Australian business culture and custom, and this acts as a significant deterrent to the use of electronic signatures. In addition, the age factor compounds this reluctance, with mature individuals often reticent to adopt a new technology.

Issues for Further Consideration

In light of the above findings, this section proposes a few measures that may address the concerns raised by participants with regard to the use of electronic signatures. However, it cannot be ascertained that these measures, if adopted, will necessarily eliminate businesses' hesitance to use electronic signatures.

Education and Awareness

Ignorance and lack of understanding of the technology was identified as a key impediment to the use of electronic signatures for contracts and commercial transactions in the Australian business community. Businesses' lack of awareness and knowledge of the technology and legislation governing the technology can be addressed by disseminating information through marketing campaigns, and education and training programmes. In this respect, the Australian Government Information Management Office (AGIMO) that overlooks the *Gatekeeper* (which provides accreditation to certification authorities (CAs) to issue digital signature certificates) can play an important role. Such campaigns can also be initiated by other bodies such as the Law Council of Australia (LCA), the Australian Corporate Lawyers Association (ACLA) and the Australian Computer Society (ACS). In fact, given that electronic signatures is a techno-legal issue, LCA/ACLA and ACS can work in collaboration to promote the use of the technology from both legal and technical aspects. It is also useful to impart to businesses that the convenience that electronic signatures provide is likely to outweigh the expenses involved in their usage. Such awareness programmes and campaigns are expected to lend confidence to businesses to use the technology.

Security Policies

Passwords are prone to misuse and security threats. However, if used properly, they can provide adequate security to the use of electronic signatures. To minimise the possibility of misuse of passwords, organisations need to strengthen their password policies and ensure that employees conform to them. The use of the Internet or an Intranet still exposes subscribers to risks of remote attacks. In order to minimise such risks towards electronic signatures, it is suggested that subscribers be encouraged to store their electronic signature on PISDs, in particular, smart cards that are nowadays available with improved security and usability features in the form of biometrics sensors. Recent advances in the field of the smart card technology include a fingerprint sensor embedded on the card itself.[1]

Amendments in the ETA

This research has identified some loopholes in the ETA.[2] If these loopholes are addressed, the legislation will strengthen businesses' confidence in electronic signatures. The following outlines a couple of suggestions with regard to the ETA:

(a) It is suggested that the ETA incorporates the definition of electronic signature and digital signature. Such amendments will help the Australian business community as well as other stakeholders understand what an electronic signature represents and also overcome the confusion between the terms *electronic* and *digital* signature. Other countries such as Hong Kong have already implemented these changes in their legislation.[3]

(b) In order to address the issue of witness, the author believes that an additional provision be included in the Act stating that witnessing can be effected using electronic signatures. Such provision is already a feature of the New Zealand's *Electronic Transactions Act 2002* and Ireland's *Electronic Commerce Act 2000,* both of which state that an electronic signature can be witnessed.[4] If included in the ETA, this provision is likely to eliminate concerns of the business community, in particular, their legal advisors who believe that electronic signatures and electronic documents cannot be witnessed.

Amendment to the Evidence Act

Currently, the *Evidence Act 1995* (Cth) outlines a set of rules and guidelines to prove electronic transactions but does not include provisions exclusively for electronic signatures. It is suggested that the *Evidence Act 1995* (Cth) or the ETA

---

[1] Once the smart card is inserted into the reader the user places his finger on the sensor area on the card. The feedback on access or denial is given through a green or red light embedded within the card. The costs of these cards currently vary from US$40–US$60. See 'A standards-based biometric smart card-at what cost?' (2008) 16(1) *Biometric Technology Today* 3. See also Denis, Praca and Claude Barral, 'From smart cards to smart objects: the road to new smart technologies' (2001) 36 (4) *Computer Networks* 381, 386.

[2] Note that one of the loopholes in the ETA had been vagueness and ambiguity in s 10, which has recently been fixed. See Chap. 6 for further details.

[3] See *Electronic Transactions (Amendment) Ordinance 2004* (HK).

[4] See *Electronic Transactions Act 2002* (NZ) s 23; *Electronic Commerce Act 2000* (Ireland) s 14.

contains a separate section on electronic signatures which explicitly states that electronic signatures are admissible in evidence in any legal proceedings, as provided in the *Electronic Communications Act 2000* (UK).

It is reiterated that the above suggested measures may address some of the concerns raised by participants. However, it cannot be said with certainty that the business community would eventually embrace the technology if such measures are implemented. Examining the effect of such measures in the event they are adopted opens a potential avenue for further research.

Conclusion

This book identified through empirical evidence the potential reasons underlying Australian businesses' hesitance to use electronic signatures for electronic contracts and commercial transactions despite a fast developing e-environment. While legislative and technological shortcomings were identified as being important factors that can make businesses hesitant to adopt electronic signatures, the perception of business stakeholders was often not supported by reference to the actual legislation and/or to the technology underlying electronic signatures. Rather, this book provides significant evidence of Australian businesses' lack of awareness and understanding of electronic signatures and the associated legislation despite significant steps undertaken by Australian authorities to facilitate their usage. It is unlikely that any perfection of either electronic signature technology or the legal environment for electronic signatures will see a greater use by the business community of such signatures until knowledge of these things becomes more pervasive. While it is possible to perfect technological systems and to improve upon legal constructs, informing businesses of these developments may however be a challenging task.

Appendices

Appendix A: How Does Public-Key Cryptography Work?

This section describes how the public-key cryptography works mathematically.[1] Let us define public as information available to everyone and private as information available to only one person. A data message usually comprises a plain text message which can comprise data in a range of formats. The data message is converted into blocks of bits of a specific length such as 64 bits.

For simplicity, suppose that the plain text data message $DM=2$, a single digit that needs to be sent as an e-mail using public-key cryptography. First, two primary numbers are chosen, say p and q. Let $p=3$, $q=5$ in this example. p and q are kept private. Let $n = p \times q = 3 \times 5 = 15$; $n=15$ where n is the product of the two primary numbers and n is public. Another product m is calculated based on the prime numbers such that $m = (p-1) \times (q-1) = (3-1) \times (5-1) = 2 \times 4 = 8$ and m is private.

Again two numbers are chosen, say a and b, which when multiplied together and divided by m leaves a remainder 1. In mathematical terms, this is called 1 mod m. Suppose a and b are the respective public and private keys. These keys enable the subscriber and the recipient to encrypt and decrypt the data message at their ends. Let $a=11$ and $b=3$ since $a \times b = 11 \times 3 = 33$ and $\frac{33}{8} = 4$ with a remainder 1 (or=1 mod 8).

Encryption

In order to encrypt DM, the recipient's public key is used. The mathematical formula used is $Z = DM^a \bmod n$. Thus, $Z = 2^{11} \bmod 15 = 2048 \bmod 15 = 8$. Since a and n are public, anyone can do this. The encrypted message $Z=8$ is then transmitted from the sender's computer to the recipient's computer.

[1] This example is adapted from an article by David Herson, 'The Changing Face of International Cryptography Policy - Part 14 - RSA and Digital Signatures' (2000) 9 *Computer Fraud & Security* 7.

DOI 10.1007/978-81-322-0743-6,

Decryption

To decrypt the message, the recipient performs the reverse process but this time using b instead of a. Thus, $DM = Z^b \bmod n = 8^3 \text{mod} 15 = 512 \text{mod} 15 = 2$. Since b is private, only the recipient of the encrypted text can decrypt the data message.

This system is known as the public-key cryptography where n and the public key a are publicly available and b; the private key is kept private.[2]

Cryptography in Digital Signatures

The process used to create a digital signature is similar to the one used in public-key cryptography. In this case, the plain text message *DM* is also sent out to the recipient along with the encryption (in this case the digital signature) to ensure that the recipient would know who has sent the message and that the digital signature ensures that the message has not been tampered.

Since the private key is available only to the sender, the encryption process this time the encryption Z of data message is done through b, the sender's private key instead of a, his/her public key.

Thus, $Z = DM^b \text{mod} n = 2^3 \text{mod} 15 = 8 \text{mod} 15 = 8$. Z, the digital signature, is public. Once digital signature is created, it is attached to *DM* and sent to the recipient:

$$\text{Sender} \xrightarrow{\text{Digital Signature}(Z)+DM} \text{Recipient}$$

The recipient receives data message *DM* along with the sender's digital signature. He/she decrypts it using the sender's public key, a, that is publicly available. Thus, $DM = Z^a \text{mod} n = 8^{11} \text{mod} 15 = 8192 \text{ mod} 15 = 2$. Given that the data message is secured by the sender's digital signature (created by the sender using his/her private key), the recipient can ascertain the security of the data message. This process of attaching a digital signature to an electronic document can be considered similar to affixing a manuscript signature to a paper document.

Note that in the above example, the private key and public key are small numbers, that is, 4 bits long, which was taken deliberately to explain the cryptographic process. However, this will not be the case in reality. In practice, when digital signatures are used, the keys are 512/1024 bits long.[3]

---

[2] Note that if both a and b are the same number, say 9 ($9 \times 9 = 1$), then the procedure will be that of symmetric-key cryptography as the public and private key will be the same and will be shared as a secret key between the sender and the recipient.

[3] Note that in some countries, the law stipulates the use of keys to be of a particular length. For example, the *Information Technology Act* 2000 (India) specifies that digital signatures will be awarded legal recognition only if they are created with private keys that are at least 1024 bits in length. See Safescrypt, *Enrollment Guide for SafeCerts: RCAI Class 3* (2002) http://www.safescrypt.com/support/india-rcaiclass3.html at 15 October 2011.

Appendix B: Electronic Signature on a Smart Card

Electronic signatures, in particular, a digital signature, can be used to sign a data message using a private key stored on a smart card. This process is best illustrated through a hypothetical example. Suppose Tim is the CEO of a company in Melbourne and wants to send an acceptance to a business proposal made to him by Jack who is the MD of a company in Perth. Tim wants to send the acceptance through an e-mail that is signed through his digital signature. First, he types the e-mail that says 'I accept your offer' and then passes or hashes[4] the e-mail through a hashing algorithm. The output is a message digest. To create his digital signature, the message digest is then locked or encrypted through Tim's private key stored on his smart card. To access his private key, Tim inserts his smart card into a smart card reader attached to the computer. The digital signature is generated and sent back to the computer which is then embedded to the data message (e-mail). Tim can now send his signed e-mail to Jack. Figure B.1 depicts this process.

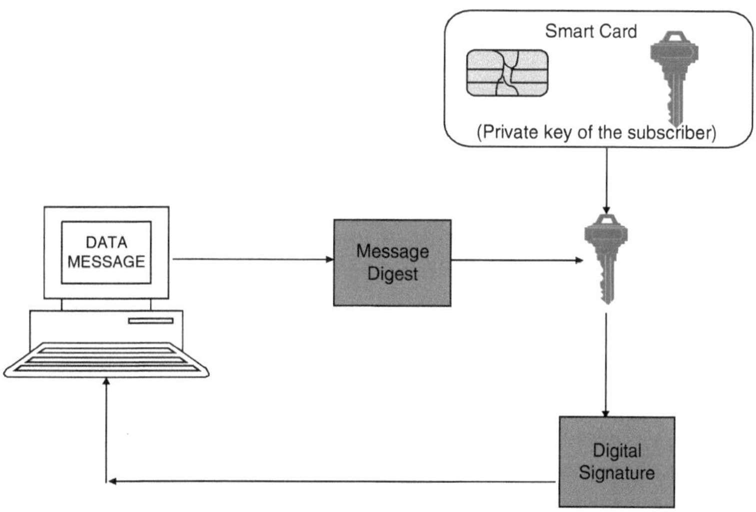

Fig. B.1 Electronic signature on a smart card

[4] It is a process whereby the data message is passed through a hashing algorithm. This is a one-way and an irreversible process. The result of this process is a number which is substantially smaller than the data message and is called a *message digest* or a *hash value*. It is virtually impossible to derive the data message from its hash value. Two similar data messages if passed through the same hashing algorithm will give the same hash value. However, if one data message is even slightly modified, the hash value will change. See Chap. 2.

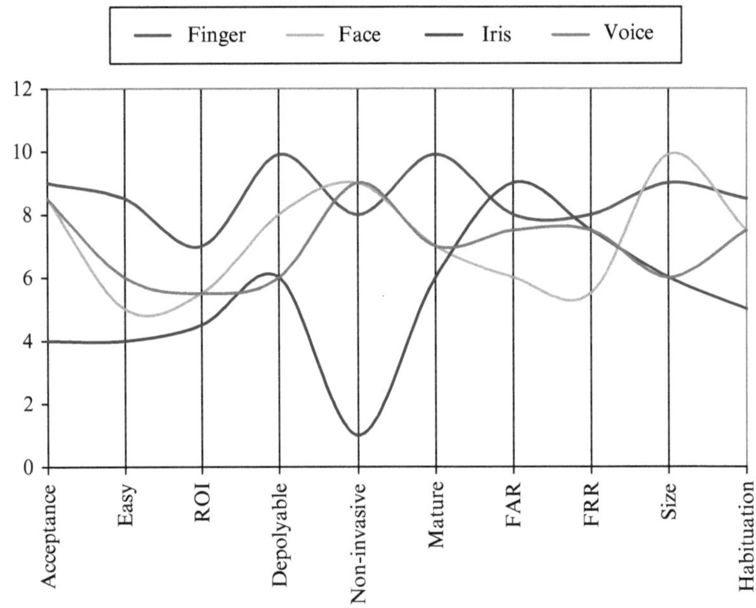

Fig. C.1 Rating of various types of biometric

Appendix C: Fingerprint: the Best Form of Biometric

There are various types of biometric. The degree of security and usability varies across the different types of biometric. According to Reid, there are ten factors that need to be taken into consideration to determine the best biometric.[5] They are as follows:

- Users willingly accept the biometric device.
- Users find it easy to use.
- Total technology costs and benefit provide a suitable return on investment.
- Technology is deployable and supportable.
- Technology is not invasive and requires the user to actively submit to its use.
- Technology is mature and reliable.
- Technology has lower probability of false acceptance (false acceptance rate).
- Technology has higher probability of false rejection (false rejection rate).
- Technology is small in size or requires little physical space.
- Users become habituated quickly to the device.

Reid compared four major types of biometrics (voice, face, iris and fingerprint) on the basis of the above ten factors. Figure C.1 depicts the rating of the four types of biometric in terms of their various features.

[5] Paul Reid, *Biometrics for Network Security* (2004) 56.

On the scale of 1–10, Reid found that fingerprint was the most appropriate biometric technology to date. It is readily acceptable by individuals, easy to use, cost-effective, easily deployable on a computer, less invasive, the oldest and most matured biometric technology, has a low false acceptance rate (FAR), requires only small physical space to operate and user-friendly. The only drawback of fingerprint found was that it has a high false rejection rate (FRR), which means that sometimes it may fail to recognise a legitimate user's fingerprint.

Bibliography

Articles/Books/Reports

Aalberts, B., & van der Hof, S. (2007). Digital signature blindness. *The EDI Law Review, 7*(1), 1–55.

Ackerman, M. S., & Davis, D. T. (2003). Privacy and security issues in e-commerce. In D. C. Jones (Ed.), *New economy handbook* (p. 215). San Diego: Academic.

American Bar Association. (1996). *Digital signature guidelines*. http://www.abanet.org/scitech/ec/isc/dsgfree.html. At 28 Jan 2006.

Anderson, J. C., & Closen, M. L. (1999). Document authentication in electronic commerce: The misleading notary public analog for digital signature certification authority. *The John Marshall Journal of Computer & Information Law, 17*(3), 833.

Ang, K. M., & Caelli, W. J. (2001, July 11–13). *Certificate based PKI and B2B e-commerce: Suitable match or not?* Paper presented at the 16th International Conference on Information Security: Trusted Information, The New Decade Challenge, Paris, France.

Angel, J. (1999). Why use digital signatures for electronic Commerce? *Journal of Information, Law and Technology, 2*. http://www2.warwick.ac.uk/fac/soc/law/elj/jilt/1999_2/angel/. At 28 Feb 2012.

Argy, P. (2007). Law of evidence: Relevance and admissibility. In S. Mason (Ed.), *Electronic evidence: Disclosure, discovery and admissibility* (p. 122). London: LexisNexis Butterworths.

Argy, P. (2006, March 30–31) *Electronic evidence, document retention and privacy*. Paper presented at the Australian Corporate Lawyers' Association (ACLA), Sydney, Australia.

Armenakis, A. A., Harris, S. G., & Mossholder, K. W. (1993). Creating readiness for organizational change. *Human Relations, 46*(6), 681.

Athanasopoulos, D., & Dye, M. J. (1999). A proposed code of professional responsibility for certification authorities. *The John Marshall Journal of Computer & Information Law, 17*(3), 1003.

Australian Bureau of Statistics. (2004). *Business use of information technology*. http://www.ausstats.abs.gov.au/Ausstats/subscriber.nsf/Lookup/BD644A4DB2920E2ACA256FC6007374F9/$File/81290_2003-04.pdf. At 17 June 2011.

Backhouse, J. (2007). Assessing the certification authorities: Guarding the guardians of secure e-commerce. *Journal of Financial Crime, 9*(3), 217.

Backhouse, J., Hsu, C., & McDonnell, A. (2003). Toward public-key infrastructure interoperability. *Communications of the ACM, 46*(6), 98.

Badger, R. (1999). The formulation of government policy for the Internet. *Communications Bulletin, 18*(3), 1.

Bakdi, I. (2006, April 19–21). *Towards a secure and practical multifunctional smart card*. Paper presented at the 7th IFIP WG 8.8/11.2 International Conference, Cardis, Tarragona, Spain.

A. Srivastava, *Electronic Signatures for B2B Contracts: Evidence from Australia*,
DOI 10.1007/978-81-322-0743-6, © Springer India 2013

Baker, S., & Yeo, M. (1999). *Survey of international electronic and digital signature initiatives*. Internet Law and Policy Forum. http://www.ilpf.org/groups/survey.htm. At 31 July 2012.

Balaban, D. (2003). Digital signature cards: For professionals only? *Card Technology, 8*(3), 28.

Barley, S. R. (1990). The alignment of technology and structure through roles and networks. *Administrative Science Quarterly, 35*(1), 61.

Barofsky, A. (2000). The European Commission's directive on electronic signatures: Technological "favoritism" towards digital signatures. *Boston College International and Comparative Law Review, 24*(1), 145.

Barry, N. (1962). *An introduction to Roman law*. Oxford: Clarendon Press.

Bazeley, P., & Richards, L. (2004). *The NVivo qualitative project book*. London: Sage.

Beale, H., & Griffiths, L. (2002). Electronic commerce: Formal requirements in commercial transactions. *Lloyd's Maritime and Commercial Law Quarterly, 4*, 467.

Beer, M. (1980). *Organisational change and development: A systems view*. Santa Monica: Goodyear.

Bell, J., et al. (2001). Electronic signature regulation. *Computer Law & Security Report, 17*(6), 399.

Bell, T., et al. (2003). Explaining cryptographic systems. *Computers in Education, 40*(3), 199.

Bergsten, E., & Goode, R. M. (1989). Legal questions and problems to be overcome. In H. B. Thomsen & S. B. Wheble (Eds.), *Trading with EDI: The legal issues* (p. 125). London: IBC Financial.

Berman, A. B. (2001). International divergence: The "keys" to signing on the digital line – The cross-border recognition of electronic contracts and digital signatures. *Syracuse Journal of International Law and Commerce, 28*, 125.

Bharvada, K. (2002). Electronic signatures, biometrics and PKI in the UK. *International Review of Law, Computers & Technology, 16*(3), 265.

Biddle, C. B. (1996). Misplaced priorities: The Utah Digital Signature Act and liability allocation in a public Key infrastructure. *San Diego Law Review, 33*, 1143.

Biddle, C. B. (1997). Legislating market winners: Digital signature laws and the electronic commerce market place. *San Diego Law Review, 34*, 1225.

Bishop, M. (2003). *Computer security: Art and science*. Boston: Addison-Wesley.

Black, S. K. (2002). *Telecommunications law in the Internet age*. San Francisco: Morgan Kaufmann Publishers. ch 9.

Blum, D. J., & Litwack, D. M. (1995). *The e-mail frontier: Emerging markets and evolving technologies*. Reading: Addison-Wesley.

Blythe, S. E. (2005). Digital signature law of the United Nations, European Union, United Kingdom and United States: Promotion of growth in e-commerce with enhanced security. *Richmond Journal of Law and Technology, 11*(2), 6.

Bohm, N., Brown, I., & Gladman, B. (2000). Electronic commerce: Who carries the risk of fraud. *Journal of Information, Law and Technology, 3*. http://www2.warwick.ac.uk/fac/soc/law/elj/jilt/2000_3/bohm. At 29 Jan 2012.

Borst, J., Preneel, B., & Rijmen, V. (2001). Cryptography on smart cards. *Computer Networks, 36*(4), 423.

Boss, A. H. (1998a). Electronic commerce and the symbiotic relationship between international and domestic Law reform. *Tulane Law Review, 72*, 1931.

Boss, A. H. (1998b). Searching for security in the law of electronic commerce. *Nova Law Review, 23*(2), 583.

Bouma, G. D., & Ling, R. (2004). *The research process* (5th ed.). Melbourne/New York: Oxford University Press.

Boyle, K. (2000). An introduction to gatekeeper: The government's public Key infrastructure. *Journal of Law and Information Science, 11*(1), 39.

Braley, S. W. (2001). Why electronic signatures can increase electronic transactions and the need for laws governing electronic signatures. *Law and Business Review of the Americas, 4*(2), 417.

Brazell, L. (2004). *Electronic signatures law and regulation*. London: Thomson/Sweet & Maxwell.

Breslin, A. J. (2001). Electronic commerce: Will it ever truly realize its global potential. *Penn State International Law Review, 20*(1), 275.

BT Today. (2008a). A standards-based biometric smart card-at what cost? *Biometric Technology Today, 16*(1), 3.

BT Today. (2008b). Fingerprint cards announces biometric payment card. *Biometric Technology Today, 16*(2), 3.
Burnett, S., & Paine, S. (2001). *RSA security's official guide to cryptography*. New York: Osborne/ McGraw-Hill.
Carnall, C. A. (2007). *Managing change in organizations* (5th ed.). Harlow: Financial Times Prentice Hall.
Carr, I. (2003). UNCITRAL & electronic signatures: A light touch at harmonisation. *Hertfordshire Law Journal, 1*(1), 14.
Cazier, J. A., & Medlin, B. D. (2006). Password security: An empirical investigation into e-commerce passwords and their crack times. *Information Systems Security, 415*(6), 5.
Charrot, T. (2001). What's wrong with public Key cryptography? *Computer Fraud & Security, 7*, 12.
Ching, L. C. (2002). Electronic signatures: A comparison of American and European legislation. *Hastings International and Comparative Law Review, 25*(2), 199.
Chong, J. (1998). A primer on digital signatures and Malaysia's Digital Signatures Act 1997. *Computer Law & Security Report, 14*(5), 322.
Christensen, S. A., & Low, R. (2003). Moving the statute of frauds to the digital age. *Australian Law Journal, 77*, 416.
Christensen, S. A., Duncan, W., & Low, R. (2002). *Moving Queensland property transactions to the digital age: Can writing and signature requirements be fulfilled electronically?* Brisbane: Centre for Commercial and Property Law, Queensland University of Technology.
Christensen, S. A., Duncan, W., & Low, R. (2003). The statute of Frauds in the digital age – Maintaining the integrity of signatures. *Murdoch University of Electronic Journal of Law, 10*(4). http://www.murdoch.edu.au/elaw/issues/v10n4/christensen104.html. At 13 June 2011.
Christensen, S. A., Mason, S., & O'Shea, K. (2006). The international judicial recognition of electronic signatures – Has your agreement been signed? *Communications Law, 11*(5), 150.
Ciocchetti, C. A. (2001). Are online business transactions executed by electronic signatures legally binding? *Duke Law and Technology Review*. http://www.law.duke.edu/journals/dltr/Articles/2001dltr0005.html. At 12 Apr 2011.
Clarke, R. (2001, June 27–29). *The fundamental inadequacies of public key infrastructure*. Paper presented at the 9th International Conference on Information Systems, Bled, Slovenia.
Cleary, E. W., & Strong, J. W. (1965). The best evidence rule: An evaluation in context. *Iowa Law Review, 51*, 825.
Coia, A. (2002). Security is not a child's play. *Card Technology, 7*(9), 30.
Collis, J., & Hussey, R. (2003). *Business research: A practical guide to undergraduate and postgraduate students* (2nd ed.). Basingstoke: Palgrave Macmillan.
Commission of the European Communities. (2006a). *Report on the operation of directive 1999/93/ EC on a community framework for electronic signatures*. http://ec.europa.eu/information_society/eeurope/i2010/docs/single_info_space/com_electronic_signatures_report_en.pdf. At 11 May 2011.
Commission of the European Communities. (2006b). *Report on the operation of directive 1999/93/ EC on a community framework for electronic signatures*. http://ec.europa.eu/information_society/eeurope/i2010/docs/single_info_space/com_electronic_signatures_report_en.pdf. At 11 May 2007.
Cooper, D. R., & Schindler, P. S. (2006). *Business research methods* (9th ed.). Boston: McGraw-Hill Irwin.
Crabtree, B. F., & Miller, W. L. (1999). *Doing qualitative research* (2nd ed.). Thousand Oaks: Sage.
Creswell, J. W. (1998). *Qualitative inquiry and research design: Choosing among five traditions*. Thousand Oaks: Sage.
Creswell, J. W. (2003). *Research design: Qualitative, quantitative and mixed methods approaches* (2nd ed.). Thousand Oaks: Sage.
Customs Cooperation Council. (1981). *Recommendation of the Customs Cooperation Council concerning the transmission and authentication of customs information which is processed by computer*. http://www.wcoomd.org. At 22 June 2011.
Davis, F. D. (1989). Perceived usefulness, perceived ease of use, and user acceptance of information technology. *MIS Quarterly, 13*(3), 319.

Davis, F. D. (1993). User acceptance of information technology: System characteristics, user perceptions and behavioral impacts. *International Journal of Man-Machine Studies, 38*(3), 475.

Davis, D. (1996, July 22–25). *Compliance defects in public-key cryptography*. Paper presented at the 6th Conference on USENIX Security Symposium, Focusing on Applications of Cryptography, San Jose, CA.

del Val, M. P., & Fuentes, C. M. (2003). Resistance to change: A literature review and empirical study. *Management Decisions, 41*(2), 148.

Denzin, N. K., & Lincoln, Y. S. (Eds.). (2000). *The handbook of qualitative research* (2nd ed.). Thousand Oaks: Sage.

Dexter, L. A. (2006). *Elite and specialized interviewing*. Colchester: ECPR.

Dey, I. (1993). *Qualitative data analysis: A user-friendly guide for social scientists*. London: Routledge.

deZwart, M. (1998). Electronic commerce: Promises, potential and proposals. *University of New South Wales Law Journal, 21*(2), 45.

Diffie, W., & Hellman, M. E. (1976). New directions in cryptography. *IEEE Transactions on Information Theory, 22*(6), 644.

Domanowski, S. (2001). E-SIGN: Paperless transactions in the new millennium. *DePaul Law Review, 51*(2), 619.

Domingo-Ferrer, J., et al. (2007). Advances in smart cards. *Computer Networks, 51*(9), 2219.

Drugs and Crime Prevention Committee, Parliament of Victoria. (2004). *Inquiry into fraud and electronic commerce*. http://www.parliament.vic.gov.au/dcpc/Reports/DCPC_FraudElectronicCommerce_05-01-2004.pdf. At 21 Mar 2012.

Dumortier, J. (2004). Legal status of qualified electronic signatures in Europe. In S. Paulus, N. Pohlmann, H. Reimer (Eds.), *ISSE 2004 Securing Electronic Business Processes*, (pp. 281–289) Wiesbaden: Vieweg.

Dumortier, J., & Eecke, P. V. (1999). The European draft directive on a common framework for electronic signature. *Computer Law & Security Report, 15*(2), 106.

Eisenhardt, K. M. (1989). Building theories from case study research. *The Academy of Management Review, 14*(4), 532.

Electronic Commerce Expert Group. (1998). *Electronic Commerce: Building the legal framework-report of the Electronic Commerce Expert Group to the Attorney General*. http://www.ag.gov.au/www/agd/agd.nsf/Page/ecommerce_Electroniccommerceexpertgroupsreport. At 15 Jan 2006.

Ellison, C., & Schneier, B. (2000). Ten risks of PKI: What you're Not being told about public Key infrastructure. *Computer Security Journal, 16*(1), 1.

Ernst, & Young. (2006). *Global information security survey 2006-achieving success in a Globalized World: Is your way secure?* http://www.naider.com/upload/ernst%20young.pdf. At 21 Mar 2012.

Fernandes, A. D. (2001). Risking "trust" in a public Key infrastructure: Old techniques of managing risk applied to new technology. *Decision Support Systems, 31*(3), 303.

Fillingham, D. (1997). A comparison of digital and handwritten signatures. *Ethics and Law on the Electronic Frontier 6*. http://swissnet.ai.mit.edu/6805/student-papers/fall97-papers/fillingham-sig.html. At 28 Jan 2012.

Fischer, J.-B., & Prouff, E. (2006, April 19–21). *Off-line group signatures with smart cards*. Paper presented at the 7th IFIP WG 8.8/11.2 International Conference, Cardis, Tarragona, Spain.

Fisher, W., & Wesolkowski, S. (1999). The social and economic costs of technology resistance. *IEEE Canadian Review* (Winter), 14.

Fisk, A. D., Rogers, W. A., & Walker, N. (1996). *Aging and skilled performance: Advances in theory and applications*. Mahwah: Lawrence Erlbaum Associates.

Fitzerald, B., et al. (2007). *Internet and e-commerce law*. Pyrmont: Thomson Law Book Co.

Fontana, A., & Frey, J. H. (2000). The interview: From structured questions to negotiated text. In N. K. Denzin & Y. S. Lincoln (Eds.), *The handbook of qualitative research* (2nd ed.). Thousand Oaks: Sage.

Ford, J. D., Ford, L. W., & McNamara, R. T. (2002). Resistance and the background conversations of change. *Journal of Organizational Change Management, 15*(2), 105.

Forder, J., & Svantesson, D. (2008). *Internet and e-commerce law*. South Melbourne: Oxford University Press.

Frances, M. (1995). Organisational change and personal mythology-the rhetoric and culture of HRM. *Personal Review, 24*(4), 58.
Freedman, A. W. (2001). The Electronic Signatures Act: Pre-empting state law by legislating contradictory technological standards. *Utah Law Review, 3*, 807.
Freedman, C., & Hardy, J. (2007). J Pereira Fernandes SA v Mehta: A 21st century email meets a 17th century statute. *Computer Law & Security Report, 23*(1), 77.
Froomkin, A. M. (1996). The essential role of trusted third parties in electronic commerce. *Oregon Law Review, 75*, 49.
Furnell, S. (2005). Authenticating ourselves: Will we ever escape the password? *Network Security, 3*, 8.
Furnell, S. (2007). An assessment of website password practices. *Computers & Security, 26*(7), 445.
Ganley, M. J. (1998). Digital signatures. *Information Security Technical Report, 2*(4), 12.
Garner, B. A. (Ed.). (2004). *Blacks law dictionary* (8th ed.). St. Paul: West Group.
Gauthreaix, C. (2001). A cursory look at the E-Sign Act. *Louisiana Bar Journal, 48*, 452.
Gelbord, B. (2000a). Signing your 011001010: The problems of digital signatures. *Communications of the ACM, 43*(12), 27.
Gelbord, B. (2000b). The dangers of digital signatures. *Communications of the ACM, 43*(12), 27.
Glaser, B. G., & Strauss, A. L. (1967). *The discovery of grounded theory: Strategies for qualitative research*. Chicago: Aldine Transaction.
Goulding, C. (2002). *Grounded theory: A practical guide for management, business and market researchers*. London: Sage.
Grady, M. F. (2006). *The law and economics of cybersecurity*. New York: Cambridge University Press.
Grandori, A., & Warner, M. (1996). *International encyclopaedia of business and management* (Vol. 5, p. 4419). London: Routledge.
Greenberg, J. A., & Baron, R. A. (2008). *Behavior in organizations*. Upper Saddle River: Pearson Prentice Hall.
Greenleaf, G. (2007). Australia's proposed ID card: Still quacking like a duck. *Computer Law & Security Report, 23*(2), 156.
Greenleaf, G. (2008). Function creep – Defined and still dangerous in Australia's revised ID card bill. *Computer Law & Security Report, 24*(1), 56.
Grindsted, A. (2005). Interactive resources used in semi-structured research interviewing. *Journal of Pragmatics, 37*(7), 1015.
Gripman, D. L. (1999). Electronic document certification: A primer on the technology behind digital signatures. *The John Marshall Journal of Computer & Information Law, 17*(3), 769.
Guillou, L. C., Ugon, M., & Quisquater, J. J. (2001). Cryptographic authentication protocols for smart cards. *Computer Networks, 36*(4), 437.
Gururajan, R., Ryle, A., & Hafeez-Baig A. (2004, May 26). *Legal and regulatory issues of implementation of electronic signatures*. Paper presented at the AusCert Asia Pacific Information Technology Security Conference, Gold Coast, Australia.
Hannan, M., & Freeman, J. (1988). Structural inertia and organizational change. In K. S. Cameron, R. I. Sutton, & D. A. Whetten (Eds.), *Readings in organizational decline: Frameworks, research and prescriptions* (p. 149). Cambridge: Ballinger.
Hartley, J. A. (2003). Electronic signatures and electronic records in cyber-contracting. *The Practical Lawyer, 49*(1), 51.
Hays, M. J. (2001). The E-Sign Act of 2000: The triumph of function over form in American contract law. *Notre Dame Law Review, 76*(4), 1183.
Hedley, S. (2006). *The law of electronic commerce and the Internet in the UK and Ireland*. London: Cavendish. ch 9.
Herda, S. (1995). Non-repudiation: Constituting evidence and proof in digital cooperation. *Computer Standards & Interfaces, 17*(1), 69.
Herson, D. (2000a). The changing face of international cryptography policy – Part 14 – RSA and digital signatures. *Computer Fraud & Security, 9*, 7.
Herson, D. (2000b). The changing face of international cryptography policy – Part 9 – Developments in the UK, US and EU. *Computer Fraud & Security, 2*, 8.
Herson, D. (2000c). The changing face of international cryptography policy – Part 15 – Trusted third parties. *Computer Fraud & Security, 11*, 6.

Hertz, R., & Imber, J. B. (1995). *Studying elites using qualitative methods*. Thousand Oaks: Sage.

Hill, S. W. B. (2001). E-mail contracts-when is a contract formed? *Journal of Law and Information Science, 12*(1), 46.

Hirchheim, R., & Newman, M. (1998). Information systems and user resistance: Theory and practice. *The Computer Journal, 31*(5), 398.

Hodkowski, W. A. (1997). The future of Internet security: how new technologies will shape the Internet and affect the law. *Computer and High Technology Law Journal, 13*(1), 217.

Holloway, C. J. (1995). Controlling digital signature services using a smart card. *Computers & Security, 14*(8), 681.

Hopkins, R. (1999). An introduction to biometrics and large scale civilian identification. *International Review of Law Computers and Technology, 13*(3), 337.

Hunt, R. (2001). Technological infrastructure for PKI and digital certification. *Computer Communications, 24*(14), 1460.

Huntley, J. (2007). Book review of electronic signatures, law and regulation by Lorna Brazell, (Thomson, Sweet & Maxwell, 2004). *International Journal of Law and Information Technology, 15*(2), 227.

Husemann, D. (2001). Standards in the smart card world. *Computer Networks, 36*(4), 473.

Ikbal, J. (2004). An introduction to cryptography. In F. T. Harold & K. Micki (Eds.), *Information security management handbook* (5th ed., p. 1333). Boca Raton: Auerbach Publications.

Jackson, M. (2003). Internet privacy. *Telecommunications Journal of Australia, 53*(2), 21.

Jackson, M., & Ligertwood, J. (2006a). Identity management: Is an identity card the solution for Australia? *Prometheus, 24*, 379.

Jackson, M., & Ligertwood, J. (2006b, October 25–26). *The health and social services access card: What will it mean for Australians?* Paper presented at the Financial Literacy, Banking and Identity Conference, Melbourne, Australia.

Jain, M. (2000). Digital signatures. *CBI Bulletin* 19.

Jancic, A., & Warren, M. J. (2006, November 26). *PKI-advantages and obstacles*. Paper presented at 2nd Australian Information Security Management Conference on Securing the Future, Perth, Australia.

Jason, R. R. (1999). The Utah Digital Signature Act as "model" legislation: A critical analysis. *The John Marshall Journal of Computer & Information Law, 17*(3), 873.

Johnson, J. M. (2001). In-depth interviewing. In J. F. Gubrium & J. A. Holstein (Eds.), *Handbook of interview research: Context & methods* (p. 103). Thousand Oaks: Sage.

Jueneman, R. R., & Robertson, R. J., Jr. (1998). Biometrics and digital signatures in electronic commerce. *Jurimetrics, 38*(3), 427.

Julià-Barcelo, R., & Vinje, T. (1998). Towards a European framework for digital signatures and encryption. *Computer Law & Security Report, 14*(2), 79.

Kahn, D. (1996). *The codebreakers: The story of secret writing*. New York: Scribner.

Kalla, M., et al. (1999). Achieving non-repudiation of web based transactions. *Journal of Systems and Software, 48*(3), 165.

Kay, S. (2001a). Security and authentication requirements in the court process: Part 1: Current security practices and requirements and survey of courts' approaches to online security in Australia and the US. *Internet Law Bulletin, 4*(1), 5.

Kay, S. (2001b). Security and authentication requirements in the court process: Part 2: Technological solutions for security and authentication in the legal environment. *Internet Law Bulletin, 4*(2), 5.

Keefe, C. P. (1997). A law student's guide to the future of transactions over the internet: A review of the digital signature guidelines. *Virginia Journal of Law and Technology, 1*. http://www.vjolt.net/vol1/issue/vol1_art6.html. At 12 Dec 2011.

Kendler, P. B. (2002). Sign on the cyberline. *Catalog Age, 19*(5), 53.

Kidd, D. L., Jr., & Daughtrey, W. H., Jr. (2000). Adapting contract law to accommodate electronic contracts: Overview and suggestions. *Rutgers Computer & Technology Law Journal, 26*(2), 215.

Kincaid, H. V., & Bright, M. (1957). Interviewing the business elite. *The American Journal of Sociology, 63*(3), 304.

King, N. (2004). Using interviews in qualitative research. In C. Cassell & G. Symon (Eds.), *Essential guide to qualitative methods in organizational research* (p. 11). Thousand Oaks: Sage.
Kingpin, J. (2000, October 12–13). *Attacks on and countermeasures for USB hardware token devices*. Paper presented at the 5th Nordic Workshop on Secure IT Systems Encouraging Co-operation, Reykjavik, Iceland.
Kiran, S., Lareau, P., & Lloyd, S. (2002). *PKI basics – A technical perspective*. PKI Forum. http://www.oasis-pki.org/pdfs/PKI_Basics-A_technical_perspective.pdf. At 31 July 2012.
Klein, J. A. (1984). Why supervisors resist employee involvement. *Harvard Business Review, 62*(5), 87.
Klein, A. (2007). Building an identity management infrastructure for today ... and tomorrow. *Information Systems Security, 16*(2), 74.
Koger, J. L. (2001). You sign, e-sign, we all fall down: Why the United States should not crown the market place as primary legislator of electronic signatures. *Transnational Law & Contemporary Problems, 11*(2), 491.
Kohnfelder, L. M. (1978). *Towards a practical public-key cryptosystem*. Bachelor's thesis, Massachusetts Institute of Technology, Cambridge.
Kotter, J. P., & Schlesigner, L. A. (1979). Choosing strategies for change. *Harvard Business Review, 57*(2), 106.
Kuechler, W., & Grupe, F. H. (2003). Digital signatures: A business view. *Information Systems Management, 20*(1), 19.
Kuhn, D. R., et al. (2001). *Introduction to public Key technology and the federal PKI infrastructure*. Gaithersburg: National Institute of Standards and Technology.
Kuner, C., et al. (2000). *An analysis of international electronic and digital signature implementation initiatives*. Internet Law and Policy Forum. http://www.ilpf.org/groups/analysis_IEDSII.htm. At 31 July 2012.
Lampe, D. C. (2001). The Uniform Electronic Transactions Act and federal ESIGN law: An overview. *Consumer Finance Law Quarterly Report, 55*, 255.
Law Commission (UK). (2001). *Electronic commerce: Formal requirements in commercial transactions*. http://lawcommission.justice.gov.uk/docs/Electronic_Commerce_Advice_Paper.pdf. At 31 July 2012.
Lee, T. W., Mitchell, T. R., & Sablynski, C. J. (2004). Qualitative research in organizational and vocational psychology, 1979–1999. *Journal of Vocational Behaviour, 55*(2), 161.
Leung, R. P. H. K., & Hui, C. K. L. (2001). Handling signature purposes in workflow systems. *Journal of Systems and Software, 55*, 245.
Lewis, R. B. (2004). NVivo 2.0 and ATLAS.ti 5.0: A comparative review of two popular qualitative data-analysis programs. *Field Methods, 16*(4), 439.
LexisNexis. *Halsbury's laws of Australia*, vol 6 (at 22 June 2008) 110 Contract, II Formation of Contract [110–1030].
Lim, L. (2001). Digital signatures for Australian businesses. *Internet Law Bulletin, 3*(8), 105.
Lim, Y. F. (2002). Digital signature, certification authorities and the law. *Murdoch University Electronic Journal of Law, 9*(3). http://www.austlii.edu.au/au/journals/MurUEJL/2002/29.html. At 20 June 2011.
Lincoln, A. (2004). Electronic signature laws and the need for uniformity in the global market. *Journal of Small and Emerging Business, 8*(1), 67.
Locke, K. (2001). *Grounded theory in management research*. Thousand Oaks: Sage.
Locke, L. F., Silverman, S., & Spirduso, W. W. (2004). *Reading and understanding research* (2nd ed.). Thousand Oaks: Sage.
Lockie, M. (2002). *Biometric technology*. Chicago: Heinemann Library.
López, A. M. (2007). Smart card-based agents for fair non-repudiation. *Computer Networks, 51*(9), 2288.
Lu, H. K. (2007). Network smart card review and analysis. *Computer Networks, 51*(9), 2234.
Maltoni, D., et al. (2003). *Handbook of fingerprint recognition*. New York: Springer.
Marshall, C., & Rossman, G. B. (2006). *Designing qualitative research* (4th ed.). Thousand Oaks: Sage.
Mason, S. (2002a). The evidential issues relating to electronic signatures – Part I. *Computer Law & Security Report, 18*(3), 175.

Mason, S. (2002b). The evidential issues relating to electronic signatures – Part II. *Computer Law & Security Report, 18*(4), 241.

Mason, S. (2006). Electronic signatures in practice. *Journal of High Technology Law, 6*(2), 148.

Mason, S. (2007). *Electronic signatures in law* (2nd ed.). Haywards Heath: Tottel Publishing.

Mason, S., & Bohm, N. (2003). The signature in electronic conveyancing: An unresolved issue? *The Conveyancer and Property Lawyer, 67*, 460.

Maxwell, J. A. (2005). *Qualitative research design: An interactive approach* (2nd ed.). Thousand Oaks: Sage.

McCracken, G. D. (1988). *The long interview*. Newbury Park: Sage.

McCullagh, A., & Caelli, W. J. (2000). Non-repudiation in the digital environment. *First Monday, 5*(8). http://firstmonday.org/issues/issue5_8/mccullagh/index.html. At 28 Jan 2012.

McCullagh, A., Little, P., & Caelli, W. J. (1998). Electronic signatures: Understand the past to develop the future. *University of New South Wales Law Journal, 21*(2), 452.

Metselaar, E. E. (1997). Assessing the willingness to change: Construction and validation of the dinamo. Free University of Amsterdam, Amsterdam quoted in Vos, J, *The role of personality and emotions in employee resistance to change*. Master thesis, Erasmus University, 2006.

Miles, M. B., & Huberman, M. A. (1994). *Qualitative data analysis: An expanded sourcebook* (2nd ed.). Thousand Oaks: Sage.

Miles, M. B., & Huberman, M. A. (Eds.). (2002). *The qualitative researcher's companion* (2nd ed.). Thousand Oaks: Sage.

Morgan, D. L. (1997). *Focus groups as qualitative research* (2nd ed.). Thousand Oaks: Sage.

Morris, K. F., & Raben, C. S. (1995) The fundamentals of change management. In D. A. Nadler, R. B. Shaw, A. E. Walton, & Associates (Eds.), *Discontinuous change: Leading organizational transformation* (p. 47). San Francisco: Jossey-Bass

M'Raïhi, D., & Yung, M. (2001). E-commerce applications of smart cards. *Computer Networks, 36*(4), 453.

Mulligan, J., & Elbirt, A. J. (2005). Desktop security and usability trade-offs: An evaluation of password management systems. *Information Systems Security, 14*(2), 10.

Myers, S. G. (1999). Potential liability under the Illinois electronic commerce security Act: Is it a risk worth taking? *The John Marshall Journal of Computer & Information Law, 17*(3), 909.

Nadler, D. A. (1993). Concepts for the management of organisational change. In C. Mabey & B. Mayon-White (Eds.), *Managing change* (p. 85). London: Paul Chapman Publishing.

Naezer, D. (1989). EDI: A European perspective. In H. B. Thomsen & S. B. Wheble (Eds.), *Trading with EDI: The legal issues*. London: IBC Financial.

Nason, J., & Golding, D. (1998). Approaching observation. In C. Cassell & G. Symon (Eds.), *Qualitative methods and analysis in organizational research: A practical guide* (p. 234). Thousand Oaks: Sage.

National Authentication Council. (2002). *Report on liability and other legal issues in the use of PKI digital certificates*. http://www.noie.gov.au/Projects/Authentication_Policy/PKI_legal_report_May2002.pdf. At 15 June 2011.

National Office for the Information Economy. (2001). *Government role in B2B e-commerce*. Department of Communications, Information Technology and the Arts. http://archive.dcita.gov.au/2001/10/b2b_e-commerce/role. At 12 Oct 2011.

National Office for the Information Economy. (2003a). *Australian business number digital signatures certificate (ABN-DSC): Broad specification*. http://www.agimo.gov.au/__data/assets/file/0019/5095/ABN-DSC-specification.pdf. At 17 Feb 2012.

National Office for the Information Economy. (2003b). *Interoperability between gatekeeper and foreign digital certificates through cross-recognising PKI domains*. http://www.agimo.gov.au/__data/assets/file/18913/crossRecPolicyV2.3.pdf. At 15 June 2011.

Nunno, R. M. (2000). Electronic signatures: Technology developments and legislative issues. *Government Information Quarterly, 17*(4), 395.

Odendahl, T., & Shaw, A. M. (2002). Interviewing elites. In J. F. Gubrium & J. A. Holstein (Eds.), *Handbook of interview research: Context & methods* (p. 299). Thousand Oaks: Sage.

Osty, M. J., & Pulcanio, M. (1999). The liability of certification authorities to relying third parties. *The John Marshall Journal of Computer & Information Law, 17*(3), 961.

Owens, L. (2002). *Hack proofing your wireless network*. Rockland: Syngress.

Pappas, C. W. (2002). Comparative US and EU approaches to E-commerce regulation: Jurisdiction, electronic contracts, electronic signatures and taxation. *Denver Journal of International Law & Policy, 31*(2), 325.

Pasley, K. (2004). Hash algorithms: From message digests to signatures. In H. F. Tipton & M. Krause (Eds.), *Information security management handbook* (5th ed., p. 1349). Boca Raton: Auerbach Publications.

Patton, M. Q. (2002). *Qualitative research & evaluation methods* (3rd ed.). Thousand Oaks: Sage.

Pearlman, B. A. (2001). Finding an appropriate global legal paradigm for the internet: United States and international responses. *Georgia Journal of International and Comparative Law, 29*(3), 597.

Peltier, T. R. (2005). Implementing an information security awareness program. *Information Systems Security, 14*(2), 37.

Perritt, H. H., Jr. (1996). Legal and technological infrastructures for electronic payment systems. *Rutgers Computer and Technology Law Journal, 22*(1), 1.

Perry, R. (2001). Digital signatures – Security issues and real-world conveyancing. *New Law Journal, 151*, 1100.

Perry, R. (2003). E-conveyancing: Problems ahead? *The Conveyancer and Property Lawyer, 67*, 215.

Phoenix, S. J. D. (1997). Cryptography, trusted third parties and escrow. *BT Technology Journal, 15*(2), 45.

Poland, B., & Pederson, A. (1998). Reading between the lines: Interpreting silences in qualitative research. *Qualitative Inquiry, 4*(2), 293.

Potter, W. J. (1996). *An analysis of thinking and research about qualitative methods*. Mahwah: Erlbaum.

Pounder, C. (1998). Further developments in the field of encryption and digital signatures. *Computers & Security, 17*(4), 308.

Praca, D., & Barral, C. (2001). From smart cards to smart objects: The road to new smart technologies. *Computer Networks, 36*(4), 381.

Preneel, B. (2007). A survey of recent developments in cryptographic algorithms for smart cards. *Computer Networks, 51*(9), 2223.

Pugh, D. (1993). Understanding and managing organisational change. In C. Mabey & B. Mayon-White (Eds.), *Managing change* (p. 108). London: Paul Chapman Publishing.

Pun, K. H., et al. (2002). Review of the electronic transactions ordinance: Can the personal identification number replace the digital signatures. *Hong Kong Law Journal, 32*, 241.

Ramage, J. R. (2001). Slow to sign online. *Pennsylvania Lawyer, 23*, 32.

Rambarran, I. A. (2002). I accept, but do they? The need for electronic signature legislation on mainland China. *The Transnational Lawyer, 15*(2), 405.

Randolph, P. A., Jr. (2001). Has e-sign murdered the statute of frauds. *Probate and Property, 15*(4), 23.

Reed, C. (1989). Authenticating electronic mail messages-some evidential problems. *The Modern Law Review, 52*(5), 649.

Reed, C. (2000). What is a signature. *Journal of Information Law and Technology, 3*. http://www2.warwick.ac.uk/fac/soc/law/elj/jilt/2000_3/reed. At 29 Jan 2012.

Reid, P. (2004). *Biometrics for network security*. Upper Saddle River: Prentice Hall PTR.

Richards, R. J. (1999). The Utah digital signature act as "Model" legislation: A critical analysis. *The John Marshall Journal of Computer & Information Law, 17*(3) http://www.jcil.org/journal/articles/217.html. At 12 Sept 2011.

Ritchie, J., & Spencer, L. (1994). Qualitative data analysis for applied policy research. In A. Bryman & R. G. Burgess (Eds.), *Analyzing qualitative data* (p. 173). London: Routledge.

Robbey, D. (1979). User attitude and management information system use. *The Academy of Management Journal, 22*(3), 527.

Roßnagel, H. (2006). On diffusion and confusion – Why electronic signatures have failed. In S. Fischer-Hübner et al. (Eds.), *Trust and privacy in digital business* (p. 71). Berlin/Heidelberg: Springer.

Roland, S. E. (2001). The Uniform Electronic Signatures in Global and National Commerce Act: Removing barriers to e-commerce or just replacing them with privacy and security issues? *Suffolk University Law Review, 35*(3), 625.

Rubin, H. J., & Rubin, I. (2005). *Qualitative interviewing: The art of hearing data* (2nd ed.). Thousand Oaks: Sage.

Rumelt, R. P. (1993). Inertia and transformation. In C. A. Montgomery (Ed.), *Resource-based and evolutionary theories of the firm* (p. 101). Boston: Kluwer.

Saripan, H., & Hamin, Z. (2011). The application of digital signature law in securing internet banking: Some preliminary evidence from Malaysia. *Procedia Computer Science, 3*, 248.

Saunders, M., Thornhill, A., & Lewis, P. (2007). *Research methods for business students* (4th ed.). Harlow: Financial Times Prentice Hall.

Scaleplus. (1999). *Explanatory memorandum to the Commonwealth Electronic Transactions Act.* http://scaleplus.law.gov.au/html/ems/0/1999/rtf/0642410364.rtf. At 21 Jan 2012.

Schapper, P., & Rivolta, D. M. (2004). *Authentication & digital signatures in e-law and security: A guide for legislators and managers.* http://siteresources.worldbank.org/INTEDEVELOPMENT/Resources/AuthenticationandDigitalSignatures.pdf. At 31 July 2012.

Schapper, P. R., Rivolta, M., & Malta, J. V. (2006). Risk and law in authentication. *Digital Evidence Journal, 3*(1), 10.

Schellekens, M. H. M. (2004). *Electronic signatures: Authentication technology from a legal perspective.* The Hague: Asser.

Schmitt, J., & Kozar, K. (1978). Management's role in information system development failures: A case study. *MIS Quarterly, 2*(2), 7.

Schneier, B. (2003). *Beyond fear: Thinking sensibly about security in an uncertain world.* New York: Copernius Books.

Schultz, E. (2002). The gap between cryptography and information security. *Computers & Security, 21*(8), 674.

Schwandt, T. A. (2001). *Dictionary of qualitative inquiry* (2nd ed.). Thousand Oaks: Sage.

Scoville, A. W. (1999). Clear signature obscure signs. *Cardozo Arts and Entertainment Law Journal, 17*(2), 345.

Sebé, F., Viejo, A., & Domingo-Ferrer, J. (2007). Secure many-to-one symbol transmission for implementation on smart cards. *Computer Networks, 51*(9), 2299.

Seddon, N. C., & Ellinghaus, M. P. (2002). *Cheshire and Fifoot's: Law of contract* (8th ed.). Chatswood: LexisNexis Butterworths.

Seidman, I. (2006). *Interviewing as qualitative research: A guide for researchers in education and the social sciences* (3rd ed.). New York: Teachers College Press.

Shelfer, K. M., et al. (2004). Smart cards. *Advances in Computers, 60*, 149.

Shuy, R. W. (2001). In-person versus telephone interviewing. In J. F. Gubrium & J. A. Holstein (Eds.), *Handbook of interview research: Context & methods* (p. 537). Thousand Oaks: Sage.

Siems, M. M. (2002). The EU directive on electronic signatures – A worldwide model or a fruitless attempt to regulate the future? *International Review of Law Computers and Technology, 16*(1), 7.

Silverman, D. (2000). *Doing qualitative research: A practical handbook* (1st ed.). Thousand Oaks: Sage.

Singleton, R. C., & Straits, B. C. (1993). *Approaches to social research* (2nd ed.). New York: Oxford University Press.

Sinisi, V. (2000). Digital signature legislation in Europe. *International Business Lawyer, 28*(11), 487.

Skevington, P. J., & Hart, T. P. (1997). Trusted third parties in electronic commerce. *BT Technology Journal, 15*(2), 39.

Smaling, A. (2002). The argumentative quality of the qualitative research report. *International Journal of Qualitative Methods, 1*(3). http://www.ualberta.ca/~iiqm/backissues/1_3Final/html/smaling.html. At 25 Jan 2012.

Smart, A. R. (2001). E-sign versus state electronic signature laws: The electronic statutory battleground. *North Carolina Banking Institute, 5*, 485.

Smedinghoff, T. J. (2005). Seven key legal requirements for creating enforceable electronic transactions. *Journal of Internet Law, 9*(4), 3.

Smith, R. E. (2002). *Authentication: From passwords to public keys.* Boston: Addison-Wesley.

Smith, G. J. H. (2007). *Internet law and regulation* (4th ed.). London: Sweet & Maxwell.

Sneddon, M. (1998). Legislating to facilitate electronic signatures and records: Exceptions, standards and the impact on the statute book. *University of New South Wales Law Journal, 21*(2), 59.

Sneddon, M. (2000). *Legal liability and e-transactions: A scoping study for the National Electronic Authentication Council.* http://unpan1.un.org/intradoc/groups/public/documents/APCITY/UNPAN014676.pdf. At 5 Dec 2012.

Solomon, M. (2003). Far from dead: Digital signatures getting new life. *Bank Technology News, 16*(2), 24.

Sommer, B., & Sommer, R. (2001). *A practical guide to behavioral research: Tools and techniques* (5th ed.). New York: Oxford University Press.

Spector, B. A. (1989). From bogged down to fired up: Inspiring organizational change. *Sloan Management Review, 30*(4), 29.

Spyrelli, C. (2002). Electronic signatures: A transatlantic bridge? An EU and US legal approach towards electronic authentication. *Journal of Information, Law and Technology, 2.* http://www2.warwick.ac.uk/fac/soc/law/elj/jilt/2002_2. At 29 Jan 2012.

Srivastava, A., & Thomson, S. B. (2006, December 7–10). *Framework analysis: A qualitative methodology for applied policy research.* Paper presented at the Australia New Zealand Academy of Management Conference (ANZAM), Canberra, Australia.

Stern, J. E. (2001). The Electronic Signatures in Global and National Commerce Act. *Berkeley Technology Law Journal, 16*(1), 391.

Stewart, D. W., Shamdasani, P. N., & Rook, D. W. (2007). *Focus groups: Theory and practice* (2nd ed.). Thousand Oaks: Sage.

Stirland, M. (2000). Identrus-the technical platform. *Information Security Technical Report, 5*(4), 84.

Stolz, J. S., & Cromie, J. D. (2011, July 12). E-commerce gets a boost with e-sign. *Business Law Today, 10*(4). http://www.abanet.org/buslaw/blt/bltmar01cromiestolz.html. At 12 July 2011.

Strauss, A. L., & Corbin, J. M. (1998). *Basics of qualitative research: Techniques and procedures for developing grounded theory* (2nd ed.). Thousand Oaks: Sage.

Stumpf, F., et al. (2007). The creation of qualified signatures with trusted platform modules. *Digital Evidence Journal, 4*(2), 81.

Sturges, J. E., & Hanrahan, K. J. (2004). Comparing telephone and face-to-face qualitative interviewing: A research note. *Qualitative Research, 4*(1), 107.

Summers, W. C., & Bosworth, E. (2004, January 5–8). *Password policy: The good, the bad, and the ugly.* Paper presented at the Winter International Symposium on Information and Communication Technologies (WISICT'04), Cancum, Mexico.

Swire, P. P., & Litan, R. E. (1998). *None of your business: World data flows, electronic commerce, and the European privacy directive.* Washington, DC: Brookings Institution Press.

Symon, G., & Cassell, C. (1998). Reflections on the use of qualitative methods. In C. Cassell & G. Symon (Eds.), *Qualitative methods and analysis in organizational research: A practical guide.* Thousand Oaks: Sage.

Tahat, H. (2005, April 6–8). *Factors affecting e-commerce contract law.* Paper presented at the 20th BILETA Conference: Over-Commoditised; Over-Centralised; Over-Observed: The New Digital Legal World? Belfast, Ireland.

Thomas, R. J. (1993). Interviewing important people in big companies. *Journal of Contemporary Ethnography, 22*(1), 80.

Thomsen, H. B., & Wheble, S. B. (Eds.). (1989). *Trading with EDI: The legal issues.* London: IBC Financial.

Thomson, S. B., & Cahoon, S. (2004, January 29–31). *Overcoming consent form obstacles.* Paper presented at the Advances in Qualitative Methods, 5th International Interdisciplinary Conference, Edmonton, AB, Canada.

Tipton, H. F., & Krause, M. (2004). *Information security management handbook* (5th ed.). Boca Raton: Auerbach Publications.

Torres, J., Izquierdo, A., & Sierra, J. M. (2007). Advances in network smart cards authentication. *Computer Networks, 51*(9), 2249.

Towle, H. K. (2001). E-signatures: Basics of the US structure. *Houston Law Review, 38*(3), 921.

Trader-Leigh, K. E. (2002). Case study: Identifying resistance in managing change. *Journal of Organizational Change Management, 15*(2), 138.

United Nations Economic Commission for Europe. (1979). *Recommendation No. 14 adopted by the working party on facilitation of international trade procedures*. http://www.unece.org/cefact/recommendations/rec14/rec14_1979_inf63.pdf. At 30 Jan 2012.

van Esch, R. (2003). Electronic signatures: A survey of the directive and the legislation in the United Kingdom and the Netherlands. In H. J. Snijders & S. Weatherill (Eds.), *E-commerce law: National and transnational topics and perspectives* (p. 27). The Hague: Kluwer Law International.

Venkatesh, V., et al. (2003). User acceptance of information technology: Toward a unified view. *MIS Quarterly, 27*(3), 425.

Vidich, A. J., & Lyman, S. M. (2000). Qualitative methods: The history in sociology and anthropology. In N. K. Denzin & Y. S. Lincoln (Eds.), *The handbook of qualitative research* (2nd ed., p. 37). Thousand Oaks: Sage.

Visoiu, D. F. (2002). Digital signature legislation in Central Europe. *International Business Lawyer, 30*(3), 109.

Vogel, H.-J. (2000). E-commerce: Directives of the European Union and implementation in German law. In D. Campbell & S. Woodley (Eds.), *E-commerce: Law and jurisdiction* (p. 29). The Hague: Kluwer Law International.

Vos, J. (2006). *The role of personality and emotions in employee resistance to change*. Master thesis, Erasmus University, Rotterdam.

Wang, M. (2006a, August 13–16). *A review of electronic signatures regulations: Do they facilitate or impede international electronic regulations*. Paper presented at the 8th International Conference on Electronic Commerce: The New E-Commerce: Innovations for Conquering Current Barriers, Obstacles and Limitations to Conducting Successful Business on the Internet, Fredericton, New Brunswick, Canada.

Wang, M. (2006b, April 6–7). *The role of economic, cultural and legal backgrounds in the ICT law-a particular examination on the regulation of electronic signatures*. Paper presented at the Global and Harmonisation in Technology Law Conference, Malta.

Wang, M. (2007a). Do the regulations on electronic signatures facilitate electronic commerce? A critical review. *Computer Law & Security Report, 23*(1), 32.

Wang, M. (2007b). The impact of information technology development on the legal concept – A particular examination on the legal concept of signatures. *International Journal of Law and Information Technology, 15*(3), 253.

Watson, M. (2001). E-commerce and e-law; is everything e-okay? Analysis of the Electronic Signature in Global and National Commerce Act. *Baylor Law Review, 53*(4), 803.

Weil, M. M., & Rosen, L. D. (1997). *TechnoStress: Coping with technology@ work@ home@ play*. New York: Wiley.

Whitman, M. E., & Mattord, H. J. (2004). *Management of information security*. Boston: Thomson Course Technology.

Winn, J. K. (2001). The emperor new clothes: The shocking truth about digital signatures and internet commerce. *Idaho Law Review, 37*(2), 353.

Wolcott, H. F. (2001). *Writing up qualitative research*. Newbury Park: Sage.

Wright, B. (1999). Electronic signatures: Making electronic signatures a reality. *Computer Law & Security Report, 15*(6), 401.

Wu, R. (2000). Electronic transactions ordinance – Building a legal framework for e-commerce in Hong Kong. *Journal of Information, Law and Technology, 1*. http://www2.warwick.ac.uk/fac/soc/law/elj/jilt/2000_1/. At 29 Jan 2012.

Wylder, J. O. (2003). Improving security from the ground up. *Information Systems Security, 11*(6), 29.

Wyrough, W. E., Jr., & Klein, R. (1998). The Electronic Signature Act of 1996: Breaking down barriers to widespread electronic commerce in Florida. *Florida State University Law Review, 24*(2), 407.

Yin, R. K. (2003). *Case study research: Design and methods* (3rd ed.). Thousand Oaks: Sage.

Zimmerman, D. (2002). Evidence in the digital age. *Law Institute Journal, 76*(2), 77.

Case Law

Bennett v Brumfitt (1867) LR 3 CP 28.
British Estate Investment Society Ltd v Jackson (HM Inspector of Taxes) (1956) TR 397.
Brydges (Town Clerk of Cheltenham) v Dix (1891) 7 TLR 215.
Butera v Director of Public Prosecutions for the State of Victoria (1987) 164 CLR 180.
Caton v Caton (1867) LR 2 HL 127.
Central Motors (Birmingham) Ltd v P A & SNP Wadsworth (1982) 133 NLJ 555, Court of Appeal (Civil Division).
Clipper Maritime Ltd v Shirlstar Container Transport Ltd (1987) 1 Lloyd's Rep. 546.
Cloud Corporation v Hasbro Inc 314 F 3d 289 (7th Cir, 2002).
Electronic Rentals Pty Ltd v Anderson (1971) 124 CLR 27.
Farrelly v Hircock (No1) (1971) QdR 341.
Faulks v Cameron (2004) NTSC 61.
Foreman v Great Western Railway Company (1878) 38 LT 851.
Good Challenger Navegante SA v Metalexportimport SA (2004) 1 Lloyd's Rep. 67.
Goodman v J Eban (1954) 1 QB 550.
Halley v O'Brien (1920) 1 IR 330.
J Pereira Fernandes S A v *Mehta* (2006) 1 WLR 1543.
Jenkins v Gaisford & Thring (1836) 3 SW & TR 93.
L'Estrange vs F Graucob Ltd (1934) 2 KB 394.
Masquerade Music Ltd v Springsteen (2001) EWCA Civ 563.
McGuren v Simpson (2004) NSWSC 35.
Newborne v Sensolid (Great Britain) Ltd (1954) 1 QB 45.
Omychund v Barker (1745) 26 ER 15.
Parker v South Eastern Railway Company (1877) 2 CPD 416.
Phillimore v Barry (1818) 1 Camp 513.
Pyror v Pyror (1860) LJR 29 NS P, M & A 114.
Re a debtor (No 2021 of 1995), Ex parte Inland Revenue Commissioners (1996) 2 All ER 345.
Re Whitley Partners Ltd (1886) LR 36 ChD 337.
Regina v Moore, Ex parte Myers (1884) 10 VLR 322.
Ringham vs Hackett and Another (1980) 124 SJ 201.
Shattuck v Klotzbach 14 Mass L Rep 360 (Mass Super Ct, 2001).
SM Integrated Transware Pte Ltd v Schenker Singapore (Pte) Ltd (2005) 2 SLR 651.
Standard Bank London Ltd v Bank of Tokyo Ltd (1995) CLC 496.
Toll (FGCT) Pty Limited v Alphapharm Pty Ltd (2004) 219 CLR 165.
Torrac Investments Pty Ltd v Australian National Airline Commission (1985) ANZ Conv. R.82.

Legislation

Australia

Corporations Act 2001 (Cth).
De Facto Relationship Act 1999 (NT).
Electronic Transactions (Northern Territory) Act 2000 (NT).
Electronic Transactions (Queensland) Act 2000 (Qld).
Electronic Transactions (Victoria) Act 2000 (Vic).
Electronic Transactions Act 1999 (Cth).
Electronic Transactions Act 2000 (ACT).
Electronic Transactions Act 2000 (NSW).
Electronic Transactions Act 2000 (SA).

Electronic Transactions Act 2000 (Tas).
Electronic Transactions Act 2003 (WA).
Evidence Act 1995 (Cth).
Limitation Act 1969 (NSW).

United Nations
UNCITRAL. *Model Law on Electronic Commerce 1996.*
UNCITRAL. *Model Law on Electronic Signatures 2001.*
United Nations Convention on the Carriage of Goods by Sea 1978 (The Hamburg Rules).
United Nations Convention on the use of Electronic Communications in International Contracts 2005.

International
Australian Courts Act 1828 (Imp).
Civil Law Act (Singapore).
Directive 1999/93/EC of the European Parliament and of the Council of 13 December 1999 on a Community Framework for Electronic Signatures [2000] OJ L13/13 (Electronic Signatures Directive).
Electronic Commerce Act 2000 (Ireland).
Electronic Communications Act 2000 (UK).
Electronic Digital Signature Law 2002 (Russia).
Electronic Signature Act 1996 (Florida).
Electronic Signatures in Global and National Commerce Act 2000 (E-Sign).
Electronic Transactions (Amendment) Ordinance 2004 (HK).
Electronic Transactions Act 1998 (Singapore).
Electronic Transactions Act 2002 (NZ).
Electronic Transactions Act 2004 (China).
Information Technology Act 2000 (India).
Statute of Frauds 1677 (Imp).
Uniform Electronic Transactions Act 1999 (UETA).
Utah Digital Signature Act 1995.
Wills Act 1837 (UK) c 26.

Internet Materials and Other Sources

ASX. *Detailed search – Prices, announcements and charts.* http://www.asx.com.au/asx/research/CompanfoSearch.jsp. At 11 May 2011.

Australian Government Information Management Office. (2008). *Gatekeeper PKI framework: Glossary.* http://www.agimo.gov.au/__data/assets/pdf_file/0003/52248/Glossary.pdf. At 12 May 2011.

Australian Government Information Management Office. (2009). *Gatekeeper PKI framework: Cross recognition policy.* http://www.finance.gov.au/e-government/security-and-authentication/gatekeeper/docs/Glossary.pdf. At 12 May 2011.

Beary, E. (1998). *The digital signature debate: Technology neutral or specific?* http://raven.cc.ukans.edu/~cybermom/CLJ/beary.htm. At 25 Aug 2011.

California Secretary of State, California Digital Signature Regulations: California Government Code Section 16.5. http://www.sos.ca.gov/digsig/code-section-16-5.htm. At 28 Jan 2012.

Canter, S. (2002, January 2). Electronic signatures – Now it's legal to sign documents electronically but should You? *PC Magazine*, 102.

Clinton, W. J., & Gore, A. (1997). *A framework for global electronic commerce.* Technology Administration. http://www.technology.gov/digeconomy/framewrk.htm. At 21 Mar 2011.

Commission of the European Communities. (2006). *Commission frustrated that people ignore digital signatures.* OUT-LAW.COM. http://www.outlaw.com/page-6751. At 22 May 2011.

Daily Mail Reporter. (2012, March 6). Lazy workers beware! Study reveals the most popular computer password (and, yes, it's 'Password1'). *Daily Mail*. http://www.dailymail.co.uk/news/article-2110924/Lazy-workers-beware-Study-reveals-popular-password-yes-Password1.html. At 20 Mar 2012.

Dearne, K. *Canberra fails e-security test: Parliamentary report 6 April 2004*. news.com.au. http://www.news.com.au/. At 15 Apr 2011.

Directory of Accredited Service Providers (2012). Australian Government Information Management Office. http://www.finance.gov.au/e-government/security-and-authentication/gatekeeper/accredited/index.html. At 21 Feb 2012.

Donovan, C. (2002). *Strong passwords*. SANS Institute. http://www.giac.org/certified_professionals/practicals/gsec/0043.php. At 15 Mar 2012.

Editorial. (2003, May 10). Online flaw a visa to thieves. *World, Herald Sun* (Melbourne), 19.

eGovernment. (2004). *Take-up of electronic signatures remains low in Germany*. epractice.eu. http://www.epractice.eu/document/1276. at 12 Mar 2008.

Electronic Frontiers Australia. (2001). *Introduction to cryptography*. http://www.efa.org.au/Issues/Crypto/crypto1.html. At 12 May 2011.

Fonseca, B. (2001, March 22). VeriSign issues false Microsoft digital certificates. *Infoworld*. http://www.infoworld.com/articles/hn/xml/01/03/22/010322hnmicroversign.html. At 22 May 2011.

Fontana, J. (2002, September 5). Microsoft patches core cryptography interfaces in Windows. *Computerworld*. http://www.computerworld.com/securitytopics/security/holes/story/0,10801,73996,00.html. At 10 Jan 2012.

Free Download Manager. *Software downloads site*. http://www.freedownloadmanager.org/download.htm. At 5 Mar 2012.

Funston, L. (2007, June). Biometric technology shines. *Australian National Security Magazine*, 28.

Hancock, B. (2002). *An introduction to qualitative research*. Trent Focus Group. http://www.trentrdsu.org.uk/cms/uploads/Qualitative%20Research.pdf. At 12 Mar 2012.

IBISWorld. (2005, April 21–27). The top 500. *Business Review Weekly*, 64.

International Chamber of Commerce. (2000). *Being coy about your age makes good e-security sense*. http://www.iccwbo.org/search/query.asp. At 25 Apr 2011.

Kearns, B. (2004). *Technology and change management*. http://www.comp.dit.ie/rfitzpatrick/MSc_Publications/2004_Brenda_Kearns.pdf. At 25 Jan 2012.

Lacey, A., & Luff, D. (2001). *Qualitative data analysis*. Trent Focus Group. http://www.trentrdsu.org.uk/cms/uploads/Qualitative%20Data%20Analysis.pdf. At 12 Mar 2012.

Legon, J. (2003, June 11). *Student hacks school, eErases class files*. CNN.com. http://www.cnn.com/2003/TECH/internet/06/10/school.hacked/index.html. At 12 Mar 2012.

Leyden, J. (2003). Office workers give away password for a cheap pen. *The Register*. http://www.theregister.co.uk/2003/04/18/office_workers_give_away_passwords/. At 21 Mar 2012.

Markillie, P. (2004, May 15). A survey of e-commerce: Unlimited opportunities? *The Economist*, 14.

Mathers, N., Fox, N., & Hunn, A. (2001). *Using interviews in a research project*. Trent Focus Group. http://faculty.uccb.ns.ca/pmacintyre/course_pages/MBA603/MBA603_files/UsingInterviews.pdf. 12 Mar 2012.

McCullagh, A. (2000). *Electronic commerce within the Australian legal environment*. Gaden Lawyers. http://www.gadens.com.au/Publications.asp?CategoryID=24&navid=4&cid=24. At 28 Jan 2012.

Meehan, M. (2001, July 9). Too late for digital certificates. *Computerworld*. http://www.computerworld.com/action/article.do?command=viewArticleTOC&specialReportId=11&articleId=61990. At 22 Dec 2011.

Merriam-Webster. (2008). *Merriam-Webster's online dictionary*. http://www.merriam-webster.com/dictionary/security. At 2 Mar 2012.

Microsoft. (2007). *MS02-048: Flaw in certificate enrolment control may cause digital certificates to be deleted*. http://support.microsoft.com/kb/323172. At 9 Jan 2012.

Murphy, K. (2004, April 27). Psst: A candy bar for your password? *IT Business, The Australian* (Melbourne), 6.

National Conference of State Legislatures. *The Uniform Electronic Transactions Act*. http://www.ncsl.org/programs/lis/CIP/ueta-statutes.htm. At 11 May 2011.

National Office for the Information Economy. (2001). *The NOIE column: Project Angus*. http://www.business.gov.au/BEP2002/NewsLetter/NewsArchivesArticle/0,1589,8048,00.html. At 15 June 2011.

OECD. (2000). *OECD guidelines for cryptography policy*. Department of Justice. http://www.justice.gov/criminal/cybercrime/oeguide.htm. At 10 June 2011.

Pornwasin, A. (2008, January 8). Drive for greater use of digital signatures. *The Nation*. http://www.nationmultimedia.com/2008/01/08/technology/technology_30061450.php. At 10 May 2011.

Prud'homme, P., & Chira-aphakul, H. (2001). *E-commerce in Thailand: A slow awakening*. Thailand Law Forum. http://thailawforum.com/articles/ecommerce.html. At 14 Dec 2011.

Ralph Waldo Emerson quotes (American Poet, Lecturer and Essayist, 1803–1882). Thinkexist.com. http://thinkexist.com/quotation/fear_always_springs_from/193238.html. At 25 Aug 2011.

Regan, K. (2003). The fine art of password protection. *E-Commerce Times*. http://www.ecommercetimes.com/story/21776.html. At 20 Mar 2012.

Safescrypt. (2002). *Enrollment guide for SafeCerts: RCAI class 3*. http://www.safescrypt.com/support/india-rcaiclass3.html. At 15 Oct 2011.

Schneier, B. (2008, March 28). Art and science: Bruce Shneier shares security ideas at museum. *Network World*. http://www.networkworld.com/news/2008/032808-schneier.html. At 20 Mar 2012.

Shark tank: Not exactly what the doctor ordered (2003). Computerworld http://blogs.computerworld.com/sharky/20030129. At 22 Mar 2012.

The Lectric Law Library's lexicon(2008). Lectric Law Library. http://www.lectlaw.com/def2/s140.htm. At 10 Mar 2012.

The Phrase Finder. http://www.phrases.org.uk/meanings/237250.html. At 14 Mar 2012.

Tuesday, V. (2002). *User indifference thwarts electronic signature effort*. Computerworld. http://www.computerworld.com/securitytopics/security/story/0,10801,67303,00.html. At 28 Jan 2012.

UNCITRAL. (1996). *Guide to enactment of the UNCITRAL model law on electronic commerce*. http://www.uncitral.org/pdf/english/texts/electcom/0589450_Ebook.pdf. at 3 July 2011.

UNCITRAL. (2001). *Guide to enactment of the UNCITRAL model law on electronic signatures*. http://www.uncitral.org/pdf/english/texts/electcom/ml-elecsige.pdf. At 5 Aug 2011.

UNCITRAL. (2005a). *2005 – United Nations convention on the use of electronic communications in international contracts*. http://www.uncitral.org/uncitral/en/uncitral_texts/electronic_commerce/2005Convention.html. At 10 June 2011.

UNCITRAL. (2005b). *Explanatory note by the UNCITRAL secretariat on the United Nations convention on the use of electronic communications in international contracts*. http://www.uncitral.org/pdf/english/texts/electcom/0657452_Ebook.pdf. At 11 June 2011.

UNCITRAL, *FAQ – UNCITRAL Texts*. http://www.uncitral.org/uncitral/en/uncitral_texts_faq.html#model. At 13 May 2011.

US Department of Education. (2008). *Federal student aid PIN*. http://www.pin.ed.gov/PINWebApp/pinindex.jsp. 11 May 2011.

VeriSign Authentication Services. (2011). *Gatekeeper digital certificates overview*. http://www.verisign.com.au/gatekeeper/overview/index.html. At 17 Feb 2012.

VeriSign. *VeriSign gatekeeper: Customs digital certificates*.http://www.verisign.com.au/gatekeeper/customs/. At 20 May 2011.

VeriSign. *VeriSign gatekeeper: Gatekeeper pricing* http://www.verisign.com.au/gatekeeper/pricing.shtml. 23 Mar 2012.

VeriSign. *VeriSign gatekeeper: Non-individual (Type 2) certificate*. http://www.verisign.com.au/gatekeeper/nonindividual.shtml. 23 Mar 2012.

Watson Jr, J. K., & Choksy, C. (2000, September 18). Digital signatures seal web deals. *InformationWeek*. http://www.informationweek.com/804/rbdigital.htm. At 30 June 2011.

Wayne Dyer Quotes (American motivational speaker and author, b 1940). WorldofQuotes.com. http://www.worldofquotes.com/author/WayneDyer/1/index.html. At 18 June 2011.

Worthington, T. (2006). *Digital evidence for lawyers and IT professional*. TomW Communications Pty Ltd. http://blog.tomw.net.au/2006/08/digital-evidence-for-lawyers-and-it.html. At 27 Feb 2012.

Index

A. Srivastava, *Electronic Signatures for B2B Contracts: Evidence from Australia*,
DOI 10.1007/978-81-322-0743-6, © Springer India 2013

MIX
Papier aus verantwortungsvollen Quellen
Paper from responsible sources
FSC® C105338

If you have any concerns about our products,
you can contact us on
ProductSafety@springernature.com

In case Publisher is established outside the EU,
the EU authorized representative is:
Springer Nature Customer Service Center GmbH
Europaplatz 3, 69115 Heidelberg, Germany

Printed by Libri Plureos GmbH
in Hamburg, Germany